BERNARD SHAW

The Road to Equality

TEN UNPUBLISHED LECTURES AND ESSAYS, 1884-1918

WITH AN INTRODUCTION BY
LOUIS CROMPTON

*Edited by Louis Crompton with
the assistance of Hilayne Cavanaugh*

BEACON PRESS   BOSTON

Contents

Editor's Preface

The preparation of these unpublished writings of Bernard Shaw for the press has not been without its small element of adventure. First there was the discovery that the British Museum collection contained a sizable number of manuscripts of lectures and essays by Shaw on economics that had not yet appeared in print. Then these writings turned out to be, not ephemeral sketches, but carefully thought out, cogently argued, and often brilliant expositions of a subject to which Shaw devoted more time and effort than any other in his long and varied career. It was also a happy chance that they had a central theme, namely, the ethics of free enterprise and the struggle for a more equal distribution of income. Moreover, most of the papers proved fairly readily transcribable. In three cases, however, difficulties arose. In one the writing showed that Shaw had struck off only a draft, though a remarkably well-organized one; in another case the handwritten manuscript was full of puzzling gaps; and in the third there was a crucial difficulty in establishing the order of a dozen separate fragments. The overcoming of these problems was in itself a kind of challenge. The reader will find a detailed account of these matters in the notes at the end of the book.

Naturally, with a writer as idiosyncratic as Shaw, the editing of a series of manuscripts written over a period of more than thirty years presents a variety of problems. Since his usage varies considerably among the ten selections I have tended to choose among the various forms the one employed in Shaw's later published writings. Thus apostrophes are omitted from most verbal contractions; -or endings are used instead of the normal British -our; compound numbers are written without hyphens; book titles, without italics; et cetera. On the other hand, Shaw's use of capitals for abstract nouns in political science is so distinctive, if erratic, that I have generally followed the individual manuscripts. I have not wide-spaced words in order to indicate italics, as Shaw does in his published works, since at no point does this style appear in these writings. Occasionally, as in the spelling of *laisser-faire*, Shaw's usage is so various both in his manuscripts and in published works that I have simply chosen the commonest spelling for the sake of consistency. Misspellings, typing errors, and obvious slips and omissions have been corrected silently and brackets used only where real doubt exists as to what Shaw intended.

I first became aware of Shaw's unpublished socialist lectures during a trip to London in 1962 to work on my book on Shaw's plays. I am indebted to the Research Council of the University of Nebraska for a grant to microfilm this material at that time. I was enabled to begin work on the edition by a Woods Fellowship awarded in the spring of 1967. The job of preparing the text was appreciably forwarded by research assistants provided by the Research Council in 1967–68, and in the spring of 1969. Mrs. Norma Byrd gave valuable aid in deciphering passages canceled by Shaw in his first drafts and in typing a preliminary transcription. At a later stage, Mrs. Hilayne Cavanaugh provided such substantial and unstinting help in collating manuscripts and establishing Shaw's usage that it seemed proper her name should appear on the title page. The extensive index has also been prepared by her. I am grateful to Dan Laurence and Stanley Rypins for answering inquiries out of their wide knowledge of Shaw and to Lloyd Hubenka of Creighton University for lightening my labor and that of my assistants very considerably by arranging to turn the original microfilm into photostats.

Introduction

1 Freedom and Equality

At the moment the youth of the world are everywhere in revolt. What does this restlessness mean? Chiefly it is a response to a respite in the Cold War, however long or short the interlude turns out to be. For twenty years, each side in the conflict has professed its belief in freedom and equality and offered as proof of its devotion to these ideals its hatred for the other side. To be anticommunist in America or anticapitalist in Russia was enough in the way of virtue. The mote was all in our brother's eye. But now the young are judging their societies by the ideal standards to which their elders have long paid lip service. And everywhere they are finding them wanting. Our rhetoric, like chickens, has come home to roost. The realities young men and women see do not reassure them. Whatever measure of personal liberty exists in America (and it is small enough by any decent standards), we have seriously neglected the problem of social equality. In Russia, on the other hand, where economic disparities are not as gross as in the United States, civil liberties can scarcely be said to exist. But it is now patently obvious that both societies fall far short of what the human spirit of our age demands.

In the West it is social justice which has been most neglected. It is fitting then that this should be the theme of these ten hitherto unpublished lectures and essays by Bernard Shaw. For sixty-six of his ninety-four years Shaw made the fight for social equality his first concern, delivering over a thousand public lectures on the theme, pouring out essays between 1890 and 1910, and then in the third decade of the twentieth century publishing the compendious *Intelligent Woman's Guide to Socialism and Capitalism*. What these new writings do is to fill

THE ROAD TO EQUALITY

in the picture from 1884 (a few months before Shaw joined the Fabian Society) until 1890, and then again from 1910 until the end of the First World War. In all, they give a remarkably lucid, systematic, and comprehensive outline of his thinking on economics. Indeed, some of his leading ideas are developed here with a clarity and emphasis hardly equaled in anything which saw print in his lifetime.

The central idea of this book is that social equality means no less than equality of income, that everyone is entitled to an equal share of the national wealth. In Shaw's early economic writings this revolutionary notion is only implicit. It is first stated boldly and nakedly in a lecture he delivered in 1910 called "The Simple Truth about Socialism," which is the pivotal chapter of this volume. Before this he had analyzed the roots of inequality in the phenomena of rent, interest, and capital gains. He had also smashed the moral pretenses of capitalism by showing how hollow was the claim that wealth went to the provident and hardworking. As Shaw shows, economic power goes first to those who are able to grab land or other natural re-annual income of our twenty-two million Negroes falls short of happenstance; but once instituted, it fights furiously to pre-serve its privileges or to augment them.

But in 1910 he defines social equality as equality of income, pure and simple. Shaw would thus find a heartening develop-ment in America's civil rights movement, which has come at last to see that what the Negro needs is not primarily courses in Swahili or medieval Nigerian history, but simply money and the things that money will buy—better food and clothing for his children and better housing and medicine for old and young alike. Shaw would, however, decry the half billion (or even three billion) the Black Manifesto has demanded as merely an-other sign of the fatal "wantlessness" of the poor, since the annual income of our twenty-two million Negroes falls short of the national average by twenty billion, and this reparation would, in his eyes, be due not once but every year.

But is social equality, so understood, compatible with liberty? For Shaw admits that such equality could only be achieved by an immense increase in the power of the state, so that the state would, in fact, become the principal employer of labor, the sole owner of land, and the prime supplier of capital. Now, when we look at this prospect from the point of view of civic freedom we are immediately faced with a paradox. "Freedom," it turns out, is the slogan inscribed on the banner of every faction in America and Western Europe today, whether it be liberal or conservative, revolutionary or counterrevolutionary. It is at one and the same time the cry of the John Bircher and the communist anarchist. Nevertheless, the paradox is resolvable on consideration. To the conservative, freedom does not usually mean intellectual, moral, and political freedom: it means freedom to pursue his private economic ends without government interference. Historically, this is what we know as *laissez-faire*. Hence the anomaly that Macaulay, if he could read Senator Goldwater, would scratch his head at his calling himself a "conservative," since the latter's notion of the function of government parallels so exactly what called itself economic "liberalism" in the 1830s. But the so-called modern liberal is as inconsistent as the modern conservative; if he fights for freedom of speech and freedom in the arts and private life, he is a decided illiberal when it comes to "free" enterprise, which he sees may be freedom for the entrepreneur and slavery for his employee. Thus we are all hybrids, so to speak, but hybrids of opposite sorts, as centaurs with human heads are the opposite of minotaurs with human legs.

Shaw never worked out an adequate theory of his own hybridism. Intellectually he was a moral liberal and an economic antiliberal or statist. In his personal ethics he belongs with the anarchists, or with Wagner, whom he hailed as the "Adam Smith" of moral philosophy. He defended Parnell, Wilde, and Casement in their moments of greatest unpopularity, scourged the British government for its treatment of the Egyptians at Denshawai, vigorously opposed stage censorship, and pleaded for the toleration of intellectual heresy "to the last bearable degree." But if Shaw was in practice a great libertarian in the tradition of Voltaire and Zola, his analysis of the relation of the state to personal liberty in his essay "Freedom and the State," printed here for the first time, is open to serious question. In this chapter he applies Adam Smith to the moral sphere, arguing that the interference of the modern state in the private life of the individual will seek its own "natural level," as goods find their natural price in a free market. He rejects the central concept of Mill's *On Liberty*, the "self-regarding act," as an "abstract superficiality" and a "cast off garment of eighteenth century sociology." According to Shaw the modern state would not interfere immoderately in the private life of the citizen because it would not be worth its while to do so and it would exhaust its energy before its interference became oppressive. The briefest reflection will, of course, reveal this view to be as wildly optimistic as Bastiat's conviction that natural economic harmonies would make for the happiness of all under economic laissez-faire.

Why then did Shaw propound it? To understand this we must understand the attitude toward the state that English egalitarians took after 1867. Before then men like Macaulay had wanted the state to become a mere policeman protecting property and to keep out of economic affairs. Shaw agreed that this traditional liberal distrust of the state was quite intelligible on historical grounds: first, the minute regulation of trade by feudal precepts was helplessly outmoded even in the eighteenth century, and secondly, the aristocracy which had controlled the state in England had notoriously abused its power to protect its economic privileges. But when the second reform bill opened the door of parliament to the lower middle and working classes, Shaw, like Matthew Arnold before him, thought conditions had radically changed. The masses would be foolish not to use their new state power to foster economic equality. The bad class state was safely dead. Where Bentham and his school had wanted to minimize state action, Shaw followed Hegel in seeing the state as a useful positive instrument, not just a necessary evil. The modern state, purged of corruption, snobbery, and incompetence by the new civil service examinations, would be the trustee for all the people and was no longer to be feared.

But what Shaw did not see is that, though such a state is indeed necessary if a nation is to move toward social equality, there must be specific constitutional safeguards, both of minority rights and of what we now call "the right to privacy." Here Mill, with his nagging fear of the "tyranny of the majority," was more realistic than the overly sanguine Shaw. Because Mill's doctrine of liberty was warped by his followers into a defense of the rights of private property (something it was never intended to be), Shaw erroneously thought of himself as a postliberal, which he wasn't. He also made a second mistake in thinking the Millites' battle for intellectual freedom had been permanently won in England, a notion the antilibertarian hysteria of the First World War soon disabused him of.

Shaw failed to grasp the need for legal protection of minorities from majority prejudice. He did, however, see one way in which the extension of state functions positively aids civil liberties. Next to freedom from arbitrary arrest, the most important aspect of freedom is the right to work—that is, the right of access to a job if a man belongs to an unpopular minority, or the right to keep it if he adopts unpopular opinions after he has been hired. After imprisonment, loss of work is the most potent sanction that can be used against a man. How are we to be sure it is not invoked illegitimately? Shaw clearly perceives in these lectures that, because of tenure regulations, civil servants, at least potentially,[1] have more liberty than private employees. Indeed, without job tenure the idea of free speech itself soon becomes a hollow figment. Judges and professors, for instance, can speak and act more freely than bank clerks and salesmen because of their "tenure," though the judges have not always been willing to defend the professors and the professors' tenure is the more shaky because it is not protected by law but only by the willingness of professional organizations to blacklist offending institutions. Under certain circumstances the hog

1. I say potentially because the federal government, which fights discrimination against America's Negro minority, actively supports it against our homosexual minority, which is almost as large. But this policy can be changed.

butcher may have a more solid guarantee of freedom of speech than the college teacher, simply because his union has a more potent sanction, in the form of the strike, at its command. To be really effective, academic tenure would have to be backed by court decisions or by provisions written into federal aid, making funds contingent on a decent standard of academic freedom. True, Congress may move the other way and attach illiberal restrictions to federal money. But all power for good is also power for evil, and the government passed much prosegregation legislation before it first experimented with integration. Federal power may compound social abuses: but without it they cannot be effectively countered at all.

We have left to last the reasons why Shaw thinks equality is a good in itself. The first is social. We cannot afford to harbor in our cities a poverty-stricken, ignorant, violent, diseased, and jobless proletariat. As citizens, such a class is a clear liability: even for the purposes of exploitation they are largely a loss, and we would do better to give them a fixed annual income and educate them up to middle-class standards. But we could, and in fact we even may, end poverty without establishing equality. The argument against this latter course is a political one. Eventually, the slogan "one man, one vote" is meaningless unless we add to it the further cry of "one man, one income." Under our present system we give one man one income, another half an income, a third no income at all, and a fourth a thousand incomes for himself alone. The wealthiest man in the United States has assets equal to the annual income of half a million Negro families. To pretend that men are political equals under such circumstances is a wild absurdity. Anyone with the money will obviously call the tune to a degree far beyond the power of a poor man. The man who owns a newspaper or television station is ten thousand times as powerful politically as the man who can only write letters to the editor. If he does not run himself, he is in a position to contribute huge sums to meet the crushing expenses of modern electioneering. Under such a system even something as basic as equality before the law is reduced to a mere mockery. The poor man charged with a crime goes undefended or is defended only by an overworked and unsympathetic public servant, and he is tried before a jury and a judge who often have a strong class bias against him. As for civil disputes between the rich and the poor, the situation is laughable. The rich man can hire expensive lawyers, secure innumerable delays, and afford costly appeals if the case goes against him, all of which are out of the question for the man without money. In brief, legal equality is a sham so long as we are not equal before the Internal Revenue Service. Finally, the effect of social inequality on tax legislation is before us. Pressed far enough, inequality of this sort can lead to the conniving of the middle class at the guillotining of the privileged by the mob, as in the case of the French Revolution.

II Shaw's New Lectures

These are the pillars of the classical egalitarian position. But how does Shaw develop his argument in detail in the lectures and essays here published for the first time? "Our Lost Honesty" looks at the distribution of wealth from the point of view of social ethics. Adam Smith had imagined trade as first arising in a primitive barter economy where goods would exchange directly according to the labor time spent producing them. Shaw turns this abstract model into a principle of social justice. In effect he calls it theft to consume more than we produce. At this point his argument is akin to Marx's use of the surplus-value theory to indict capitalists as robbers of primary producers. But Shaw's Marxism is not here the harshly vituperative Marxism of, say, his *Unsocial Socialist*, despite the fact that this lecture (delivered in May, 1884) was written so soon after the novel. All the spleen of the earlier work has vanished, and the argument is now developed with sparkling humor. Shaw playfully compares the capitalist to the highwayman as a work-maker and a risk-taker, dissolving the moral prestige of the first in laughter by showing that the encomiums traditionally delivered in honor of the entrepreneur fit the rogue just as neatly. Not since Mandeville has economic logic cavorted so gaily.

Having indicted modern society, Shaw then asks, in "The New Radicalism," what hope lies in England's two historic parties. The prospects, he finds, are dim. Each plays up the misery of the poor when it is out of office, then when elected does nothing to basically change the system. The Gladstonian Liberals, preoccupied with Home Rule, ignore the fact that what the Irish peasant really suffers from is poverty, and that the English worker is often worse off than his Irish cousin. The Radicals attack the monarchy or propose to make peasant tenants into proprietors, or town tenants into owners, without realizing that this will only play into the hands of the Tories by increasing the voting power of the landowning class, while leaving farm laborers and the civil proletariat unprotected. The latter, unconvinced that the Liberal businessman has his interest at heart any more than the squire, does not vote at all. While partisanship masquerades as statesmanship in national politics, the unemployed face starvation and revolution threatens. (Shaw wrote his essay only a few weeks before the "Bloody Sunday" riots in Trafalgar Square in 1887.) Morally, revolutionary violence is quite justified. The conservative ethical objection to it is hypocritical, since the present system, just as much as any revolution, rests on the power of soldiers' bayonets and the police. But practically it is inadvisable, since the problem of industrial reorganization is not solvable by such means. Salvation can only come through the state providing jobs for the workless, paying a decent minimum wage, taxing landlords out of existence, and developing government-owned industries.

In "Freedom and the State," Shaw develops the theory of the benevolent "natural level" of state interference with the private lives of its citizens we have already criticized. "From Lassalle to the Fabians," by contrast, deals not with party politics or theory but with the personalities and history of European socialism since 1848. This brings to the stage Ferdinand Lassalle. Without this vivid sketch we would hardly have realized how much Shaw admired Lassalle or the extent to which he was influenced by his thinking. For Lassalle and not Marx seems to have been the chief link between Shaw and the German Hegelians. Lassalle saw the state as divided into hostile classes, so that the next to uppermost always enlisted the aid of those below to overthrow the class in power, then coalesced with it, and finally itself underwent supplantation. This meant the proletariat would inevitably replace the bourgeoisie, just as the latter had replaced the feudal nobility: the final classless state would then be the custodian of the good of the whole nation. What attracted Shaw to Lassalle, apart from his heroic temper, was the breadth of his cultural vision, especially his perception that the coming of social democracy would mean not only radical economic change but also completely new conceptions of the family, of religion, of manners, and of personal honor.

After Lassalle's death, Shaw gives us the history of Marx and the First International, up to the dissolution of that body at the fall of the Paris Commune. The drama of the collapse of the Commune obviously made a great impression on Shaw. First, he was revolted by the brutality of its suppression and the hypocrisy of the propaganda of the anti-Communards. Secondly, it convinced him of the folly of premature revolts by well-intentioned workers without the administrative ability to run a government. Much of Shaw's distrust for "barricade socialism" and his belief that Fabian planning was the sine qua non of social change sprang from the grim lesson of the Commune. With these grisly events behind, Shaw concludes with a series of lighthearted personal vignettes of himself and his fellow workers in the Social-Democratic Federation and the Fabian Society: Bax, Hyndman, Frost, Champion, Joynes, Aveling, and a half dozen others.

Shortly before 1890 Shaw seems to have dallied with the idea of producing a formal textbook on economics from a collectivist point of view, to be called "Technical Socialism." In the excerpt from this unpublished treatise, included under the title "Capital and Wages" in this collection, he tackles the question of the practical limits of private and public ownership. There is, he thinks, no a priori rule as to what should be private or public property: obviously a pocket watch cannot be used collectively or Big Ben privately appropriated. But "Private Property" as an economic system means first and essentially private property in land. Here private property is quite illegitimate, since land, being both limited in amount and indestructible, has all the characteristics of the kind of property that must not be monopolized by the few to the deprivation of the many. The system may be tolerable as a way of opening up new countries, but in developed states fertile land, along with business and housing sites, should be appropriated by the government and held as the possession of the nation as a whole as soon as the political machinery is fully enough grown to allow for this. As for the traditional argument in defense of capitalism, that only by underpaying the masses and letting the wealth pile up in the hands of the few can venture capital be obtained, Shaw responds by offering the new Social-Democratic State as the chief source of capital.

Having dealt with land, Shaw goes on to the question of wages and profits. In new countries wages will be high since men will not take for their labor less than they can make as cultivators of good free land. However, as population grows, a landless proletariat will eventually have to sell themselves more cheaply in the open market, depressing wages generally. This fall in wages will cause profits on productive land to rise correspondingly, further enriching the landowning class. Capitalization temporarily raises wages by increasing the demand for labor, but once the land is improved, this demand will fall off, causing wages to sink, while the increased productivity will make profits rise again. Thus the rich get richer, the poor poorer. This is not necessarily a law of nature however. Shaw avoids the pessimism of Malthus by arguing that the increase in productivity actually outdoes the rise in population so that only maldistribution of the national product keeps the workers' condition from improving proportionately.

But if socialism is technically feasible, is it compatible with human nature as it exists in the world today? Opponents have objected that humanity is not idealistic or altruistic enough to make such a system work. In "Socialism and Human Nature," Shaw admits that mankind often does appear to be outrageously

selfish· exploitive employers, parasitic shareholders, and rack-
renting landlords do exist. But Shaw maintains that the case for
socialism is even stronger if we assume men are by instinct
fiercely selfish than if we assume they are disinterested. For if
this bad propensity is intrinsic, socialism is all the more necessary, legislated social equality being in fact the only bulwark we
have against man's enslavement of man. However, the capitalist
system does not uniquely reflect human nature: it was not something the human race willed and consciously invented but something we stumbled into. And whatever the apparent economic
evidence, it is absurd to label any human propensities as specifically wicked. Vices and virtues spring from the same root,
and the same characteristic leads in certain circumstances to evil
and in others to good. The sensible thing is to organize society
so men's natural tendencies will do least harm. Since the present
system in fact invites men to viciousness, we are mistakenly led
to believe that self-renunciation is the highest morality: hence
England's dismal Puritanism and its cult of sacrifice. Should the
workers tolerate this state of affairs? No, they should be prepared to fight rather than put up with it, since significant
change will only come under the threat of revolution. They
must realize that parliament is made up of unscrupulous aristocrats, hypocritical plutocrats, and well-intentioned philanthropists, whose willingness to condone the present state of affairs
is the consequence of their cowardice. Socialists must make
these truths clear even at the risk of losing the approbation of
respectable society.

But are not state enterprises notoriously corrupt and inefficient, as the government's conduct of the Crimean War, for
instance, seemed to show? In "Bureaucracy and Jobbery,"
Shaw answers that private business is also full of bribery, and
that the high rate of business failures testifies to its blunders,
which often go unpublicized, while government fiascoes are
always ruthlessly exposed. Moreover, the real outrages in
times of national emergency are the profits of private speculators who take advantage of the crises to corner markets. Nor
is the objection that state officials are always insolent valid.

Most "official" insolence is really "class" insolence. The police behave quite differently to a vagrant and to a rich man.

These considerations lead Shaw once more to a general consideration of human social psychology. Men's characters are fixed at birth, but their behavior is determined by their situations and by circumstances. There are no intrinsic differences between the rich and the poor. A chimney sweep who comes into money will clean himself up; an officer on active duty may get dirtier than the sweep. Nor is the natural diversity of personal tastes an impediment to social equality. Fox hunters, cardinals, successful businessmen, and undergraduates all associate on terms of equality even now. Men are not naturally good or bad, but mixed. Every man has his breaking point under temptation. The wise thing to do is to change society to reduce temptation, and to make the worst kind of commercial scoundrelism impossible.

How then do we go about establishing social equality? Twenty years later, in "The Simple Truth about Socialism," Shaw gives his startling answer: Socialism means simply equality of income. Outrageous as the idea sounds, Shaw points out that in certain social classes such equality already exists; i.e., all English judges, all policemen, and all military officers of a certain rank get the same pay irrespective of their individual merits or talents. Indeed, the absurdity of our present system comes home to us when we try to estimate a man's worth in monetary terms. How does one decide if a boxer is worth more or less than an archbishop? The question is unanswerable. But we could, of course, have equality between members of the same class but marked distinctions between different classes. We are then faced with the question: is a class system necessary or desirable? In an aristocracy, inequality is deemed necessary in order to produce the illusion that rulers are a different order of beings from the governed. Clearly, however, this is an idea that modern democracy does not countenance. On the other hand, social democracy can, by the opposite device of monetary equality, insure that bureaucrats do not treat ordinary citizens as social inferiors.

But quite apart from the impossibility of assessing personal merit, the practical bad effects of inequality are patent. First, there is the problem of malproduction. The nation builds stables for racehorses before it clears its slums or feeds its children. However, if we rationalized production, most of the advantages of wealth would disappear, since luxury trades would vanish. The only advantage remaining would be that a rich man would not have to work at all. But social parasitism, once defensible as an incentive to saving, is no longer necessary, since the state can now provide its own capital. "Benefit of capital" as a means of escaping work must go the way of "benefit of clergy" as a means of escaping hanging. Secondly, equality is the only solution to the political problem. At present, even where universal suffrage exists, the governments of Europe are in fact wealthy oligarchies. But while poverty holds sway, this is at least preferable to government by the poor, who are so cramped and penurious in their thinking as to make incompetent legislators. Finally, equality is also desirable biologically, since without the abolition of classes and the creation of intermarriageability the advent of the Superman will be seriously delayed. Shaw, in concluding, admits that absolute equality of income seemed too radical a proposal for the Fabians to make in the eighteen-nineties; but now that men have begun to catch up with their other proposals, it is the logical next step to take.

Four years later, shortly after the outbreak of the First World War, Shaw delivered a series of lectures on "The Redistribution of Income," parts of which are now published here. In these he deals with three questions: whether inequality is justified by social utility, whether money is an indispensable incentive to enterprise, and what mechanisms are promoting equality of income in society today. Once again, Shaw argues that inequality is indefensible: the manager and the manual laborer are both necessary to any enterprise. The supply-and-demand system, however, hopelessly cheats the lower classes by depressing wages. We must educate human beings, not to create classes, but because education is a good in itself. Industry does not need idols; people seek leadership and follow it because they feel a need for it. In an imaginary debate between a railway traffic manager and a porter, Shaw wittily reduces all the common arguments for wage differentials to absurdity.

Nor is money the important incentive people think it is. If it were an overruling influence on people's lives, we would not have a rich minority and a poor majority, when the people have the political power to expropriate the wealth of the rich. Much good is done in the world with no regard for money at all, though most dishonorable deeds require payment. Nor is the capitalist wage system an incentive to think. The moment a laborer thinks about his condition and speaks out he risks punishment as a seditious rebel. So little is money the main concern in life that very few men ever work at becoming millionaires. Nor has Marx's demonstration that workers are being robbed of surplus value ever really moved the masses. In order to produce a revolutionary mood you have to reduce wages below mere subsistence to a starvation level. The poor suffer from "wantlessness" more than from cupidity. A pittance will buy them off and reduce them to quiescence.

Meanwhile, what are the prospects for change? The suffering caused by the present system is so great that violence would be perfectly justified morally, but it would not work practically. Indeed, the most hopeful sign lies in the results not of socialist preaching but of Trade Union action. Unions are gradually raising the wages of unskilled labor to the level of skilled. This will go on, producing a highly desirable "leveling up" of minimal incomes. Eventually a national minimum wage will be established, and at last wages themselves will be superseded by an annual salary which will in effect be an equal share of the national product. But men will not be free not to work: neither tramps nor gentlemen will exist in the new society.

As rising wages threaten marginal businesses, the government will have to decide whether to let them go under or, if they are essential ones, whether to subsidize them out of the profits of other concerns. In the meantime, governments can contribute to the movement toward equality by taxing large incomes and forcing landlords and plant owners finally to sell out to them.

All this would be robbery if a private person did it, but in fact governments have to proceed this way if social equality is to be achieved; they are the only agents in the community capable of doing the job. This step-by-step approach is not ideal or heroic: but it is the one practical road to Utopia.

The last lecture in this book, originally given in 1918 under the title "The Soil and Climate for a Labor Party," touches a totally new subject, socialism and culture. Readers of Shaw's dramas will note its numerous connections with the preface to *Heartbreak House*, the play he had just finished. As the play sprang out of the milieu of the early years of the First World War, so the lecture reflects the mood of its closing months. It shows, above all, the shock felt by Shaw and the British intelligentsia on finding themselves suddenly face to face with a public which had suddenly become antilibertarian and antihumanitarian after nearly a hundred years in which radical leaders had been able to count on popular sympathy. This disappearance of Victorian cosmopolitan liberalism was dramatically signalized, above all, by the imprisonment, in 1917, of Bertrand Russell for his criticism of England's war policy.

What had happened to change things? Shaw's answer was that reform movements have no roots because their principles do not get incorporated into the teaching of our schools and universities. As the most notable example of this failure, Shaw points out that the great liberal movement in German culture from Goethe's *Faust* to Wagner's *Parsifal* had left German politics and militarism untouched in the day of the Kaiser. Similarly, Queen Victoria was in the long run the victor in the struggle for men's allegiance in the nineteenth century because her morals and prejudices remained the teaching of the schools.

Shaw is saying that intellectual advances are lost as soon as they are won unless they are incorporated into genuine "cultural revolutions," that is, into the educational system. At present modern education has not advanced the course of social progress at all: it has thrown it back by creating a mass readership for the yellow press. The obvious taste these masses have shown for jingoist conservatism has destroyed the myth of a liberal majority and revealed to reactionaries that the mob can more easily be used to threaten intellectuals than entrenched interests. The mob, at war, has thrown off liberty with relief, supported censorship, shut up cultural institutions, abolished elections, ended cabinet responsibility and established a dictatorship. Yet, secondary education is necessary. The best way, Shaw thinks, would be for the young to educate themselves as the Fabians did, through what we would now call "Free Universities." The learners must employ the teachers and be imbued with the will to learn. Otherwise education is a waste. All real education is, and must be, controversial. We need "a new Reformation far more radical than Luther's."

But if the World War was catastrophic for civil liberties, Shaw thought it had helped to open the road to equality. First, the government had controlled prices. Then, when essential industries were faced with losses, it had taxed the industry as a whole, which amounted exactly to the pooling of economic rent Shaw had advocated in 1914. Secondly, in organizing the army the government had faced most of the problems of socialist planning, though unfortunately the army is an institution dedicated to the perpetuation of caste, not to the creation of equality. But whatever these achievements may mean, we must not count on simply blundering into socialism. The policy of muddling through has made a hell of Europe for four years. Socialism will have to be a carefully thought out way of life with a positive, scientific religion behind it as carefully rationalized by theologians, sociologists, and philosophers as medieval feudalism was. It must also hold out greater attractions to the young than dull Fabian tracts. Above all, it should make an appeal to people's artistic sense and to their desire for a rich joyous life, with as much freedom as possible in the moral sphere, where the police should interfere only to suppress acts clearly definable as destructive crimes. Men should not be free to be idle and thus throw the necessary work of society on others, but they should be given a free choice of occupation. Incentive is no problem since the capacity for a certain job is usually in itself an incentive to exercise it. Only in filling the highest political office is it sensible to depart from the principle of letting men work at what they want to. For leadership, it is necessary to draft the reluctant man and discourage mere demagogues, political hacks, and routineers.

III   Shaw's Economic Theory

The general reader may want to turn to Shaw's own words after a glance at the advice on page xxxvi. Those with a special interest in the broad outlines of his economic thinking may find that the following analysis helps them to see it in perspective and in relation to the other economic theories of his age. Apart from his work as a socialist, Shaw, of course, had half a dozen other careers, from playwright to music critic. But even within the special area of economic reform the range of his interests was astonishing. Not only was he a practical working municipal councilor, a platform speaker and open-air agitator, and a tract writer on such problems as city government, fiscal policy, and imperialism, but he was also the Fabian Society's leading expert on economic theory. For this latter role, Shaw qualified himself in his early middle age by poring over economic treatises and debating their ideas in what we would now think of as graduate seminars, conducted by men with university training, though not directly under university auspices.

Four main currents shaped nineteenth-century socialism in England—Utopian, Christian, Marxist, and Fabian. To understand Shaw it is necessary to grasp his relation to each of them. Least significant in this connection are the Utopians. In his published writings Shaw nearly always dismissed them deprecatingly as impractical dreamers. It is surprising, after this, to discover among the unpublished manuscripts in the British Museum an unfinished essay in which Shaw speaks with genuine appreciation of the achievements of Saint-Simon, Fourier, and Owen. Fourier he praises as a satirist and for his grasp of the dialectics of history. Owen, on the other hand, was the first to see clearly the connection between poverty and crime, and to realize how much the workingman's personal behavior was worsened by the degrading environment of the new industrialism. But it is for Saint-Simon that Shaw saves his greatest praise. The French Revolution, the first great attempt in history to rationalize human social institutions, was more than half a failure:

> We know well enough by this time that the Kingdom of Reason came to nothing after all but the Kingdom of Commercial Respectability; that eternal justice stopped short at the protection of the commercially respectable; that universal equality was satisfied by the establishment of "freedom of contract"; that the inalienable rights of man turned out to be the inalienable right of the middle class to whatever they could get hold of without deductions for the benefit of an aristocracy of birth; and that the enforcement of the "social contract" of Rousseau was left in the hands of a makeshift of a republic partly democratic, partly commercial, but in neither particularly respectable. The great thinkers of the nineteenth century were no more able than their predecessors to overleap the walls of their epoch.

All the more reason, Shaw thinks, for recognizing the stroke of genius by which Saint-Simon, in his *Letters from Geneva,* perceived the crucial fact that the revolution involved the rights not just of *two* parties, but *three*—"the Nobility, the Mercantility, and the disinherited laborers"—and his prescience in declaring later, in 1816, that the science of politics would eventually be merged into the science of economics.

Still, "Utopian socialism" meant mainly Quixotic attempts by hopeful enthusiasts to found model communities, a program Shaw thought missed the fundamental fact that the whole economic system of the state must be reformed. Consequently, "Utopian" has for Shaw a largely pejorative connotation in connection with socialism. His feeling for the Christian Socialists, on the other hand, was markedly warmer. The reasons for this are complex. Marx had denounced religion, and revolutionary British groups like the Social-Democratic Federation and Socialist League were hostile to the clergy. Shaw, however, after his early manhood, was never a rationalist or secularist at heart. Like Tolstoy he reread, and found an antiproperty bias in, the Christian Gospels. Like Carlyle, he believed that ultimately social instincts, to be vital and courageous, must rest, not on logic or self-interest, but on religious convictions. Shaw thus belongs to the tradition, of which Carlyle and Ruskin were leaders, of men who aimed not to discard theology but to purge it of supernaturalism, Biblical literalism, and popular salvationism and then to mate it with modern science and social ideals.

Thus when Maurice's disciple, Stewart Headlam, revived the Christian Socialist movement in 1877, Shaw was able to enter into cordial personal relations with him and other clergymen like Clifford, Fleming, and Henry Carey Shuttleworth. He was keenly appreciative of the work Anglo-Catholic priests did in the East End to improve slum housing and end the prostitution which sprang from the underpayment of women. Like them he regarded *Past and Present* as a powerful attack on laissez-faire, and set beside it *Unto This Last, Munera Pulveris, Ethics of the Dust,* and *Fors Clavigera* as classics of nineteenth-century social thought. All this helps explain why there is a distinct flavor of the pulpit about Shaw's writings that we do not find in the other Fabians. Indeed, there are times when they take on a veritable neo-Calvinist tinge, as in his denunciations of idleness and luxury, or in his theory of history, which is not optimistic like Marx's, but colored by the Old Testament (and Carlylean) idea that national calamities are God's (that is, history's) punishment for national sins of social negligence.

But socialism for Shaw was more than a religion; it had also to be "scientific." Where was this scientific basis to come from? The Utopians and Christians alike were woefully lacking on the economic side of their thinking. Willian Irvine has pointed to Mill as the master of Shaw and the Fabians in economics. It is, of course, true enough that Mill approaches Shaw on such questions as land nationalization, inheritance, and unionization. But a chasm still yawns between them. Mill, for instance, believes staunchly in the necessity of competition and money incentives. But more important than any question of theory is the contrast in mood. Those who see the incipient Fabian in Mill overlook the cloud of gloom that hangs over his final "Chapters on Socialism," in which radical schemes of social betterment are condemned as impractical in the face of immutable economic laws. It is true that the idea—"this is unjust"—plays about the writings of the classical economists from Ricardo on. Shaw himself comments on the mood of "suppressed rebellion" that underlies Mill's abstract analyses. But such discontent is usually stifled by the countervailing conviction—"this is inevitable." Carlyle likened the typical mid-nineteenth-century economist to a goose held enchanted within a chalk circle, and indeed there is more than a little perversity in the apparent satisfaction even progressives like Mill take in demonstrating that fundamental economic changes, though desirable, are impossible.

The man who ended this habit was Marx. Shaw thought there was something sublime in the way Marx faced down the pessimists, dismissing the "immutable" economic relations of the nineteenth century as part of a vast dissolving panorama which was only a fleeting moment of history. Was Marx, then, the sought-after master of the keys Shaw needed? He was both an optimist and, *par excellence*, the giant of European "scientific" socialism. For a while in 1883 and 1884 Shaw seems to have been willing to adopt Marxism as a tentative creed. But he soon ran into intellectual difficulties. To begin with, at the very center of Marxism was the labor theory of value. It is easy to see what attracted Marx to this theory, which, after all, had been formulated and universally accepted by the classical economists. If labor is the sole creator of value, then it follows that the capitalist, in taking from the worker the "surplus value" he has created above and beyond his subsistence wage, is guilty of a kind of theft, a point Marx rubbed in ruthlessly.

But by the mid-eighties the labor theory of value was fast going out of fashion in non-Marxist circles. When he tried to defend Marx against his most formidable academic critics, Shaw found that a new theory of value, based on supply and demand, worked out by Stanley Jevons in 1871, had swept the labor theory from the field in central Europe and was rapidly gaining ground elsewhere. After a spirited exchange with W. H. Wicksteed, he abandoned the Marxist position for Jevons's. Nor was he able to accept Marx's theory of class warfare. In Shaw's eyes the crucial political conflict in England was not between the poor and wealthy. The rich employed a large army of retainers and gave business to workers in luxury trades, all of whom tended to vote conservative, seeing their welfare bound up with their employers' and patrons'. Finally, Shaw rejected the idea that a society's art, religion, and morals could be entirely deduced from economic relations. Of Marx he wrote, "He was a born materialist, and when he attempted to carve a theory with the tools of a born metaphysician, he cut his fingers." Shaw was unremitting in his scorn of moral idealists who did not see the importance of economics, but he did not believe it determined the ultimate direction of the human spirit. Indeed, Shaw as a voluntarist, vitalist, and immaterialist was not a determinist at all.

Yet, while refusing to become a dogmatic Marxist to whom Marx was a Messiah or Pope, Shaw adamantly refused to join his detractors. Though he rejected its theoretical basis, he avowed that he never took up a book that was better worth reading than *Capital*. But what Shaw chiefly admired Marx for was his hatred of social unjustice and his determination, through research, to expose England's social degradation. Ironically, what he admired in Marx the would-be "scientist" is exactly what he admired in the Christian Socialists—the quality of his moral protest. For Shaw, Marx is not the founder of modern socialist theory but the last of the Old Testament Jewish Prophets, a latter-day Amos or Micah.

Still, the rejection of Marxist orthodoxy left Shaw in an embarrassed position. Socialism was desperately in need of new economic foundations if it was not to be discredited on the scientific side by professional economists. But Jevons was not a socialist, nor was his new value theory one that led obviously to socialist conclusions. What was to be done? Shaw's tactic was to return once more to the classical economists. One pillar of

Ricardian theory had collapsed, carrying Marxism with it, but two others were still standing to provide Shaw with the support he needed. These were, respectively, the "law of economic rent" and the so-called iron law of wages. The clue to the socialist adaptation of the first Shaw found in Henry George. In *Progress and Poverty* (1879) George had raised the question: why did poverty increase so dramatically in the nineteenth century, during a time of unprecedented industrial and technological progress? He noted that misery was most evident in older, more highly developed countries, and that even in comparatively new lands like the United States it tended to be most prevalent in the largest cities and in the longest settled regions.

Ricardo had, in fact, given the reason in formulating his famous law of economic rent. Early settlers would find an abundance of free good land. Later ones would be forced to move to less fertile and remote regions, or alternatively could obtain prime sites by paying the first owners a premium in the form of the difference between their yield and the yield of the best land still available. The growth of population drove up the demand and raised rents as men were pushed further into the "margin of cultivation." Landlords could then retire as idle rentiers on the gain of this "economic rent" they had done nothing to earn. Later, their heirs would enjoy this advantage ad infinitum, the further increase in population actually increasing it. Moreover, as farming skills and productivity improved, the extra yield would, according to Ricardo, go to the landlord by the same law. The same rise in rents would occur with central business or housing. The classical economists had all recognized this phenomenon and accepted it merely as a law of nature. But George, who had seen the cycle develop with dramatic quickness in San Francisco in the seventies, took the radical step of asking whether man's sense of natural justice could be satisfied with letting a lucky few preempt valuable soil, building lots, or mines and then pass these advantages on to their descendants. He proposed to recover this "economic rent" for the state by a single tax on land values, so that the unearned increment would be shared by all citizens.

On the issue of land, Shaw's analysis of "The Economic Basis of Socialism," which opens the *Fabian Essays* of 1889 is pure George. George, however, was not a socialist, and distrusted state power. Shaw, by contrast, rejects George's "single tax" in favor of the nationalization of land and, because he treats capitalist profits as another form of economic rent, of industry. As the agent for this task, Shaw, under the influence of Lassalle and Hegel, proposes the state, now democratized through universal suffrage, and hence the appropriate instrument for the redistribution of wealth. Private entrepreneurs may develop new businesses and create new wants, but as soon as their undertakings become of national significance, like the railways, or the coal and steel industry, the state would take over.

Shaw also borrowed heavily from George's theory of wages. The so-called wage fund theory taught by the orthodox economists maintained that wages could be calculated simply by dividing the amount of capital available by the number of workers. As against this, George argued that wages depend first of all on the workers' productivity and are in fact created by the workers themselves. The wage fund theory held that wages, being proportional to capital, must rise or sink as capital increases or decreases. But George shows that in a new country, where capital is scarce, wages will also be high, since, as we saw, men will not sell their services for less than they can get from working free land. In his essay on "Capital and Wages," Shaw follows George to his final conclusion: as population grows, landless men will have to sell themselves more and more cheaply on the free market, depressing wages generally. Here Shaw goes beyond Ricardo, who had held that wages would indeed fall as population rose, but that the laborer's efforts would at least gain him a subsistence wage. Why so, asks Shaw? Dropping Ricardo's labor theory of value for Jevons's new doctrine of "final utility," Shaw demonstrates that labor, under this principle, suffers the same fate as other commodities. According to Jevons, prices are set, not by the work that goes into a commodity, but by the usefulness (as measured by the demand) for finally, cooperatives, when they hired outside workers, tended to do so at supply-and-demand rates and hence became exploiters of labor in their turn.

These, Shaw thought, were ineffective halfway measures. But various groups, notably the anarchists, were proposing solutions at least as radical as the Fabians'. Shaw thoroughly agreed with the disciples of Bakunin and Kropotkin that the bourgeois state was a hypocritical fraud whose vaunted ideal of law and order boiled down in the last analysis to their willingness to use the police and soldiery to protect property and class privileges. But the individual anarchists who simply wanted to do away with the state and leave every man king on his own plot of land were open to the same criticism as other distributionists, while the Communist anarchists, who favored pooling the resources of the community and letting men take freely what they needed for their sustenance entertained, held, Shaw was convinced, a wildly unrealistic view of human nature. For men had been so corrupted by the present traditions of social morality, which made work a disgrace and a life of idleness the greatest good, that, for a generation at least, stern coercion by the state might well be necessary to reeducate men to the view that it was immoral to be a consumer in society unless one was a producer as well.

Through all these arguments it will be noted that the law of economic rent runs as a leitmotif. (Shaw followed Mill in calling it the *pons asinorum* of political economy.) How then were its inequalities to be dealt with? Shaw's solution was for the state to collect rents, which would thus go not into private pockets but into public coffers. Eventually, this meant expropriating the landowning class. Such a move, in turn, raised the hotly debated question of whether or not they should be compensated. Here Shaw took the affirmative, holding that, since the state could not very well take over all the land at once, piecemeal expropriation would discriminate invidiously against those landlords first to be bought out. Shaw proposed instead to compensate each landlord and at the same time to raise the money for the compensation by taxing the landlord class as a

whole. By this means the landowners would, so to speak, buy
each other out and get more nearly equal treatment. At the end
of the process all rental receipts from farms, apartments, business sites, and mines would go to the state and be applied to
the welfare of the nation as a whole.

Rising taxes would in turn make landlords increasingly eager
to sell out to the state. Shaw saw a similar transfer of control
taking place in industry under the pressure of rising wages.
When high wages absorbed profits, marginal industries would
be forced to declare bankruptcy or seek support from the
state. If their operation proved necessary for the public good,
then the state would give them grants out of the profits of
better situated businesses, factories, or mines. Shaw thought
the trend toward state ownership was also being accelerated
by two new economic developments: the replacement of the
old capitalist-entrepreneur by the joint-stock company, and
the growth of trusts and cartels. The managers of a joint-stock
company would not ultimately care whether their salaries were
paid by a board of directors or the government. Indeed, they
might find a positive advantage in working for the state, since
their style of living would then be of their own choosing. As
for trusts, it was not *big* business that appalled Shaw so much
as *little* business. He positively preferred the ruthlessness of
the John D. Rockefellers and the Krupps to the narrow petti-
ness of the Pumblechooks and Snopeses. Wealth educated men;
poverty and the desperate attempt to escape from it stunted and
warped them. Far from disliking cartels, Shaw welcomed their
development, holding that this made for better organization
and more efficiency. When the business grew to monopoly size,
it could then be taken over by the government as a national
service.

Shaw's program as it appears in these pages was designed on
the premise that Europe would develop on the pattern of 1890–
1914, that is, with the eventual replacement of the remaining
feudal empires by parliamentary democracies. After the war,
as Yeats put it, "things fell apart" as democratic governments
collapsed, and the age of the dictators was succeeded by a sec-

ond holocaust. The third quarter of the twentieth century has, by contrast, witnessed an amazing renaissance of parliamentary democracy in Europe. Indeed, despite the failure of democratic experiments in the Third World and the rise of a whole new concept of civilization in the East, the domestic situations in English-speaking America and Europe today are remarkably like what forward-looking thinkers hoped for in 1918. We have been given, in other words, a scarcely-to-be-looked-for second chance. The other unforeseen development is the vanishing, under the inspiration of television advertising, of the "wantless-ness" of the poor which drove so many nineteenth-century reformers to despair. Standing, then, in a position not too unlike our own, Shaw saw a way to the future which might bypass revolution, though he was willing to face a revolution if the path were blocked. We are ahead of him only with respect to our welfare system, which is the hospital care necessary to patch up the worst consequences of social inequality. But we are beginning to grow as disgusted with welfare as Shaw and his co-workers were with charity. Equality, backed by a willing-ness of the state to force men to work, has everything to be said for it as an alternative.

A NOTE TO THE READER

The lectures and essays in this book are printed in their pre-sumed chronological order. The reader who wants to compre-hend the gist of Shaw's thinking about social equality and is not a Shaw specialist is advised to omit Shaw's discussion of British party politics in chapter two and his technical analysis of capital and wages in chapter seven on first reading and to come back to them if and when his interests dictate. Probably the most expeditious way to understand Shaw is to read chapters one, four, and five first and then the final sequence—eight, nine, and ten.

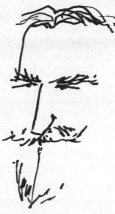

1   Our Lost Honesty

Shaw first became interested in eco-
nomics on hearing Henry George, the
author of Progress and Poverty, *speak*
on Land Nationalisation and the Single
Tax on September 5, 1882. The next
year he wrote his Marxist novel, The Unsocial Socialist, *and*
attended meetings of H. M. Hyndman's Social-Democratic Fed-
eration, without however, joining that body. On May 22, 1884,
he spoke to the Bedford Debating Society, under the presi-
dency of the Reverend Stopford Brooke, on his new faith. The
frontispiece of the holograph of his lecture bears the notation
in Shaw's hand, "MS of Lecture That the Socialist Movement
is Only the Assertion of Our Lost Honesty." This speech ante-
dates Shaw's election to the Fabian Society by about three and
a half months.

The proposition which I have to submit to you is That the
Socialistic Movement is only the Assertion of our Lost Honesty.
It will immediately occur to some of you that my notion of
Honesty must be a very strange one. I venture to say, however,
that Honesty is not a subjective impression of yours or mine,
but a condition of social life capable of exact definition. It
means that when one man has worked an hour for another,
that other shall work not less than an hour for him. Among
individuals, each of whom works for himself—produces everything he needs for himself—no question of honesty rises. But
this only occurs in Robinson Crusoe communities of one, because it is a wasteful arrangement. A man can fell trees better
than a woman. A woman can knit stockings better than a man.
Suppose the man can fell two trees whilst the woman is felling
one; and that the woman can knit two pairs of stockings whilst

the man is knitting one. Suppose further that the time occupied by the man in felling the two trees, and by the woman in knitting the two pairs of stockings is one hour. Now if each produces for himself and herself respectively, when the woman wants a tree to burn and a pair of stockings to wear, it will take her an hour to fell the tree, and half an hour to knit the stockings—one hour and a half in all. And the man, under the same necessity, will spend half an hour in felling his tree, and one hour in knitting his stockings—also one hour and a half in all. It costs the man and woman three hours labor to supply themselves with fuel and hosiery. But they can save an hour of this by each working for the other. They require between them two trees and two pairs of stockings. The man can fell the two trees, and the woman knit the four stockings in an hour each. Let them do so, and exchange a tree against a pair of stockings. Each is now supplied as well as before, although they have only worked two hours instead of three. They have gained half an hour's leisure each, and neither has gained it at the expense of the other. The woman has worked half an hour for the man, and he has worked half an hour for her. This is the state of things which the Socialistic movement aims at establishing. Socialism is neither the organization of labor by the State, nor the abolition of competition, nor an equal division of all existing wealth, nor the assertion that one man is as good as another and a great deal better, nor the better housing of the poor, nor a differential income tax, nor a barricade fight in the streets, as many persons seem to believe. These things may be steps towards Socialism, or inevitable results of it, or accidents of it, or mere historical associations with the idea of a change of system; but the essential principle of Socialism is that men shall honestly labor for those who labor for them, each man replacing what he consumes, none profiting at his fellows' expense, and all profiting alike by the most economical division of labor, as in the case of the stockings and the firewood. And if, in that case, the man by threatening to withhold from the woman the use of the axe, or the woman by threatening to withhold the use of her knitting needles, or on any pretext whatever the one force the other to do the largest share of the work necessary to both of them, then Socialism arises as the protest against that unfair proportion and endeavors to adjust it anew. Socialism is loud and earnest just now because the just proportion has been so flagrantly upset that large numbers of able-bodied persons are openly living in idleness and luxury, whilst others, in spite of unremitting toil, cannot attain to even a brute's standard of comfort. This fact shews that some men do not replace what they consume, or, if we call that which a man produces his property, that men take away the property of other men without giving anything in return.

We sometimes use the word "honest" to describe a truthful man or a chaste woman. But we do not describe untruthful men or unchaste women as "dishonest." We should not be understood if we did so. We call them by shorter names; and whenever we speak of a dishonest man or woman we are understood to mean that they are thieves. What is a thief? A thief is one who takes your property and gives you nothing in exchange. It does not follow that everyone who takes your property and gives you nothing in exchange is a thief, because, if you are generous, or charitable, or ostentatious, or in love, you may often consent to such an arrangement, as happens when you make a present, for example. But when your property is taken from you against your will, you are robbed; and the person who takes it is a thief. I have said that the thief takes your property and gives you nothing in exchange. But a thief may give you something in exchange which is of less value than the property he takes. He may take five shillings from you for an article worth only half a crown. In that case he robs you, not of five shillings, but of two and sixpence. But he is none the less a thief because he does not rob you of the whole five shillings. Again, he may give you in exchange something that you dont want. For example, a highwayman of the Claude Duval type gave you, in exchange for your purse, a dash of romance to enliven your prosaic life; a model of address and horsemanship which he assured you was the finest possible model; a gallantry and elegance in conversation which improved your manners (the genius of Fielding has preserved a specimen or two for us); and opportunities of studying the effect of handsome dresses upon other people. All this, if you believed in it and wanted it, was very good value for the contents of an ordinary purse. The highwayman in Tom Jones who relieved Miss Western of her jewels with such grace and wit that she declined to prosecute him, did not really rob her at all. As she liked his gallantry, it had a value in use for her; and as she consented to give him her jewels, it had also a value in exchange. The requisite economic conditions of fair barter being thus complied with, the highwayman was not in that particular transaction a thief. But he robbed the other passengers. They did not appreciate his gallantry, nor did they feel edified by his example. He gave them in exchange for their money the spectacle of a dashing highwayman, which, agreeable as it is on the stage or in a chromolithograph in a juvenile periodical, is about the last thing which any man would desire to witness in a lonely place on a dark night. He gave them something which they didnt want, took something from them against their wills which they did want, and was therefore a thief. I must beg you not to conclude hastily that, because highwaymen of the Duval type no longer exist, the example I have just cited is irrelevant to the social questions of our own time. On the contrary, it is confidently and commonly asserted by many people that the exhibition of personal graces and accomplishments by certain classes of the community is a sufficient return for the property which they forcibly take from certain other classes. The methods of the highway robber are worthy of still further consideration from this point of view.

His profession, for example, was one which involved a considerable outlay of capital, and thereby gave employment to many workmen, and wages to many a poor household. Besides his ordinary human necessities, he required a good horse and weapons. He therefore gave employment to stock raisers, drovers, horse dealers, corn chandlers, agricultural laborers, ostlers, innkeepers, tanners, saddlers, miners, smelters, blacksmiths, whitesmiths, locksmiths, woodcutters, charcoal burners, powder millers, cutlers, carriers, constables, jailers, judges, juries, lawyers, and hangmen, all of whom were to some extent thrown out of employment by his suppression. To us it may seem an act of gross ingratitude and perverse impolicy to hang such a public benefactor. We defend our capitalists on the ground that they are immense employers of labor. In other words, we praise a man for giving a great deal of trouble to other people; and the more trouble he gives the more we praise him. When he employs such a vast number of people from morning to night that it is obvious that he cannot possibly replace the thousandth fraction of the labor he consumes —when he is an open and shameless thief, in short, then, instead of treating him as a public nuisance, we generally send him to parliament to make laws in favor of thieves and thieving. As we are certainly not wilfully anxious to set up such men for the sake of wantonly outraging public morality, we must have in us some idea that a man who forces another to work for him confers a favor on him. Monstrous as this paradox seems, it is tenable in a slave holding state. No man will take the trouble to govern a slave unless he derives some benefit from the labor of that slave. If the slave is useless to him, he will sell him to someone who needs his services. If no one needs them, the slave will be cast out and must die of starvation unless he can find a master, because the masters will let none but their slaves use the sources from which the subsistence of man must be drawn by labor. Hence the slave is under the most desperate necessity to find a master; and where slaves are so plenty that they become a drug in the slave market, they are driven to look upon whoever will take them into servitude as their benefactor, and upon themselves as very lucky in being saved by him from starvation. This is the origin of the popular impression that a great employer of labor is a public benefactor.

England is a slave state in which the slaves are so plenty and so helpless that they are no longer bought and sold in the market as chattels. They are a drug there. No one will buy a slave nowadays—not because he thinks it wrong to do so, but because he can get him for nothing, often without the trouble of asking.

An intelligent inhabitant of Mars, if told that England was a
country in which men who consumed what they did not replace were honored as benefactors to those who produced what
was so consumed, would at once infer that slavery must be an
institution in England, and would set down a person who
should assert that slavery had been abolished there, as either a
fool or a liar. A second paradox which arises in a slave state is
that an idle man, by becoming a worker, inflicts injury on
his fellow creatures. For instance, if a slaveholder, tired of in-
action, does the work of a slave, he throws that slave out of
employment, and consequently deprives him of his means of
subsistence. In England today every lady or gentleman who
volunteers to teach in a school, to sing or play at a concert, to
act as secretary to a society, or to act in any honorary capacity,
injures some professional teacher, artist, or man of business who
would otherwise be engaged and paid for the work. The amateur, in a free and honest community, would benefit the professional (supposing such distinctions still existed) by relieving him
of his duties. In a slave state, relieving him of his duties means
depriving him of his pay, and consequently starving him. Yet
another paradox. In a slave state, where slaves are a drug in the
market, the more extravagant and luxurious the masters are, the
better for the slaves. The master's need is the slave's opportunity. The prodigal needs a host of slaves, and he throws his
land open to them to raise food from on condition that they
will raise all that he desires in addition to what they absolutely
need for themselves. The more he desires, the greater will be
the number of slaves whom he will thus enable to subsist. The
less he desires, the fewer slaves will he enable to exist. Idleness
and luxury thus become virtues in slaveholders. The poor always hate and despise the abstemious aristocrat, and applaud
the spendthrift. The professional man everywhere hates the
amateur who takes a share of his work from him. Such feelings
are perfectly reasonable. Economists have successfully shown
that luxury, and the existence of a rich and idle class in an
honest and free community are unmitigated evils. Persons who
imagine that the English nation is an honest and free community

naturally believe that the economists have shown that the
English poor are mistaken in their admiration of spendthrifts.
Those who know that England is a slave state know that the
poor are right. It is a hackneyed trick of smatterers in economics to prove that breaking a window, though it gives
the glazier a job, does not benefit the community. Yet, if I
could do so with impunity, I would unhesitatingly smash the
windows of every private house rented at a hundred a year and
upwards. In a free and honest community, I should be only
wantonly giving the workers a great deal of unnecessary
trouble. In London I should be the means of forcing the owners
of the materials of production to give an additional number of
slaves access to them, provided I could push my destruction
beyond the point at which it could be remedied by making the
already employed slaves work harder, which I might only too
easily do. Conversely, if I, for example, believing as I do that
tobacco is a nuisance, induced the human race to abandon its
use tomorrow; instead of relieving mankind of a burden of
pernicious toil, I should, by depriving the slave holding class of
one of their incentives to employ slaves, be forcing thousands
of girls now employed in cigar manufacture into prostitution,
and throwing hundreds of thousands of persons employed in
tobacco planting, pipe making, paper making, carrying, distributing, and so forth, destitute upon the streets. The only
possible principle for a dishonest community is "Evil, be thou
my good."

Let us return to our instructive highwayman. It must not be
supposed that because he consumed what he did not replace,
his lot was therefore an easy and a happy one. Consider his
risk! The modern speculator often complains that he risks his
capital at every venture. The highwayman, at every venture,
risked not only his capital, but his life. His anxieties were fearful: only reckless or desperate men took to the road. When he
robbed the Dover mail, he had to face the blunderbuss of the
guard; the pistols of the passengers, with the certainty, if captured, of being flung into a loathsome jail and hung, and the
possibility that, after all, the mail might prove not worth rob-

bing. Will anyone pretend that the risks of the holders of London and North Western Railway stock are comparable to these? Yet we not only hang the highwayman and reward the shareholder, but we sometimes allege that we reward the shareholder for his risk. As both run their risk with the same object —that of escaping their natural liability to replace what they consume—it is not plain that we should treat them on different principles. If our principle be to reward risk, we should give the greater reward to the man who runs the greater risk—to the highwayman in the present case. And we should reward more highly than either the wretches who for a miserable wage are doing at all seasons and at all hours the dangerous work of coupling the London and North Western trains. But we do nothing of the sort. Risk, being unproductive of any benefit to the human race, and thus having no value in use, can have no value in exchange, and cannot therefore be bought or sold. Every man runs risks every day of his life from epidemics, lightning, fire, malice of man and beast, accidental poisoning, and the perils of the streets. No man expects to be paid for running these risks, nor could be paid if he did expect it. A gentleman who wishes to break his neck fashionably may bribe a guide to show him the way to the summit of the Matterhorn. This is a perfectly fair transaction, as the man who is paid for running a risk runs it for the sake of the man who pays him; and the man who runs the risk for its own sake gets nothing but the risk in exchange. A railway shareholder who claims his dividend as reward for risk, or insurance against it, assumes a position analogous to that which a member of the Alpine Club would occupy if he should force a guide to climb the Matterhorn, remain safely in his hotel meanwhile, and subsequently ask the guide to pay him for the risk he had run in his hotel from an avalanche. It is difficult to say how men first conceived the idea that a man deserves payment for running a risk for his own profit or gratification. But it has been encouraged by the popular method of interpreting political economy. For example, Adam Smith, in the 10th chapter of the 1st book of Wealth of Nations, writes, "The ordinary rate of profit always rises more or less with the risk." Adam Smith here simply stated a fact which he had observed. But it is customary to take every economist's statement of fact as propositions in ethics, and the ordinary interpretation of the above passage is, "It is right that man should trade for the sake of profits; and every trader is justified in extorting profit in proportion to the risk he runs of someone else making the profit out of him instead of he out of someone else." When the spread of education brings our standard works on political economy within the ken of all classes, this way of reading them may become even more inconvenient than it is at present. John Stuart Mill, in the 7th Chapter of the 2nd book of his Principles of Political Economy, says, "Day-laborers, where the laboring class mainly consists of them, are usually improvident: they spend carelessly to the full extent of their means, and let the future shift for itself." As soon as the day-laborers begin to read Mill, they will probably in imitation of their so-called betters, assert that he has proved that it is their duty to be reckless, and that the exercise of any forethought on their part would be a violation of the laws of political economy.

Let us return for a moment to our highwayman, in order that we may give him due credit for the valuable individual qualities which his profession required. To rob a mail coach single-handed must have required a degree of hardihood which few except born masters of men possess. Such hardihood, with the endurance of mental anxiety and bodily fatigue which must have accompanied them, are qualities which may be said to be the very roots of the tree of liberty. It seems a pity to discourage them by hanging their possessors. But no quality, however attractive its associations may be, is to be encouraged for its own sake, irrespective of the use to which it is put. The manipulative dexterity which we admire and reward in a locksmith when he secures our safes for us, we dread and punish in the burglar when he breaks our safes open. We can imagine an Archbishop, addressing a young man about to enter on an honorable career, earnestly exhorting him in the words of the great preacher, "Whatsoever thy hand findeth to do, do it with thy might." (Eccl. IX:10.) Can you imagine the Archbishop saying this to a prizefighter? Our admiration of individual qualities is so entirely relative to their effects, that there is hardly one such quality for which there are not two names in current use, each name denoting a mental attitude towards the quality directly the reverse of that indicated by its synonym. A man speaks of his firmness: his wife speaks of his obstinacy. Both mean the same thing objectively. Prudence and avarice are two names for one quality. So are discretion and cowardice. So are propriety and prejudice. So are sound conservatism and pig-headed obstructiveness. So are devoted courage and savage ferocity. So are conscientiousness and squeamishness. And so, in the present day, are order and anarchy. Without multiplying instances, it is plain that no objection or recommendation to any system of social intercourse can be based on the allegation that it encourages or checks any individual qualities whatever. All objections must rest fundamentally on proof that the system encourages or permits individual qualities to act against the welfare of the society as a whole. All recommendations must rest fundamentally on proof that the system restrains individual qualities from so acting, and encourages or, at least, permits them to promote the welfare of the society as a whole. For the same reasons no private course of action can be defended on the ground that remarkable individual qualities are needed to carry it out. The highwayman may be brave, resolute, sagacious, persevering, and even abstinent; but we punish him whenever he exercises these qualities in order to consume what he does not replace. And that which is no defence for the highwayman is no defence for the capitalist and landlord, if they too consume what they do not replace. Let it be understood, however, that we do not punish them for these qualities, but rather for the extraneous quality of dishonesty. A man may exercise all the cardinal virtues honestly as well as dishonestly; and hence we run no danger of discouraging the cardinal virtues by punishing dishonesty. In fact, I have already pointed out that they rank as virtues only on condition of their being exercised honestly. On the other hand, this need not debar our highwayman from calling witnesses to character in order to obtain mitigation of punishment. The popular notion that a well behaved thief is only adding hypocrisy to his other vices is too obviously only an explosion of resentment at the success with which he has imposed on us. If the thief, by giving donations to charitable institutions with the money he has stolen, by patronizing artists, or initiating public improvements, has made unintentional public benefactors of his victims, I apprehend that the public may take a more favorable view of his case than if he had been as anti-social in spending his wealth as in acquiring it. They might even go so far as to let him off scot free. But only on the clear understanding that if they catch him at it again, he need look for no mercy. Any greater leniency than may be consistent with the stamping out of thieving would be an act of rigor towards the rest of the community.

The old commandment against thieving is simply "Thou shalt not steal." This is explicit enough so long as the community who make it a law keep in sight the principle of stealing, which is always that of consuming a product which you do not replace, against the will of the producer. But, though the principle remains constant, the practice varies in its forms; and eventually the constant association of the more direct and unmistakeable of these forms with the words stealing and theft tends to limit the application of such words until they no longer suggest the principle, but only the most easily recognizable forms of the practice. "Thief" no longer suggests a man who steals, but only a man who steals in some particular way. The burglar, the pickpocket, and the shoplifter, exercising their vigilance and address in order to seize and consume products which they do not replace, are stigmatized and punished as thieves. The idle shareholder, consuming the labor of the persons employed by his company, could probably recover damages against any person who should so stigmatize him. Nevertheless he is a thief. The difference between him and the burglar is not at all one of principle, but consists in the fact that when a burglar retires from business (into prison or otherwise) there is so much less burglary in the community. But a shareholder can do no good by withdrawing from his position. If he sells out his shares, he simply puts another thief in the place he formerly occupied. If he forfeits his share and washes his hands of the whole business (supposing that were possible), there will only be so much the more plunder for the other shareholders to divide. "Besides," say the shareholders in their own defence, "idle as we are, but for us the railway would never have been made at all. Without capital, none of the great triumphs of modern engineering could have been carried out. We are necessaries of life, and as such must be paid for. Thieves are not necessary, and therefore there is a wide distinction between us and the thieves." This argument is so absurd that a great many persons are certain to be immensely taken with it, and therefore it may be as well to meet it by granting that capital is necessary to great engineering schemes, and simply pointing out that shareholders are not capital. The point at issue is not whether capital is necessary, but whether capital*ists* are necessary. Let us take the case of a railway, and examine the necessary conditions of making it, in order that we may see whether the intervention of the capitalist is one of those conditions.

In the first place, one man employed in raising food must be able to raise more than is sufficient to keep him alive. Otherwise men would be wholly occupied in food raising, and would have no time for any other work. As soon as the bounty of Nature or the greater economy of the arts of production enable each man to produce the necessaries of life for himself and another, a body of, say, a thousand men, can set five hundred of their number to work from which no return is possible for a long period. Let us suppose that railways have been invented, and their advantages to a community demonstrated. Our thousand men, without other capital than their strength and skill, can at once commence operations. Five hundred, working according to their tastes and capacities as miners, mechanics, surveyors, navigators, founders, engineers, and so forth, can produce all the plant and apply it to the completion of the railway. Whilst so employed, they are fed and clothed by the other five hundred, the incentive to this bargain being the benefit which the railway will ultimately confer upon the whole thousand. In this scheme there is no room for an idle shareholder who wants to eat his cake and have it too. From the procuring of the first scrap of metal from the earth to the pulling of the lever which starts the train, the entire enterprise is due solely to the labor of men working upon the material of Nature. Let us suppose further that it takes five years to make the railway. It may seem hard to the thousand men that they must work for five years without any available return for their labor. But it does not at all matter whether they think it hard or not. Five years expenditure of labor without return is Nature's price for the railway; and if the thousand do not think the terms good enough, they must go without. They might like to be paid for waiting; but Nature will not pay them. They might equally like Nature to save them the trouble of making the railway by enabling them to fly, but as she will not give the necessary wings they must submit to the hardship of providing speedy transit by their own labor. I do not deny that it is a hardship. I sympathize deeply with the idle shareholder who likes his sovereigns to breed as his chickens do. But if they wont breed, I cannot help him. I can only offer him my sympathy, point out that I labor under a similar disadvantage, and recommend him to set to work at once and put a good face upon the niggardliness of Nature.

Although there is no other way of making a railway than that which I have just sketched, there are certain established methods by which the dead loss to the community of five years labor may be made a source of considerable revenue to individuals who have the power of standing between the natural material and the laborer. If an individual, for instance, owns the land from which the food has to be raised, the metals dug, and across which the railway must run, the community cannot make the railway unless he chooses. They will be conscious of their own helplessness in the matter, and the effect of this will be practically that the initiative in undertaking the railway will be left to him. Now, assuming that it is his object to enrich himself at the expense of others—assuming, in short, that he is a modern gentleman, he will deal with the five hundred food producers first, saying nothing whatever to them about the railway, but merely stipulating that, on condition of his permitting them to use his land (which they absolutely must do, or else starve) they shall produce in addition to their own subsistence, subsistence for five hundred other men besides himself, and hand that stock of food over to him as rent. This done, the five hundred others are absolutely at his mercy, as he has their food in his possession. So he makes his own terms with them; and these terms are, that when the railway is made they shall continue to work just as hard as before, and that the increase in production which will result from the greater economy of the railway system shall all go into his pocket. When the railway is finished, the workers are no better off, and he is enormously richer. If he has not sufficient energy to carry out this gigantic theft single handed, he can at any stage sell his power to any person who by a similar abuse has become possessed of the means to buy it. Or he may sell it in shares to a number of persons desirous of thieving on the co-operative system. In a modern industrial state the transaction becomes intricately involved and disguised by transfers of this kind. My typical thousand workers become millions, and my typical monopolist of land thousands of monopolists of food, machinery, and special kinds of skill. But the method by which the laborers are forced to surrender the increment of their labor to idle persons is essentially the same, and never becomes, and never can become, a natural necessity to the construction of railways.

Though there is no place for the idle in any industrial enterprise, there are places of very different degrees of comfort for the workers concerned; and the common practice of rewarding certain kinds of work more than others would appeal strongly to our common sense if it were so carried out as to give the highest reward to the most disagreeable work. For example, it seems reasonable that the man who works like a water rat in the sewers of this city at the risk of his life should be more highly paid for his work than the President of the Royal Academy. We know that this is not the case, and that as a rule the more disagreeable any particular kind of labor is, the cheaper it is; and the public seem satisfied that it should be so. In the case of our railroad, it would be considered unfair to pay the navigator[1] as much for an hour's labor as the engineer. But the duration of time consumed is the only common measure by which work can be valued, and as the labor of the navigator is quite as necessary to the completion of the railway as the labor of the engineer—as, in other words, the engineer's occupation depends quite as absolutely on the navigator as that of the navigator depends on the engineer, there is no reason why one should receive a larger share of the fruit of their joint labor than the other. If a man has sufficient talent to be an engineer, he will qualify himself for the sake of escaping the drudgery of the navvy. If he has not sufficient talent, he had better remain a navvy. The effect of providing an artificial incentive to the mastery of the more highly skilled professions is merely to crowd them with men who have no natural aptitude for them, and who pursue them because they are lucrative or genteel. It drives into the medical profession, the church, and the bar, many ablebodied men who might be employed more suitably to their abilities in working for the macadamization of the land by breaking stones. The education of an engineer costs more than that of a navvy, and as he cannot defray this cost himself, the expense of it falls ultimately on the community, who have a right to expect that he shall repay them by exercising a higher skill than the navvy, who has been self-supporting from his boy-hood, and who owes the community comparatively little. The reward of the engineer's personal exertion in the course of his studies consists in the lighter labor of after years, the gratification of his preference for engineering, and the social considera-tion which his superior culture necessarily commands. Artificial class distinctions disguise natural inequalities to such an extent that they undoubtedly produce a considerable levelling among us, and the removal of this levelling influence might at first sub-divide our loose classifications with a suddenness that might give

1. In England a "navigator" or "navvy" is a unskilled workman, or "ditch-digger."—Ed.

us an impression that society was going to pieces. But we should
soon find our places by our own specific gravity. A more serious objection, from the point of view of the comfortable classes,
would be the impossibility of carrying the division of labor so
far as to throw unskilled labor of the most repulsive kind upon
one despised class. But if the disagreeable labor of a city had to
be shared by all alike, there would certainly follow, first, a
reduction in the quantity to be done owing to individuals'
becoming considerate, as they always do when they have themselves to consider; and, secondly, the intervention of labor saving machinery, by means of which necessary labor may easily
be rendered tolerable to all who are not unreasonably squeamish.

If six hours useful labor exchanges for six hours labor, ten
hours for ten hours, and so forth without regard to the degree
of skill involved, the result is Socialism. If, on the contrary, a
man is fed according to the capacity of his brain instead of that
of his stomach, the result is Individualism, founded on the idea
that the dog who jumps highest shall get the largest bone. If it
be agreed that the greatest among you shall be master of all the
rest, as a mother is the ruler of her child, the result is Despotism. If it be clearly perceived that the greatest among you
shall be servant to all the rest, as a good mother is the servant
and not the tyrant of her child, the result is Christianity, only to
be attained, after Socialism has become a matter of course, by
the utter denial and rejection of Christ in the common sense of
the words. And if you have no discoverable principle whatever, but mere anarchy as of sheep going astray, every one not
to his own way, but wherever the rest happen to shove him, the
result is the present state of things. The lot of a young man of
the middle class today is a sad one. He may, if he be pretty well
off or clever, qualify himself as a doctor, and minister to thieves,
or help them to bring idlers into the world. Or he may become
a lawyer, and, when thieves fall out, come by what is not his
own. Or he may become a clergyman, and explain from the
pulpit that the principles of Moses, Jeremiah, and Christ, were
in the main identical with those of the Postmaster General. If he
be poor, and unable to succeed in a competitive examination for
government appointment, he becomes an office boy at fifteen,

and thenceforth for a pittance which may fail him at any financial crisis, counts the money of thieves and gamblers for the rest of his abject life, they being so absolutely his masters that he dare not write a letter to a newspaper or take part in a public meeting without their approval. In his early manhood he joins the ranks of the volunteers, and learns to protect his master's interests against his own. Later on he marries, and his wife enters on her career as a nursery drudge. All this constitutes what he calls his respectability, which he jealously guards and hands on to his son, who sometimes brings down his grey hairs with sorrow to the grave by preferring to take his chance of a field marshal's baton by enlisting in the artillery. I should recommend him to become a Socialist instead. He would probably repudiate my advice, as those who owe least to the present system are generally the most afraid of losing that little by doing anything to upset it.

In conclusion, I may remark that there is no necessity for any person to become a Socialist, or to trouble himself or herself about the movement in any way. Even the poor and miserable like to be told that their misery cannot be helped, as the assurance relieves them from the troublesome responsibility of doing anything to better themselves. Much more do the prosperous like to be told that their prosperity is equally inevitable. It is thus that the standard fatalist economy is popular with all classes, and Socialism only acceptable to the few who have a superabundance of energy to work off, and who appreciate the luxury of what is called honest indignation. But the socialist economy is at bottom equally fatalistic. Evolution does not cease because the majority do not understand Darwin or believe in him; and you may have the lowest opinion of Karl Marx and his school without retarding in the least the operation of the forces which they have invited your attention to. If those forces happen to grind you to powder—which is quite possible—you may console yourself with the reflection, that, insofar as you have been a true child of your century, and have been faithful to its principles and moved by its aspirations, the sooner you are ground to powder the better the world will be for those whom you leave behind.

II   The New Radicalism

Shaw's diary for October 8, 1887, con-
tains the note, "Began article on 'The
New Radicalism' for one of the re-
views." Further notes indicate that he
worked on the article steadily up until
October 18. For whatever reason the piece seems never to have
been published. The Liberals had resigned in 1885 after the fall
of Khartoum. They won the next general election, but Glad-
stone's first Home Rule Bill of 1886 split the party and brought
to power a Conservative-Unionist government under Lord Salis-
bury that held office until 1892.

It is perhaps only candid to say at the outset that the new
Radicalism is Socialism. To call it so would be needless cruelty
to the many progressively minded persons who cannot bear
the name, though they are clamoring for the thing more or less
intelligently at every political discussion, public or private, in
England. By progressively minded persons I do not mean Radicals only; for even the progressively minded person is apt to
call himself after the party of his father or his uncle, and enrol
himself as Conservative, Liberal, Radical, or what not, rather
by the accident of birth than by appropriate conviction. Much
less confusion arises from this than might be expected; for none
of the recognized political parties stand committed to any principle that would not be applauded by all mankind, so that in
effect there are no appropriate convictions to clash. All are for
liberty, for order, for the cultivation of a manly independence
of character in the units of the people, and, generally, for the
true interests of the English people. In the sacred names of these
will your Liberal pass Coercion Acts when in office, and shriek
at them when out; your Conservative in the like vicissitude will

interfere with private enterprise wholesale and then preach laisser-faire as passionately as Mr Herbert Spencer or his *reductio ad absurdum* Mr Auberon Herbert; and your Radical will in the same breath denounce landlordism and advocate measures for turning all the leaseholders in the country into landlords; and all this without shocking the public sense of political consistency. This would be amusing to the Socialist if it cost nothing in human suffering. Even as it is, he can hardly help chuckling as he sees his calumniators writhing under irresistible economic pressure into a blundering, half grandmotherly, half despotic interference with individualism, coming upon the platform to talk of thrift, self-help, co-operation, temperance, and steady industry, and then going into the cabinet to pass Factory Acts, Truck Acts, Mines Regulation Acts, Education Acts, Employers' Liability Acts, Allotment Acts, every one of which would be monstrous violations of political principle and individual liberty if the workers whom they shield were really in the free and independent position implied by the speeches about thrift, industry, and so on. Occasionally Mr Leonard Courtney, or some obscurer politician who, in a bygone paroxysm of self-culture, has read Mill's Essay on Liberty, rises to protest that "self-regarding actions" should not be interfered with, and is greeted with a cheer from some belated amateur of Manchester economics, who was taught in his youth to believe that government must not meddle with industry, and who fears that the world has been going mad ever since. But "self-regarding actions" and the notion that two such vital organs as the industrial and governmental can act independently in the body politic, have gone the way of other superstitions; and those who still harp on them cut a melancholy figure even in the eyes of their venal supporter, the plutocrat turned parliament man, though he perhaps is actuated rather by an instinctive sense that political principle cannot in the long run be friendly to plutocratic interests, than by any perception of the unsoundness of the form in which the principle is presented. However that may be, the fact remains that with the exception of a few obsolete doctrinaires of whom the most sincere and

consistent, Mr Auberon Herbert, is admittedly the most hopelessly impossible politician among us, there is not, outside the
ranks of socialism, a man in our public life who has a policy, as
distinct from a programme, to offer either to the well-to-do
class or to the vast proletariat whose spoliation and degradation
are called the wealth and prosperity of England.

The worst of it is that there is now no public man who will
face the workers and say, "Your position is atrocious; but I
have no remedy. I do not see any way out; and I believe there
is no such way: the poor we must have always with us." The
average public man only alludes to the misery of the people
when his party is out of office; and then his remedy is to put
that party into office. When the people, by way of trying something new, try that remedy, the subject of their grievances is
promptly dropped until the ousted party takes it up. Meanwhile the men in power become eloquent about thrift, industry,
and sobriety, as the true remedies for poverty. The elevation of
the masses, it is pointed out, can never be achieved without the
elevation of the units; and whilst the units save nothing, shirk
work, and are addicted to drink, such elevation is impossible. Of
the ignorance, folly, and mendacity of all this as applied to the
case of men living, not on the full fruit of their own labor; but
on the fragment of it that they are allowed to keep as the market price of their strength and skill, commodities which are now
so cheap that unemployed men are constantly offering them for
nothing but their bare brute subsistence, and cannot find a purchaser even at that, the workers are angrily conscious, though,
being no economists, they cannot explain the matter, nor indeed, if they could, would their complacent counsellors to thrift
either understand or attend to them. And so, at any given time,
there are in practical politics only two received positions as to
the misery of the people. One—the Ministerial theory—is that it
is greatly exaggerated, and that the people have themselves to
thank for it. The other—the Opposition theory—is that it is all
the fault of the government, and can be at once dealt with by
turning them out. Today we have the misery of the Irish
peasant well to the front. Mr Balfour's theory is that the Irish

people would be perfectly happy and contented if his opponents would only let them alone. Sir William Harcourt's theory is that nothing better could be expected with Mr Balfour instead of Sir William Harcourt as Secretary for Ireland. And so the St Stephen's merry-go-round twirls away, with music of percussion instruments on the head of the Irish peasant.

Nothing that is occurring just at present so effectively illustrates the atrocious frivolity of ordinary politics as the sincere enthusiasm with which English party men are advocating Home Rule in a home-ruled country where nevertheless the real evils that oppress the Irish are too common to be worth a party man's notice. The Irishman may be excused for attributing his misery to foreign rule: the two phenomena coexist in Ireland; and their true relation, for all he knows, may be that of cause and effect. But what is to be said of the Englishman, who, if he lives in any of our vortices of population, need not walk a mile to see, among hordes of desperately industrious people, such sordid squalor and grinding poverty as these fighting tenant farmers across St George's channel do not believe possible. If the Unionists dared, they might point to the English laborer as a terrible example of the depths to which Home Rule can sink a people. It is evident that Home Rule by itself can do nothing; and it is equally evident that its English advocates have no idea beyond Home Rule—would even protest with all their might against that total repudiation of proprietary claims without which the propertyless Irishman can never hope to be free. In short, Home Rule is not a policy, or part of one: it is a monomania; and that, it would seem, is just why it has made such way. Mr Parnell and his followers, for instance, have held their way as pure monomaniacs. If they have an ulterior policy, they have kept it to themselves with unexampled reticence. To this day, no man can point to a single statesman in the Irish parliamentary party. True, they may be only waiting until the lists are prepared for them at College Green; but in the meantime one can only guess that Mr Parnell would lead the Conservative party against Mr Davitt, and that the whole business of the state would have to be provisionally entrusted to a cabinet of

disbanded agitators, with Mr Arthur O'Connor to tell them
what to do.

It cannot be said, however, that Home Rule is peculiar in
respect of being pursued as a monomania. It is our habit to
proceed from monomania to monomania in the order in which
they turn up on the list called the party programme, or on the
orders of the day in the House of Commons. We gain by this
plan intense concentration: what we lose is all certainty as to
the direction in which we are proceeding, and as to the remoter
results of our measures. Tradition and habit count for a great
deal; but their effect is to turn the old parties topsy turvy. The
Conservative is by habit and tradition a strengthener of the
hands of the government; but his persistence in this after the
state has become democratic makes a state socialist of him. The
Radical is by tradition and habit an upholder of the rights of
the individual against state authority; and his persistence after
the enfranchised individual has become a unit of the state makes
him an individualist reactionist. On the whole, what with our
old traditions and new circumstances; our plutocrat legislators
trained in nothing but the art of organizing the labor of the
masses for the benefit of the classes; our acceptance of hero worship, monomania, and partisanship as policy and statecraft; and
our ideal cabinet consisting of a lord, a smart debater, a block-
head, and a successful tradesman (representing gentility, brains,
the national character, and our great industries) with the necessary padding of experienced office seekers to do the hard work,
it is not wonderful that the Opposition is never at a loss to
substantiate the charges of vulgarity, imbecility, cruelty, mismanagement and muddle upon which it demands the dismissal
of the Government, and on which it will in due course be dismissed when it has had its turn of office. Naturally, men of
character and ability turn their backs on practical politics, and
are absorbed by science, philosophy, literature, or the fine arts.
Socialism greatly covets these men; but at present it has nothing to offer them but preaching the same weary sermon at the
street corner on Sunday morning in summer, and at the workman's club, very ill ventilated and occasionally not too clean,

on Sunday evenings all the year round. Ordinary people neglect the simple and obvious political duty of registering their claim to vote except when they are urged to do it, and all the trouble undertaken by the agents of interested parties. The wage worker, as yet unaccustomed to his vote and unconscious of its power, chooses between the Whig brewer and the Tory lordling, or whatever else the offered alternatives may be, with the frankest disbelief in the political superstition that the Liberal is the popular as opposed to the Conservative or anti-popular party. And the average man of business, as well as the average economist, regards it as a truism that the State, by its inherent predisposition to jobbery, corruption, extravagance, and official incompetence, must not be allowed to undertake a bakery for the starving unemployed, but must rigidly restrict itself to imperial diplomacy, and the maintenance of an armed force to prevent the unemployed setting up bakeries for themselves. And the whole confusion is accurately reflected by the newspapers. Even those which are on the brink of socialism, and are alternately dipping their toes in the rising flood, and recoiling to try whether some sort of embankment cannot be made out of the ten commandments, repeatedly lose their heads and mistake the shore for the sea. For example, last session, some section of the Scotch landlords complained bitterly that certain other landlords had ousted them in the division of the spoils of the cultivator. Dick Turpin, in fact, had outwitted Tom King. Yet some of the most sincerely popular journals were almost as indignant at the woes of Tom King as at those of the victims of the Bodyke evictions. The disappointment of a section of the proprietary class still seemed to them to have a prior claim on an assembly overwhelmed with business that urgently concerned the whole nation.

Meanwhile, the winter is upon us, and the unemployed are with us. The unemployed are socialists in summer, revolutionists in winter. Mr Giffen has proved to them that if they were all skilled men in full work at full wages, they would be better off than if they had happened to be their own grandfathers. But "ifs and ans" not being pots and pans, that will not pass

with them. Mr Giffen also tells them that the capital to which
they look for employment is going abroad at the rate of from
forty to sixty million pounds sterling per annum, and that "the
question to be investigated is not that of the diminution, but of
the increase, of our investments abroad." "There is no question
at all," he adds, "of the nation bringing home capital," though
there certainly is grave question of the nation bringing home
Polish Jews and Germans to compete in the labor market, not
to mention its own increasing brood. Nobody believes that the
foreigner will continue to send us his raw material to be manufactured here now that the huge rent of our natural abundance
of iron and coal is disappearing as the exhaustion of the easier
pits makes the working more expensive, and the discovery of
fresh stores of mineral wealth in America and elsewhere so
raises the margin of cultivation that coal mines have been abandoned in England as well as farms. Our start in the organization
of industry is gone now: we had no patent of our system; and
the foreigner copies it as he requires it. Theoretically, it is easy
to resort to emigration and send the worker after the capital,
leaving England, with a population of proprietors and their
attendants, to sink to the level of Monaco. Practically, it is impossible, because capital can flourish in climates where Englishmen die. These facts are naturally kept before the workers by
the socialist leaders, and it is probable that the first remedy that
will occur to the ruling classes is the strict gagging and incar-
ceration of the socialist leaders. Fortunately, such a step will no
more stop the publication of the evil than it will avert the evil
itself. Protectionists, Fair Traders, and Cobdenites blunder on
the truth at every step of their controversies. In the same way,
when the socialist draws for his audience, with unfailing effect,
the tell tale comparison between the death rates of the idle rich
and of the industrious poor, he is only doing what the insurance
companies and the sanitary reforms would be doing with greater
authority if he were safe in Holloway Gaol. He is teaching his
demonstrations of the futility of Whig reforms to the Tories,
his indictment of Conservative abuses to the Whigs, knowing
that they will keep them before the public for party purposes if

he be silenced, and deepening the conviction of the people that
there is no way out of the present miserable muddle except
through socialism. Under these disquieting circumstances, how
are the unemployed to be appeased? Certainly not with words—
not even words of which they recognize the good sense—when
hunger and cold are gnawing them. Probably every person in
the gallery of the Exeter Theatre knew the danger of rushing
to the doors in a panic as well as we who read the wise reflec-
tions of the press after the event. But that did not enable them
to sit still with the fire licking their flesh. And what hope does
any established political party hold out to these men? Is the
hope of a "revival of trade," which all parties resort to, accompanied by a convincing exposition of any newly discovered
natural spring of wealth which will bring back to our market
the nations who have learned to buy their coal and iron elsewhere, or any new development of skill, knowledge, or natural
aptitude that will enable the badly educated and slum deteri-
orated English worker to beat back the German and American
in the workshop and counting house? Is there even any evidence
that the public men who are so glib upon trade revivals and
depressions really know what they are talking about? Then
come the old fashioned so-called Radical remedies for the
hunger of the people. There is the abolition of that terrible million (in round numbers) thrown away on the Royal Family,
and that monstrous £15,000 a year to the Archbishop of Canterbury, and the perpetual pensions. But the socialist has been
at work; and the workman, formerly aghast at these sums, now
contemptuously tolerates them in their insignificance beside the
great perpetual pension of two hundred millions a year to the
idle landlords; two hundred and fifty millions to the idle capitalists, not to mention three hundred and fifty millions to the
active capitalists, employers, salaried, official, and professional
classes, who do not start fair in the race for earnings with the
wage worker. Then there is the church to be disestablished;
but here again you have your workman alive at last to the fact
that disestablishment would not add the endowment to his
wages, even if it were ostensibly applied to make education

"free," but to rent and interest, upon which, in the long run,
all taxation ultimately falls. To disendow public churches in
order to endow private ones,—perhaps to endow racecourses
and brothels (popularly supposed to be the favorite objects of
expenditure among the proprietary classes) is as little to the
workman's taste as any political work can be; for he never was
in the least enthusiastic about the disestablishment except when
he was persuaded by some public orator of average economic
ignorance that the Church's income would be added to his own
and those of his mates. The constitution of the House of Lords
is so revoltingly anomalous even to the meanest intelligence
that an enthusiastic approval of its abolition is generally obtain-
able as a matter of intellectual conviction from all popular
audiences. But the applause sometimes increases when the orator
proceeds to suggest the abolition of the House of Commons,
that being practically a chamber of landlords, railway lords,
beer lords, mine lords, newspaper lords, and money lords, every
one of whom is personally interested in reducing the workman's
share of the annual produce of the national industry so that the
shares taken as rent, interest, and profit may be the greater.
Whilst these men govern, the House of Lords does not greatly
matter, since they govern that too, in the long run. Such Conservative measures as the establishment of peasant proprietorship interest the people more, because they pretend to touch the
industrial question, which is now the only question that the
people care about. But English artisans, unskilled in agriculture,
trained to co-operate in a system of production by minutely
subdivided labor, and therefore individually incapable of any
complete act of production, meet the socialists more than half
way in their denunciations of any such foolish attempt to begin
individualism all over again. A far better bait for our town
populations is ordinary co-operation, which is the only method
of realizing socialism without legislation still supported by economists of any credit. It is however not only impracticable but
theoretically unsound. Its impracticability lies in the impossibility of bodies of workmen succeeding in modern industry without capital or credit. Credit they cannot obtain, because under

existing conditions commercial credit attaches only to property
and to individual skill in what is called "employing" or "ex-
ploiting," according to the point of view of the speaker. Capital
they can only obtain by saving out of their wages. Now the
wage workers of this country are estimated at about 14 millions
including women and children. The trades unionists, who are
the *haute volée* of this class, number only 600,000 men, and
their ordinary wages run from eighteen to thirty shillings a
week. To work as hard as these men work and yet save a shilling a week out of the wage is only possible either to heroes or
to men with whom saving is a disease and meanness a morbid
luxury: yet it would take the hero or miser nearly forty years
to save £100 in this way. If he successfully hastened the process
by using his first accumulations to set up as a sweater, he would
eventually extend his business and do what he could to prevent
co-operation. But let it be granted that a body of exceptionally
situated workmen do succeed in acquiring the capital necessary
to start a co-operative business. Let it even be assumed that they
purchase the freehold of their premises, and so escape the usual
confiscation of the good will of their business by the landlord
at the expiration of the lease. If they now succeed, their business extends; and they require additional labor to carry it on.
Naturally, instead of admitting the additional men as co-
operators, they simply hire them for wages and sweat them in
the usual fashion. Before long, if the concern still prospers, they
will hire wage workers or salaried men to do their own share of
the work. This completes the metamorphosis of the industrious
co-operator into an idle joint stock capitalist, in which condition he is held up as an example of the benefits of thrift, instead
of the fatality with which our individualist system overrules all
valuable industrial qualities for evil, the reward of success being
invariably that power of living at free quarters without effort
which paralyses all individual incentive to effort. Co-operation,
in short, is one of the quack remedies suggested by the fact
that property is directly mischievous to all except the proprietors. Hence the advocate of peasant proprietorship proposes
to make the tenant farmer a present of his own farm. The social

reformer who sees the great ground landlords swallowing the London leaseholder can see nothing for it but to make the leaseholder a landlord. Just so the co-operator, aghast at the way in which capitalism grinds the worker, is convinced that the way out of the difficulty is to make every workman a capitalist.

Here then is the position. The status quo is intolerable: the mildest conservative assents to that as promptly as the rabidest anarchist. Republicanism, democracy, and the old-fashioned radical programme are useless without socialism. Protection does not protect the worker, and is economically ridiculous. Free Trade without socialism is theoretically certain to throw England out of cultivation in the long run, unless her workers achieve the physical impossibility of producing more and consuming less than any other nation in the world market. Malthusianism is more impracticable than ever now that it is evident that population is pressing, not on the means of subsistence, but on what used to be called the wage fund before economists grew ashamed of the misrepresentations based on it, and dropped it. In short, there is nothing for it but socialism; and the new Radicalism is simply practical socialism as opposed to the catastrophic Utopian Socialism of which we are all—not without reason—so much afraid.

The way to realize socialism in this country has been hidden by the tradition which insists on bloodshed as an indispensable formality on occasions of social revolution. Sentimental socialists entertain this notion quite as obstinately as their opponents; and unfortunately, though a reasonable politician can dispose of it to the perfect satisfaction of any working class audience in five minutes, it is generally combated by ridiculous homilies intended to prove that all shedding of blood and destruction of property is immoral. Coming from the advocates of a commercial system in which employers have to be forced by legal penalties to take the simplest and cheapest precautions against the maiming and poisoning of their workpeople, in which the proprietor calls bludgeon and bayonet to his aid without the smallest scruple whenever the proletarian hesitates before he yields to the landlord the food for which his own children are crying, and within which every separate state is armed to the teeth and in chronic danger of war, these homilies are justly derided as Pecksniffian; and if there were no better arguments against a rising and rush, the rising and the rush would have been accomplished by this time. But the fact is that the application of the Garibaldian method is very limited. A fight settles nothing except which party is to have its own way afterwards. Consequently it is useless to fight until you know your own way. What restrains the socialist from violence at present is not the reflection—"Suppose we should be beaten," but "Suppose we should be victorious! What then?" Evidently the precipitation of the most tremendous job that ever appalled a statesman, with productive industry interrupted in a country living from hand to mouth, and the people out of control, impatient for the anticipated millennium, and quite unfamiliar with the necessary measures, many of which would seem to them treacherous attempts to reestablish the state of things they had just been at the trouble of upsetting. It is with something between a laugh and a shudder that one tries to imagine a too successful agitator beginning his collectivist Utopia the day after the revolution. Fortunately the really influential socialists know this, and are able to explain to the workers the necessity for patience, which they are willing enough to admit, though they will not hear of forbearance. For example, the moment they are convinced that the millionaire took his million by force from them without rendering them any equivalent, they will not be restrained from taking it back by protests against plunder which only seem to them to fortify their case. But if some person of whose candor and sympathy they entertain no doubt explains to them that the millionaire at any given moment may very possibly not possess a twopenny piece or a loaf of bread, and that his million simply means his power to take about £140 out of what they and their fellows are going to produce next day—if they be further reminded that the accumulated wealth available for popular consumption, though it seems inexhaustible when heaped together in the hands of a few persons, would not give a quota worth scrambling for if it were divided among the millions—that, in short, though we have a prosperous class among us, we are a miserably poor nation, then the workers who are inclined to try a rush come to their senses; admit that a rush would not settle the matter; and demand what is the practical thing to do. This is the position of affairs at present; and the socialists are recruiting extensively among people of all classes who held aloof before because they understood a baptism of fire and blood to be an essential preliminary to the realization of the socialist ideal. At the same time, the old radicals, alarmed by the secessions from their ranks to those of the socialists, and in particular by the action of the Northumberland miners in practically repudiating as useless their own non-socialist representatives in the House of Commons, are seeking a programme sufficiently socialistic in everything but the name to enable them to dish their rivals. The question is, what is this neo-radicalism to be?

In the first place, it must be a continuous policy for developing our existing institutions into socialistic ones, and not a catastrophic policy for simultaneously destroying existing institutions and replacing them with a ready-made Utopia. Our industries are at present partly individualistic, partly collectivist, partly communistic: no scheme has yet been suggested of which there is not a nucleus in working order among us. The individualistic industries are those which are left to the private enterprise of the proprietary class and of the professional employers who, for the sake of profit (excess of the total produce over wages + rent + interest), undertake the exploitation of the separate properties. The collectivist industries are those which, like the postal and telegraph services, are organized by the state, but depend on payments by individuals for the services rendered. Practically this is a tolerably convenient system, though it is theoretically unjust, as it compels, for instance, the writers of letters and telegrams to defray the whole cost of an institution which enormously benefits people who never write at all. The provision of penny, halfpenny, and farthing dinners in board schools is another eminently successful experiment in collectivism. Education in board schools is collectivist as far as the school pence pay for it, communist as far as it falls on the

rates. Our purely communist institutions are surprisingly extensive considering the number of presumably educated persons
who are still ready to make themselves conspicuously foolish by
making speeches about "the livid spectre of communism." Our
national defences, our police, our street paving and lighting, our
bridges and embankments are provided at the common charge,
and enjoyed alike by the industrious citizen and the thriftless
vagabond. Of these three systems, the only one that has proved
incorrigibly mischievous is the individualistic private enterprise
system. Collectivism and communism have been so successful
that, in spite of the flagrant corruption and mismanagement
which disgraces those public departments where the officials are
practically irresponsible and irremoveable, the most extreme individualists cannot deny the growing faith in State enterprise
which they are hopelessly deploring. A movement for the re-
sumption of tolls and turnpikes would be scouted as retrograde.
A proposal to abolish board school dinners on the ground that
the private cookshops would cater more efficiently for the
children would stamp its author as a fool. The gentlemen who
occasionally protest against the post office monopoly, and point
out that private enterprise could easily carry ounce letters
within the four mile radius for a farthing apiece are ignorant of
the doctrine of comparative profits, and have no idea that carrying the letters of the nation at the cheapest rate is not compatible with carrying each separate letter at the lowest charge that
will cover the expense of its particular transmission. The extent
to which private enterprise in carrying goods, with its charges
for freight varying capriciously according to the circumstances
of various railway companies, hampers trade in this country,
compared to the way in which the uniform rates of the German State railways have facilitated it abroad, has set on foot an
agitation for "nationalization" of railways here and in America
which will end in the establishment of the collectivist system in
all our traffic departments.

   We have then communism successfully established among us
and showing no sign of giving place to private enterprise. We
have collectivism established, growing, popular, and beating

private enterprise at all points where the competition of the two is not arbitrarily restrained. We have private enterprise execrated by the people, and only prevented from grinding them out of existence by a number of anomalous statutes of the Factory Acts type, which are anti-individualistic without being socialistic, and which operate so confusedly that they are sometimes almost as great a nuisance to those whom they protect as to those whom they restrain. This is inevitable on anti-individualist non-socialist lines, since the State from that point of view practically says, "We shall neither organize the national industry ourselves nor let you alone when you organize it." Private enterprise cannot retort by threatening to leave the State to organize for itself; for State organization is so certain to vanquish it in competition that it will submit to almost any molestation in the shape of Factory Acts on condition that it is to be protected from state competition in spite of all sound economic principles. Nothing indeed is more stimulating to the ironic sense than the preposterous appeals to free contract, free competition, free trade, and laisser-faire in support of this outrageous protection allowed to the monopoly of industrial organization by private proprietors against the people organized as the State. Of course the secret of it has been that the State has not hitherto been the people organized for economic production and just distribution, but the proprietors organized to keep up rent, interest, and profit, and keep down wages. But the extension of the franchise has changed that; and there are plenty of propagandists on foot making the people conscious of the power the change has given them. The first thumb rule of legislation that they will sweep away is the dogma that the State must not compete with private enterprise. It was sound class economy; but it was utterly rotten national economy; and the new rule will be that it is the duty of the State to compete with all its might in every department of production until the maxima of industrial efficiency and national welfare are attained. In this process the political organization now controlled by the enfranchised workers will become an industrial organization; and the moment the workers have an industrial organization under their control and therefore operating in their interest, they are masters of the situation.

The conditions to be observed in bringing this about are: one, since the parliamentary method is the only one we understand or believe in, the policy must be initiated in parliament; two, that since the industrial machinery must be kept constantly working whilst it is being readjusted, the series of changes must be gradual, so as not to throw the machine out of gear; three, that work must be provided for the unemployed at once, as their case admits of no delay and their temper is growing daily more threatening.

The moment there is any question of developing our political organs into industrial organs, it becomes evident that nothing can be done at first with the Imperial parliament. It cannot do its present duties, much less the additional ones that such a change would impose upon it. The new industrial organs must be developments of the corporations, municipal councils, vestries, boards of works, boards of guardians, and the like, already situated at the centres of population throughout the country. Of these as compared with the central organ, the worker has no great opinion so far, since under existing circumstances they mean little more to him than oppression, corruption, and incompetence nearer home. Consequently he is not so enthusiastic as he ought to be on the subject of Local Self-Government, which is really the question of all questions in practical politics today, and will be the great charter of the New Radicalism. But when the far reaching socialistic nature of a complete measure is explained to him, he will probably make a point of it as obstinately as his grandfather made a point of the Reform Bill of 1832. What, then, would be a complete and satisfactory measure of local self-government? Simply one that would enable local authorities, elected by adult suffrage without poverty disqualification of any kind (the pauper's is the most valuable of votes), to engage in all departments of industry in full competition with private enterprise, hampered only by the necessary Local Government Board regulations as to hours of labor, overtime, and possibly a minimum wage, but aided by powers of taxing rent, and of compulsorily acquiring land for its purposes at a reasonable price from the present private holders. In short, that they might do in all departments of public industry what they are now allowed to do in a few by special acts which have been practically subject to the veto of the representatives of the private proprietors, and which of course have only been allowed to pass on condition of maintaining the system of protection of private and proprietary as against public and proletarian interests. Such a measure would meet the conditions laid down above. It would not only be parliamentary; but its title of "Local Self-Government" is already familiar and reputed innocent by politicians of established credit. Yet it is a measure that would finally effect the revolution which all who are not living in a fool's paradise know to be inevitable—witness Mr Giffen's remarkable declaration even in the midst of a paroxysm of statistical optimism that "no one can contemplate the present condition of the masses of the people without desiring something like a revolution for the better." It would be gradual in its operation, as the local authorities could only extend their business step by step, beginning with those works the public character of which is recognized by custom, such as gas supply, water supply, tramways and the like, these also being the fittest to absorb not only the unemployed, among whom there are always plenty of laborers, but those already employed persons who are being ground to premature death in sweaters' dens, their rescue from which is no less important than provision for those who cannot find even a sweater to employ them. And as the sweater would thus find his wretched occupation of slavedriving paid by piecework gone, municipal employment would have to be found for him too. But this would hit the large employers, part of whose profits are wrung for them by the sweater out of the poorest class of workers; and these employers, finding themselves compelled to outbid the municipal wage in order to win the workers back, would make a terrible outcry about their imminent ruin and the destruction of their trades. But as they could not outvote the workers at the municipal elections, they would at last take the economically sound position that their profits must be maintained and that the increase in wages must be met by reducing the landlord's rent and the capitalist's interest, which would be perfectly satisfactory to those employers who, working with borrowed capital, were really making nothing but the value of their skill as managers—the rent of their ability, as it has been appropriately called. Eventually the municipality would outbid the landlords and capitalists for the services of these "employers." Meanwhile a grievous lamentation would go up from the landlords and capitalists—the livers on absolutely unearned incomes. With the employers unable to pay the old rents, with the rate of interest falling, with the municipality on the other hand deliberately and remorselessly throwing taxation specially on rent and interest, the infamous, useless, selfish profession of idle lady or gentleman would grow more and more precarious until finally it would become impossible, and all might say, with Hamlet, "Then is the world grown honest." The squeezing out of this class would be free from the cruelty which attends similar processes today when they occur as the accidents of competitive private enterprise. At worst, the "ruined" gentlefolk could fall no further than into municipal employment: the abysses into which they now fall daily—the sweater's den, the copyist's seat in the British Museum library, or the streets—would be filled up.

III Freedom and the State

The occasion of this "chapter" is uncertain. The reference to the July 1888 issue of Commonweal *suggests that it was probably written a few months after that date. Possibly these are the opening pages of the book on socialism that Shaw's diary mentions he was writing for Sutton's University Series on November 14, 1888. The manuscript is headed "Socialism and Property." Since, however, that designation is broad enough to cover most of the lectures and essays in this collection I have taken the liberty of giving it a new and more specific title.*

There is no divine right of property. Nothing is so completely a man's own that he may do what he likes with it. His very limbs, intimately as they belong to him, he may not use to the injury of society, much less his knife, his stick, or "anything that is his." Not only may he not use them malevolently: he must not use them even carelessly and indifferently except at his own peril if harm ensue. Exceptionally dangerous substances, such as poisons and explosives, he can only obtain and possess under exceptionally stringent conditions.

Nevertheless, as it is obviously well that each man should labor without fear of being deprived of the use and enjoyment of the product of their labor—as in the nature of things he would not labor at all without some such incentive, it may be said that a man has a natural right to own the product of his labor. The term natural right, if old fashioned, is as much to the purpose as any modern expression of the same meaning. But this natural right of the individual is still subject to all the limitations imposed by the rights of his fellows. A person may not make a weapon and then slay another with it on the ground that the weapon was his and he had a right to use it as he pleased. Nor would he at all mitigate his punishment by proving that the contrivance and fashioning of the weapon had cost him great ingenuity, laboriously acquired skill, toil, abstinence or self-denial. All these things, admirable as they are when exercised towards a good end, are but a diabolic malignity when exercised murderously; and a simpleton who committed homicide in a moment of passion with a stone snatched from the roadside would be more willingly pardoned. The natural right of property goes no further than this—that "every man has freedom to do all that he wills" with his own "provided he infringes not the equal freedom of any other man."[1]

The freedom here affirmed is a barren one. It passed for something when men believed that there were certain actions, called "self-regarding," which affected only the person performing them. But the minute division of labor in modern communities with the consequent interdependence of the individuals forming it; the extension of sanitary science and of the knowledge of heredity; the pressure upon space in modern cities and the complexity of the organization needed to subsist their huge populations, have swept away the "self-regarding action" into the limbo of decaying superstitions. There is no conceivable human action of which it can now be confidently affirmed that it will affect no one except the agent, or that the agent's freedom to do it will "infringe not the equal freedom of any other man." Consequently "freedom" in this sense may be dismissed as a mere dialectical figment, of which the very expositions—Stuart Mill's Essay on Liberty and Mr Spencer's Social Statics, for example —are now patent reductions to absurdity. Theoretically, since there are no indifferent actions, there is for every man a rigid line of conduct from which he cannot swerve one hair's breadth in the minutest detail without injury to the community; and if the community could ascertain that line it would be justified in compelling him to keep to that line, to the entire abolition of his "freedom." Conscientious educated men seek the guidance

1. Herbert Spencer, Social Statics, London, 1867.

of that line throughout their lives, and never for a moment think
of themselves as free agents.

So much for the theory of "liberty." Like other abstract
superficialities it has done good service in its day. At present it
is a cast off garment of eighteenth century sociology, and is
being fast worn out by the "individualist anarchists," of whom
more later on. But it must not be hastily inferred that because
there is no such thing as socially indifferent conduct, every
action of a man's life can be dictated and supervised by the collective wisdom, a conclusion to which the collective folly is apt
to rush headlong. It is true that such dictation is carried to a
much greater extent than most people seem aware of. It is still
common for persons to rise during discussions of socialism to
object that it would lead to society dictating what individuals
should eat, drink, and wear. It is evident on such occasions that
the objector sincerely believes that he is at present free in these
particulars. Facetious socialists are accustomed to dispel this
illusion by challenging him to walk from Piccadilly to Hyde
Park corner on any fine afternoon in May or June, wearing a
white hat turned up with green, and carrying a scarlet umbrella.
There are many parts of the kingdom where even yet only
persons of exceptional independence of character dare to be
teetotallers; and, outside a few of our great towns, the difficulties of the vegetarian are insuperable by the average man. Every
woman who voluntarily wears a strait corset and high heels not
only gratifies her own vanity; but helps to force corsets and
high heels upon other women who abhor them. For though a
duchess may wear what she likes, and a ragpicker must wear
what she can, the ordinary woman must appear in the drawingroom, or behind the counter, or in the workroom wearing, not
what she likes to wear, but what she is expected to wear. A law
forbidding high heels and stays, if it could be enforced, would
be denounced as an outrageous violation of a woman's liberty to
wear what she pleases. But as the woman has practically no
such liberty, it might very conceivably be found that the effect
of the law was to confer on sensible women the power of leaving off a uniform which they detested. The notion that the

absence of legislation means the absence of compulsion is an old fallacy of anarchism. Society at present dictates the wearing of garments that are sanitarily indefensible, and enforces its dictates by refusal of employment, dismissal, social ostracism, and refusal of admission into places of entertainment, public and private. If an effectively democratic state ventured to legislate on the subject, its laws would at least not be deliberately destructive of the health of the mothers of democracy.

But these speculations, though they may have a suggestive side for the people who are unduly alarmed at the prospect of increased State Regulation do not throw much light on its abstract limits. Theoretically, the right of the community, organized as a democratic State, to interfere with the individual is boundless. Practically the State has neither time, capacity, nor inclination to relieve the individual of more than a small share of the responsibility of guiding his own conduct. He must do most of this according to his own light and at his proper peril as to the criminal law and public opinion. If the industrial, sanitary, and educational conditions of life in the community are brought to such a point that a man without more than the average force of character can, if he chooses, maintain himself in such health and happiness as he can reasonably hope to enjoy, then the guidance of his private life is that part of the State work which must be delegated to himself. He cannot expect powers to summon a jury to settle petty differences between himself and his wife, or a meeting of the vestry to find lodgings for him; and the central parliament would certainly decline to spend a setting in choosing a wife for him. And as he cannot expect it, so he need not fear it. Interference with him costs something, and so will not be undertaken gratuitously or at a loss. Indeed State Interference is a most difficult thing to bring about, even on the part of the meddlesome, officious, and jealous oligarchies who have brought the name of State into disrepute. Even the Russian or Austrian governments could no more dictate every detail of private conduct than a postman could read all the letters he delivers, even if he had an official right to open them. It is evident that there is a natural limit to State Interference just as there is a natural limit to the quantity of work that can be done in a day; and if Adam Smith were alive in these days of democratic States, it is probable that he would advocate a policy of allowing State Interference to find its natural level as well as value in exchange.

As to Property and Liberty then, every man's property is the property of the State, which it can dispose of as it pleases, whether he will or no. And every man's liberty is the liberty of the State, which it can curtail or extend as it pleases, whether he will or no. But the object of the State is to secure his welfare coordinately with that of every other member;[2] and it will "naturally" secure that welfare at the least possible trouble to itself. Now the individual is seeking his own welfare no less than the State, so that no opposition of interests arises between him and it until he seeks it in such a way as to unfairly affect the welfare of others. Up to this point he will be doing the State's work; and the State, recognizing him as the right man in the right place, will not interfere with him; and so, though subject to a State recognizing no theoretic limit to its right of interference, he will enjoy all the liberty and property that even Mr Herbert Spencer claims for him. At that point, the State steps in to prevent his infringing the equal welfare of his fellows, an interference which is not only countenanced but demanded by individualist sociologists. Thus it appears that the acceptance of the State as supreme and the individual as merely its tenant and delegate is quite as consistent with freedom of action and security of possession as the individualist doctrine that the liberty and property of the individual are paramount, and that the activity of the State must be jealously restricted to the protection of these.

A trivial, but representative instance of the groundless alarm created by such a proposal as that all private property ought to be abolished, and all ownership to vest in the State, may be taken from a speech against Socialism by Mr Charles Bradlaugh,

2. This is true only of a Democratic State, and would have been absurdly false of any State known to or contemplated by Ricardo or the 18th century economists.

who produced from his pocket a watch, and explained that it
had been presented to him by his father-in-law. The audience,
a very sympathetic one, felt the full force of the almost sacred
right which a man has to the possession of a token of personal
esteem and affection. Under Socialism, the lecturer proceeded
to say, this watch would be no longer *my* watch. The impression conveyed to the audience was that any person might
snatch the watch on the ground that it was not Mr Bradlaugh's
property, and deprive him of it without redress. Mr Bradlaugh
might, however, unreservedly accept the socialistic position
without any fear of such deprivation. In the event dreaded by
his audience, his reply to the footpad would be simple. "You
say that this watch is not mine, because private property is
abolished. *I* say, on the same ground, that it is not yours. It is
the property of the State; and I am the individual custodian of
it. If you have been appointed custodian in my place, shew me
your credentials. If you have none, then I shall hale you before
the magistrate for having attempted to steal the State's watch
from its lawful custodian." The incident, in short, would terminate exactly as it would terminate at present. The notion that
the "abolition of private property" would enable a dishonest
person to deprive another with impunity of a watch, or that the
State would "resume" watches from individuals except, as it
does now, by way of distraint for unpaid taxes, is only an example of the danger of applying the rough and ready tests of
"common sense" to conceptions of which an adequate sense is
as yet by no means common.

The above examination of Liberty, Property, Natural Rights
of the Individual, and Limits of State Interference will seem
tedious and trivial to those who can see right through to the
realities of the situation at one glance. But it is the traditional
English beginning. The older economists loved to think that
good order in a community is spontaneous, and will always arise
if the government will only let things alone. It is worth while
shewing that they were false to their own theory when they
deprecated State Interference, since, as we have seen, that also
tends to regulate itself spontaneously, and has a beneficial

"natural level" as much as prices or wages have. It is plain on the face of it that their dogma that industry should be placed outside the sphere of the State was a demand for the protection of private employers against public competition, and was just as contrary to the principle of Free Trade as their protection against foreign competition. We also see that the inconsistency was inevitable, because to them the State meant a close oligarchy of landed proprietors, placed by economic necessity in irreconcilable hostility to the people. But the perfect State was even then at least thinkable, though it took a Hegel to think it; and democracy has since then advanced with such strides that even those who have no faith in it recognize that it has now gained a momentum that must carry it to its goal of the real State, to the imminent conditions of which all the political conclusions of the "classic" economy as to the sphere of the State must now be adjusted. Those conclusions were in the main valid under existing circumstances before 1832. After that date they became superstitions, though not altogether inexcuseable or discreditable superstitions for about forty years. Subsequent extensions of the franchise have so far advanced their obsolescence that those who now repeat them lay themselves fairly open to the charge of empty pedantry. But this does not mean that either the fundamental assumptions or the deductive method of the old economists are to be thrown overboard. The socialist economist, with his constant reference to history still makes those assumptions, and still proceeds deductively. He, too, can express himself in the old terminology of Liberty, Property, Natural Rights, and Natural Prices on occasion. The pupil of the Ricardian schools need not fear that the socialist has any design to pull up by the roots all that his academic pastors have implanted in him.[3] And, as we have seen, he can for the sake of those who still care for such exercises, deduce from the Economic Harmonies the dogma of unlimited State Interference quite as cogently as his forerunners deduced the dogma of laisser-faire.

Although the claims of the individual as against the State

3. This sentence was canceled by Shaw.—ED.

were never carried by the more eminent individualist economists to the doctrinaire extremes of the vulgarizers of the
Ricardian economy, yet it is true that the proprietary classes
and the employers have in this century set up a claim to exemption from all legal and moral responsibility in dealing with land
and capital, and in hiring labor, alleging in explanation of such
an unprecedented and impudent claim that their own interests
led them to buy as cheaply and sell as dearly as possible, and
that according to the laws of political economy—or the laws
of supply and demand, as they sometimes phrased it—such buying and selling must lead to the best attainable results and so
might be taken as a compendium of the whole duty of man in
commerce. Whenever this claim was advanced, it was scouted
by humanitarians, and found impracticable by statesmen. Factory Acts holding capitalists and employers to heavy penalties
for driving inhuman bargains with their workmen, and regulat-
ing the conditions under which such bargains might be made,
were clamored for and passed; but it seems to have been supposed that these Acts were, as the capitalists and employers
alleged, breaches of the laws of political economy. It was then
argued that since these laws could be broken, they could hardly
be, as economists had pretended, as inevitable as the law of
gravitation. One statesman spoke of banishing them to Saturn;
and the science of economics finally lost all authority with
English legislators. This, however, is due to the fact that since
the repeal of the Corn Laws in 1846, no proposals supported
mainly by economic demonstrations have reached parliament,
and consequently no party has been interested in rehabilitating
the authority of the science. Social Democracy, strong on its
economic side, is destined to effect this before long; and in the
meantime they are making it generally understood that no such
thing as a breach of the laws of political economy has really
taken place; and that, for example, Ricardo's dictum that [wages
always fall to a subsistence level] was not a law authorizing
capitalists and employers to starve and flog young children
into working upwards of twelve hours a day.

Still, the notion yet prevails that the investment and administration of capital is somehow privileged and outside the ordinary law; and newspaper editors, with just economics enough to confute the cruder sort of Protectionist, every now and then shake their heads over Truck Acts, Employers' Liability Acts and the like, as violations of Free Contract. It is therefore necessary to insist that a member of a community should no more be allowed to use his land or capital without regard to the welfare of others than so to use a knife or a gun, and that it has never been demonstrated that a purely selfish policy in regard to them will produce all the effects of an alert benevolence and sense of social duty. What has been demonstrated is that if he were wholly bent on using his property so as to produce wares of the greatest possible values in exchange, he would give employment to a sufficient number of workers to exhaust its productive capacity. From this it has been carelessly inferred that he would cause his estate to support the greatest possible number of persons. But this obviously does not follow. He will exhaust the productive capacity of the estate; but in order to save wages and have as large a surplus for himself as possible, he will employ the smallest number of workers that will suffice, besides exacting from them the longest and most assiduous toil, and paying them the smallest wage that they can be forced to submit to. The surplus, though it may be sufficient to maintain half a dozen families in reasonable comfort, he may spend on superfluities for himself. Many persons use their property at present in such a way that the work is done by women who work fifteen hours a day for three farthings an hour. The surplus, or difference between the three farthings returned to the women and the wealth they produce every hour, is of course very considerable; and it is frequently spent in senseless extravagance by the proprietor at the West End of London whilst the women are drudging in hopeless misery at the East. This is the state of things which unrestricted private control of land and capital always tends to produce. Not only would the State be justified in compelling the proprietor to forego a portion of the surplus in order to add it to the wages of the women, but it is bound to do so from the moment that the welfare of the working class is admitted to be of equal importance with that of the proprietary class an equality now admitted in theory but unfortunately still most grossly ignored in practice. The holders of land and capital then are in no sense exempt from the obligations which restrict the use of other objects of property. Nay, since the abuse of land and capital leads to evil consequences more far reaching and terrible than the abuse of anything else that a man can possess, their proprietors should be held to stricter conditions and called to sterner account than the holder of stocks of poisons and explosives, between whose interests and that of the public there is far closer harmony.

To those who have never attempted any economic analysis of our society—that is, to the great majority—the statements that proprietors of land and capital claim exemption from all moral and legal responsibility in dealing with them, and that the consequences are the inevitable and terrible consequences of anarchy, will seem extravagant. A moment's consideration will shew that they are undeniable. No candid person with an ordinary knowledge of affairs will dispute the fact that when a citizen finds himself in possession of capital, he invests it without the slightest reference to any consideration except the security and the rate of interest. If he simply leaves it with his banker on deposit, he takes the interest blindfold. If he places the capital for himself, he compares the various industrial enterprises in which shares are to be had, solely to ascertain which shares are on the whole the safest, the cheapest, and the most lucrative. He does not dream of comparing the conditions under which his capital will be employed. Whether the shares are in a distillery or in a bakery; whether the enterprise is a match factory or a tramway company in which the employees are ground down systematically and unscrupulously to an appalling depth of drudgery and poverty, or a well ordered industrial colony famous for the pleasant relations existing between the employers and workmen, is a matter absolutely indifferent to the ordinary investor. If there were the slightest preference, the market prices of the shares would shew it at once: the avoided shares would be cheaper than the desired ones. That they are not so can be ascertained by a glance at the money column of any newspaper. Shares in concerns conducted by notorious sweaters are sought for neither more nor less than in the enterprises of the best employers in the country. Investors of irreproachable private character, who would be incapable of inconsiderately walking into a neighbor's drawingroom on a muddy day without first carefully wiping their boots, will shamelessly hold out their capital on the stock exchange impartially between the sordid rascal and the truly valiant captain of industry, crying "Which bids highest?" This is anarchy, pure and simple; and its consequences are all the consequences of anarchy. Compulsory prostitution, disease, premature death, incest, social corruption untraceable and unspeakable, stand recorded against it in the reports of the parliamentary commissions which have inquired into the Factory System, the Employment of Children, the Housing of the Poor, the Sweating System, and are still the themes of our Factory Inspectors, the Labor Correspondent of the Board of Trade, and the unofficial philanthropists and agitators who have devoted themselves to the work of rousing the public conscience on the subject. It seems strange to those who do not know the historical bearings of the question that any other results could ever have been expected from anarchy. But periods of anarchy are constantly being produced under despotisms by society outgrowing the decrees of its government, which finally become so impracticable that no law at all is felt to be better than such laws as exist. Laisser-faire, laisser-aller, and away with your decrees becomes the cry; and optimistic treatises on the superiority of "natural law" to despotic regulation find a ready sale. This is what happened to industry in the eighteenth century. In the middle ages, the merchant and craft guilds in the towns, and the village manors with their communal traditions in the country sufficed for the organization of an industry chiefly agricultural, producing mainly for home consumption, and using machinery and division of labor only to an extent which now seems insignificant. Industry managed to shift with this system until the eighteenth century, when an

industrial revolution, incomparably more momentous than the
political revolutions to which historians have hitherto given
much greater prominence, was brought about by the introduction of the factory system, the invention of a practicable steam
engine, and such typical developments of machinery as the
substitution of the jenny for the spinning wheel. The minute
regulations of the mediæval crafts were as impossible of application to the industries thus transformed as the discipline of an
ancient Roman galley would be to a modern ironclad. And
just as, when ships grew big, navigators threw away their oars
and trusted to the winds and stars, so "the great industry"
threw away the mediæval regulations and trusted to competition. The change suited everyone except the proletariat. Competition rents were higher than customary rents; so the landlord
was well pleased: competition profits were higher than customary
profits; so the employers did not complain. And so for a time
anarchy came into credit. But competition wages were terrible;
and if the workers had had any direct political power, or had
clearly understood what was taking place, this most atrocious of
human institutions could not have been maintained. It must
be borne in mind that the old customary wage was not a
competition wage, but a subsistence wage—that it fluctuated,
not with the demand and supply of labor, but with the price of
provisions. The various classes into which society was divided
in the middle ages had each a certain standard of comfort and
freedom, approved of as just and fitting by public opinion, and
on occasion, enforced by law. If the agricultural laborer took
advantage of competition to get wages high enough to enable
his wife to strut in a silver girdle, the law, scandalized, forbad
his employer to offer him more than the customary wage—that
is, the wage sufficient to maintain him in the comfort recognized
as fit for a person of his condition. But on the other hand, he
was never reduced by competition to the state of the miserable
helots of our own time. When in the time of the Tudors the
laborers began to find that it was not always possible to find
employment, they were punished savagely for begging until it
became apparent that, with all the good will in the world to

work, they could not always help themselves. When that was recognized, it was admitted that they had a right to subsistence; and the famous Poor Law of Elizabeth was passed. This Poor Law, with its liberality as to outdoor relief, stood between the worker and the lowest depths of the competition wage until 1834. It involved oppressive laws of settlement[4] and was abundantly mischievous and demoralizing in its operation, as the capitalist classes had no difficulty in shewing when the Reform Bill of 1832 brought its abolition within the field of practical politics; but every objection to it might have been met by a genuine workhouse system for organizing the labor of the unemployed. This, however, would have involved State organization of industry in competition with private enterprise; and for that thin end of the Socialist wedge the conditions were not then ripe. The Poor Law was practically abolished; and the unemployed worker now found that the alternative to starvation was the breaking up of his house, separation from his wife and children, and virtual imprisonment under conditions to which many poor persons have preferred death. The workers were now for the first time openly and remorselessly left to competition wages alone.

It is to be noted that the great economists who advocated the fullest freedom of competition never realized what this meant. Adam Smith assumed that there was a "natural price" of labor fixed by the cost of the subsistence of the laborer according to the standard of comfort of his class. Ricardo took the same view, which seemed to agree with his theory that the exchange value of anything is fixed by the labor expended in producing it.[5] It is sufficiently evident, however, that the only reason why the

4. See Adam Smith, Wealth of Nations.

5. A theory now admitted to be literally preposterous. See Jevons, A New Theory of Political Economy, 1871, and all subsequent standard works on the subject. However, it is proper to mention here that the most thoroughgoing advocate of this unlucky theory was the famous socialist Karl Marx. See Das Kapital, Book I, 1867. Those who are curious on this point may consult Mr P. H. Wickstead's article in To-Day for October, 1884, and a review of Das Kapital by the present writer in The National Reformer, August 7, 14, and 21, 1887.

value of an ordinary commodity does not sink below its cost of production is because no person will produce it at a loss; and the supply is therefore checked before that point is reached. But the peculiarity of labor as a commodity is that its production is practically involuntary, fresh laborers being produced in an increasing ratio even when the price or wage of their labor has fallen so far beneath subsistence point as to create a shocking mortality in the laboring class as compared with the holders of property. Labor is offered on the market at a price which means lifelong misery and premature death to the laborer: yet it will not always fetch even this; and the unsuccessful applicant falls into the ranks of the unemployed, the value of his labor being nothing. Malthus saw this so clearly that he saw nothing but ruin for the workers if the output of them—that is, the increase of population—was not restricted. The Ricardians took this up eagerly when it became undeniable that free competition did not tend to secure to the worker the "natural wage" of Adam Smith; and thenceforth the workers were assured that if they would only be prudent enough to limit the increase of their own class so as to maintain the value at a comfortable wage, they would be comfortable; and that if they did not choose to do so, their misery was their own fault. But even if this had been good sense and sound economics, the mischief was already done; and when the old poor law was done away with, the workers felt that they were being pushed over the abyss. Riots, outrages, armed risings, and the great social-democratic agitation known as Chartism kept the country in constant disturbance for ten years; and at last capitalism surrendered its claim to the profits of irresponsible and unlimited competition, and submitted to the first effective Factory Act. Some of its provisions would seem incredibly inhuman if they were not known to be mitigations of conditions yet more inhuman. In some of the largest industries they curtailed the working day, directly for women and children, and indirectly for men (to whose labor the co-operation of women and children was indispensable) besides insisting on certain precautions against disease and misconduct. This relieved the pressure somewhat; and the impulse given to industry by the discoveries of gold in Australia and California, an impulse which England's advanced industrial organization, her natural treasury of iron and coal, and the throwing open of her ports to free imports in 1846, enabled her to take the fullest advantage of, so that for a time she became the great manufacturer of the world's raw material, and the volume of her trade increased "by leaps and bounds." In other countries the workers paid dearly for England's prosperity; but within her own confines the increased demand for labor sent up the value of labor; and the workers, by determined combination in Trades Unions secured an increase of wages which still further relieved the strain. Chartism collapsed; and the political activity of the working class subsided into Trade Unionism until the exhaustion of the impulse, the inevitable increase of population, and the copying by other nations of the English system, with the discovery by them of stores of mineral wealth not inferior to what hers had been even before economists had begun to shake their heads over the inroads made upon them in the course of time,[6] made the old pressure felt again, with the result, which we are now witnessing, of a revival of Chartism in the more developed form of avowed Social Democracy.

It must not be supposed, however, that it was possible by merely relieving the pressure to prevent the resistance of the workers from wrecking the whole social machine. If there had not been a large safety valve open, the minor explosions which were consequently occurring would have attained irresistible concentration. This safety valve was the path to comparative freedom across the Atlantic. As it was the discovery of America which burst the mediæval organization of industry, so was it the free soil of America to which the hardier and more adventurous sufferers from the competitive system escaped when life in the old country became intolerable. Emigration and colonization not only relieved the pressure directly by withdrawing competitors from the labor market: it led to the gold discoveries

6. See Jevons, [The] Coal [Question], 1865.

which, as we have seen, so greatly stimulated the demand in
that market as far as England was concerned. After the abolition
of the old Poor Law, the rush of emigrants became fast and
furious.

For the repression of the minor explosions or "half revolutions" the system provided its own remedy, by reducing the
mass of the laboring population to a condition of destitution
in which they were ready to do anything they could get a living by doing. The Sheffield sawgrinder only asked a few shillings extra wage for doing work that killed him with the utmost
certainty at an age which was his employer's prime of life. The
woman in the whitelead factory at present cannot obtain a
penny extra in consideration of the fact that her occupation
involves slow—and not even very slow—poisoning. People who
sacrifice their own claims thus recklessly are not in a position
to consider the effects of their action on the claims of others.
Therefore the capitalist and landlord have never found any
difficulty in procuring soldiers, policemen, bailiffs, "emergency
men" for a trifling wage, to repress by armed force the insur-
rections of the more desperate sections of the proletariat, and
to exact the share of their labor claimed by property. Such
repression is always carried out in the name of "law and order,"
with the result that the phrase, printed thus—"law'norder,"[7]
has become one of the stock jokes of the journals which advocate the claims of labor. The rioter attacks, not the proprietor,
but the policeman; and the policeman, however disposed to
sympathize with the man of his own class, must defend himself
against his assailant, and finally must fight, not for his own
class in the State, but for his own side in the battle, which,
being the best drilled, best equipped, and best fed, besides being free from the fear of subsequent punishment, generally wins
the day. And as even those who most deeply feel that the claims
of the insurgents are just, and the opposition to them selfish
and hypocritical, know so well how impotent an insurrectionary
mob is to reconstruct after destroying, that when a rising is re-

7. See Commonweal, July, 1888.

solved upon it very seldom secures a leader of any weight except by the expedient (well known in the secret history of such attempts) of providing him with a body guard instructed to shoot him if he flinches.[8]

The proprietary class witness all this without comprehending it. To it, a riot or insurrection is a mere ebullition of rascaldom; the misery of the proletariat an illustration of the saying "Ye have the poor with you always"; the evils of civilization to be accounted for by original sin, drink, overpopulation, and a hundred other causes. The custom of disposing of land and capital wherever it will bring the highest rent and interest is justified by those who reflect about it at all by the idea that since everybody does it the selfishness of each is neutralized by the selfishness of all the rest—a crude amateur version of the "economic harmonies" of Bastiat, a French economist who assured the proprietary classes that to doubt that their implanted instincts would work out beneficially was to doubt, in effect, the goodness of God.[9] A true comprehension of the situation can only be arrived at by an economic analysis of existing society.[10]

Meanwhile, the subject of Socialism and Individual Liberty and Property may be summed up thus.

The abstract propositions that the property of the individual is the property of the State; that the liberty of the individual is at the disposal of the State; that individual liberty and private property should be totally abolished; and that the right of the State to interfere with the individual is unlimited, are found, when reduced to practice, to be perfectly consistent with all the freedom of action, possession and enjoyment which so extreme an individualist as Mr Herbert Spencer claims for the individual. The conclusion suggested, however, is not that these abstract propositions are valid, but that, like the abstract prop-

8. Newport Rising.

9. Bastiat is himself a curious example of the fact that a man may be very intelligent and yet in the deepest sense a fool.

10. Shaw's MS here continues, "An outline of that analysis, the achievement of which even by experts is as yet a novelty, will be found in the next chapter."—Ed.

ositions to which they seemed at first sight contrary, they are by themselves perfectly barren. If two men are heard to profess themselves, one a thorough going defender of Liberty and Property, and the other bent on the destruction of both, it is impossible to infer from those statements what their religious creed, political party, or personal conduct may be. It cannot even be affirmed that they differ on any of the three. An expert might guess from abstract *a priori* declarations that such a man was either a Tory or a Socialist; such another either a Whig or an Anarchist; and a third either a Catholic or a Communist. When the doubt lies between such practical extremes as these, it is plain that the declaration throws just light enough to make darkness visible.

It further appears that the faith in competition as an automatic regulator of industrial organization acts without the slightest reference to human welfare; and that industry was only abandoned to it when it had attained a development in which the minute supervision and regulation of the middle ages became impracticable. The result, as we have seen, was anarchy, with all its consequences, which all the Factory Acts, Trade Acts, Trade Union Shop rules and other infringements of individual freedom of action which competition immediately produced to an extent that would have amazed the members of the mediæval guilds, could not alleviate sufficiently to make the condition of the masses tolerable. Even as lately as 1886 Mr Robert Giffen, in a paper expressly written and extensively circulated in order to put the most favorable complexion on the position of the proletariat, admitted that, "the condition was such as to justify a revolution for the better."[11] To extricate society from this condition is the problem of which Socialism professes to be a solution. As it is evidently an economic problem, it is useless to attempt to understand either the problem or the remedy without first carefully analysing the economic conditions of the situation.

11. Essays in Finance.

IV   The New Politics: From Lassalle to the Fabians

In the fall of 1889, the Fabian Society presented a course of historical lectures under the general title, "A Century of Social Movements," on Friday evenings at Willis' Rooms, King Street, beginning on October 4. William Clarke spoke on "Early Radicalism," Frank Podmore on "Early Socialism," Graham Wallas on "The Chartist Movement," Hubert Bland on "The Protest of Literature and Sentiment," and Annie Besant on "The Trades Union Movement." Shaw's lecture, the final one of the series, was delivered on December 20, and was called "The New Politics." I have added the phrase "From Lassalle to the Fabians" to indicate more clearly the special period Shaw covers.

Most of you have at one time or another entertained some idea of going on the stage. You will therefore have been led to notice that the actor's profession is recruited in two ways. First, there are the actors who are born to it, but who are not therefore by any means born actors. Second, there are those geniuses who have broken out of the respectable bounds of ordinary middle class life, and forced themselves upon a reluctant stage in obedience to an irresistible vocation. These are the actors who, whether successful or not, have at least a theory of acting, a consciousness of its social function, a conviction of its utility. But the actor who has merely taken the employment that lies nearest to the hand of a member of a theatrical family— who is an actor because his father was a manager, his mother a useful provincial Lady Macbeth, and his brother, who in a higher social sphere would have entered the Church, an unassuming walking gentleman: such a one may be as void of

any comprehension of the drama as an ordinary bank clerk is
of the theory of banking, or a Mint porter of the mechanism of
exchange and Gresham's law. Let us call him a routine actor,
since acting is to him only a routine, learned by rule of thumb.
Now when the routine actor finds himself in the same company with the actors by vocation, he does not open his arms to
them. He regards them much as Christian regarded Formalist
and Hypocrisy when they came into the path by burglariously
climbing over the wall, instead of having entered it at the beginning through the strait gate. He clepes them "amateurs," and,
with swinish phrase, soils their addition. He notes their ignorance
of routine, which he knows to be indispensable, and cannot see
the utility of their ideals, which, indeed, do not present themselves to his mind as ideals, but merely as ineptitudes, fads, or
affectations. And no reconciliation is possible until the idealist
has justified himself by success, which rarely arrives until he
has become a master of routine.

As on the stage, so on the political platform. You have the
routine politician and the idealist agitator; you have the same
mistrust separating them, and the same conditions of reconciliation. The routine politician is not necessarily a mere com-
plier with the habits of a political family, unless indeed he is
influentially connected, and the family is the Barnacle family.
A mechanic with some capacity for business and hard work
will by mere natural selection evolve from simple member of
his Trade Union to committee man, Trades Councillor, delegate to Trades Congress, member of Political Council, labor
candidate, and finally, perhaps, member of parliament. A middle
class gentleman of means and social ambition, will aim at a
seat in parliament or on those minor representative bodies
which are the stepping stones to full public life, solely to acquire personal distinction; and if he has only money enough, he
must be remarkably deficient in plausibility if he cannot induce
some constituency to accept him as a candidate on the ground
that he is perhaps a hair's breadth better than the next best man
rich enough to bear the expenses of registration and election,
although at any given meeting of the citizens whom he has

kindly offered to represent, he may be patently the most foolish and ignorant person in the room. Thus, assuming that the routine politician is not a rogue, which he sometimes is, and which, I am sorry to say, he always tends more or less to become, his presence and activity in the political arena can be accounted for completely by mere business capacity or riches, associated with the requisite degree of energy and ambition. Public spirit, social instinct, even common humanity in its elementary manifestation of pity for suffering: all these, and the political ideal which they create, may be entirely lacking, the substitute for them being a certain fear of the observed effects of them in other people, such fear being described as "respect for public opinion." In this way the people make progress with unprogressive instruments, and purify public life with corrupt ones, much as Samson slew his thousands with the jawbone of a pacific ass. Still, it is not desirable to fight with asses' jawbones when better weapons are to be had, even at the risk of hurting the feelings of the ass, and enduring his reproach of inconstancy and ingratitude; and the people, whilst insisting on the routine of politics, will in the long run prefer the idealist politician who has acquired the indispensable routine, to the routine politician who is incapable of conceiving an ideal.

Among the social movements of the century which our Fabian historians of "A Century of Social Movements" have carefully left out of their otherwise admirable survey of mankind since the French Revolution was the Revolution of 1848. What the Chartist made of that in England, Mr Graham Wallas has told us. In France it was a half Republican, half Utopian movement. In Germany it was what we should call merely a Constitutional movement, aiming, for instance, at inducing the sovereign, backed by the nobility and the army, to confer on the free German a constitutional right to have his visiting card printed without first obtaining a license from the official Censor of the Press. In Berlin the famous March revolution extracted the most satisfactory constitutional pledges from King Frederick William IV. During the following November the King, happening to be displeased with the National Assembly, prac

tically dissolved it. The President declared that the dissolution
was unconstitutional, and refused to leave the chair. Thereupon
the military considerately carried the chair out, President and
all, and deposited it in the street, much as Captain Boldwig
removed Mr Pickwick to the pound. Meanwhile, the King declared that Berlin was in a state of siege; the civic guard was disarmed; all clubs and associations, Fabian and other, were closed;
open air meetings were forbidden; the carrying of weapons was
prohibited; newspapers and pamphlets were placed under police
supervision; and all contraventions of these highly constitutional
regulations were dealt with by court martial. Hereupon it became apparent to logical persons that if constitutionalism meant
anything, and the March revolution had really been a revolution, there was nothing for it now but to take up arms and
fight.

Among the logical persons who not only formed this conclusion, but ventured to act on it, was a certain amateur barrister who was then conducting a *cause célèbre* at Dusseldorff.
He was a Jew, twentythree years of age, a student of philosophy, and a friend of Marx, Engels, Wolff and others of the
small circle of Hegelians who are our spiritual fathers. Mr
Bland has shewn us how socialism lay implicit in German
philosophy; but whereas the Englishmen named by Mr Bland
continued for the most part to sublimate their socialism to such
a degree that respectable society mistook it for orthodox ser-
monizing against worldliness, I need only mention the Jew
barrister's name—Ferdinand Lassalle—to convince you that no
such mistake was possible in his case. Well, Lassalle called the
citizens of Dusseldorff to arms by public placard; and the citizens of Dusseldorff, with complete unanimity, refused to come.
The result was that Lassalle found himself in the situation
which the corrupt Latinity of our day describes as "in quod."
Not that he was convicted of the charge brought against him of
exciting armed opposition to the Executive power. On the
contrary, he was acquitted; but to release him on that ground
would obviously have been a concession to constitutionalism;
and he did his six months accordingly. Nothing more came of

that business just then, but I shall dwell, for our present purpose, for a moment or two on the remarkable speech by which
he gained what may, in the phrase we use after unfavorable
bye-elections, be called the "moral victory" of his acquittal. Instead of posing as an outraged constitutionalist, he declared at
once that his standpoint was altogether a revolutionary one,
and that his deepest convictions were those of a Republican
and Social Democrat. He then proceeded to vindicate his intellectual position with absolute candor; and, as aforesaid, the
court rose to the occasion and acquitted him. Now here was a
perfect example of the idealist politician forcing his way into
politics from the study instead of creeping into them through
the caucus, and at once coming brilliantly to grief from the
practical point of view, because he was not a routine politician
and therefore did not know that the average man has not the
remotest intention of taking up arms for a constitutional
theory the moment it is demonstrated to him on a placard that
he ought to. But the failure mattered little. As Lassalle himself
said to the court, "History can forgive all errors and all convictions, but not want of conviction."

Fourteen years later, there was another constitutional crisis in
Prussia. King William I, known to us all as Franco-Prussian
conqueror, Kaiser, and continental Grand Old Man, came to
the throne, and promptly put forward his one idea, an Army
Reorganization Scheme. The Diet, Liberal in a political sense,
but the reverse in a pecuniary one, refused supplies. The King
dissolved it, and found a more obdurate one elected in its place.
In fact, the more the King dissolved his Diet, the more Liberal
it became. And so matters stood at a deadlock. Routine politicians were decidedly at a discount. Then Lassalle, who had
long ago won his *cause célèbre* and returned to his philosophic
studies, was remembered as the man who had come out not only
with a shibboleth, but with convictions, intellectually arranged.
The routine politicians wanted to be able to *prove* that the
King's action was unconstitutional; and here was the man to
shew them how to do it. To their disgust, Lassalle, now himself
equipped with the only virtue of routine politics, the virtue of

recognizing facts, told them that the constitution of a country meant the net balance of effective forces in that country, and that if the King, supported by the army and the nobility, could override the parliament, then the Prussian constitution was in fact monarchical and aristocratic, and not parliamentary. This was a blow to the routine politicians, who, though they recognized facts, as I have said, yet generally made the recognition an excuse for not facing them. The invitation to Lassalle had really meant, "We recognize the facts: shew us how to dodge them." But Ferdinand was no Fabian. He faced the facts; and the facts being favorable to the classes, the classes were for the moment delighted with him. However, when he proceeded to invite the Chambers also to face the facts by refusing to meet, and thus compel the King to carry on his absolutism in the face of Europe without the mask of constitutionalism, the classes reverted to their old opinion of him. For they thought that no monarch in the year 1862 could dare to defy public opinion and political tradition so far as to drop all pretence of constitutional methods. Just so did our own shibboleth swallowers suppose in 1887 that no government dare suppress the right of public meeting in London. The King of Prussia asked the advice of Herr von Bismarck. Herr von Bismarck was of opinion that the King's private opinion, with the army to back it, was worth any quantity of unarmed public opinion. The King, heartily agreeing with him, declared that he would act on his own responsibility for the good of the nation; and for four years he, in the phrase of American individualism, did what he darn pleased, and thereby proved the soundness of Lassalle's contention that constitutional right is simply might and nothing else. The middle class supposed that what he meant was that might is right, trying to fit the new idea with an old catchword, just as people who want to open a new drawer without the proper key try all their old ones on it. But Lassalle, who said "The sword is never right," knew better than that.

At this time the unfortunate workers of Germany were in a position which needs no explanation among us. They had nothing to hope for from the King, nothing from the Conservative party, and nothing from the great Liberal party—the National Liberal party as it called itself in anticipation of the National Liberal Club. It is true that the Liberals had offered to make the Democrats "honorary members" of the Liberal party; but the offer, though magnanimous, was not substantial enough to satisfy proletarian aspiration. Again, Herr Schulze-Delitzsch urged upon them the all-sufficiency of co-operation, and pointed to his 200,000 co-operators with their capital of £2,000,000 as the beginning of a millennium in which everybody should live on dividends. The luckier mechanics and the small tradesmen listened to Schulze; but the ordinary wage worker was not interested, knowing that any scheme that involved saving, on however modest a scale, has no hope in it for the man who has less than enough to live on. At a loss for a new idea, the workingmen turned from the routine politicians to the men of ideas. They asked Lassalle to say something on the situation. The world was beginning, in fact, to be curious as to the meaning of that declaration of his in 1848 that he was by his very innermost convictions an advocate of a Social-Democratic Republic. He answered them in the famous "Open Letter" which inspired Mr Hyndman, twenty years later, with the idea of publishing an open letter to Samuel Smith, M.P. This letter of Lassalle's contained the essence of "the new politics" which are my subject this evening; and in it he surveyed the situation in the abstract with the comprehensiveness of a philosopher, and in the concrete with the science of the historian and economist; whilst his plan of campaign again shewed that he knew as much of the inevitable routine of politics as was of any practical use to one whose aims were essentially revolutionary.

First, as a philosopher, he took the conception of the perfect State as worked out in the abstract by Hegel—the conception in which all discordant categories negate themselves by their own immanent contradictions until a final category is reached which reconciles all contradictions. Thus, if the State is a structure of hostile classes, then at any moment the uppermost class is the common oppressor of all the rest. Then the uppermost-but-one, high enough to be powerful in itself, and able to

count on the assistance of all the classes beneath it in opposing
the uppermost, turns on its oppressor, overthrows it and ab-
sorbs its units, thus becoming itself the uppermost and the common enemy. In its turn it is overthrown and absorbed by the
class beneath it; and the process continues until the turn of the
lowest class comes. When *its* revolt is accomplished, there is
only one class: that is to say, there no longer exists any such
thing as class, and so you get the perfect State, the criterion of
perfection being equality. How Lassalle traced this process in
history we all know. The feudal aristocracy was the uppermost
class, or Second Estate, the King being technically the First
Estate. The Third Estate is the middle or commercial class,
made enormously rich and powerful by the productivity given
to its capital by the introduction of machinery and steam power
in the last century. The middle class, thus reinforced, overthrew
the feudal class in 1789 with the assistance of the laboring class
or Fourth Estate. The final step, the overthrow of the middle
class by the laboring class, remains to be accomplished; and the
accomplishment of it was the object proposed by Lassalle, as it
is the object proposed by the Fabian Society.

The bare statement of this abstract theory, and of its verifica-
tion in history, cannot produce an adequate picture of the
mental attitude of Lassalle. Many persons are quite ready to
assent to the theory without accepting any of the implications
which were obvious to him. For instance, Mr Bellamy, the
author of Looking Backwards, would probably endorse it unhesitatingly. Yet Mr Bellamy is so little able to conceive what
the overthrow of the middle class means, that his fictitious
perfect State is a thoroughly businesslike commercial Utopia
in which every man is what a respectable Bostonian is today,
and every young woman a realization of the ideal young lady
heroine of the late Anthony Trollope. Like a true middle class
man, Mr Bellamy believes that middle class piety, middle class
family institutions, middle class morals are valid for all classes
and for all time—that middle class standards of right and wrong
are set up in heaven as our standards of length are set up in
Trafalgar Square and at Greenwich observatory. Lassalle was

under no such illusion. He knew that the disappearance of the middle class meant the passing away of its God, its Church, its code of manners, its family institutions, its standards of glory in nations, of honor in gentlemen and of womanliness in ladies —in short, of everything that it holds most sacred. All these were to him but the crumbling cement that still held the class structure together. And he made no secret of it. "My friends," he once said, "I am not one of the pious"; and he took care that there should be no mistake about his meaning.

Lassalle's analysis of the conditions required for the emancipation of the laborer began with Ricardo's co-ordination of the observations of the earlier economists into a complete synthesis of the economics of private property. Ricardo, from the middle class point of view, saw in his work a reassuring proof that private property, if not interfered with, would solve the problem of keeping the population fed by making it the interest of the proprietors to pay every worker enough to provide him with subsistence. Lassalle, looking at it from the worker's point of view, saw that a proof that private property must condemn the laborer to perpetual toil for no more than the bare subsistence necessary to set him on his legs for his day's work was also a proof that under private property the laborer could never improve his condition. For it is only by acquiring capital that a man prospers under private property; and it is only by saving that a man can acquire capital. But a man cannot save out of a bare subsistence wage; and the laborer, being restricted to such a wage by the operation of the Ricardian law, cannot save, therefore cannot acquire capital, therefore cannot improve his condition. Thus, for Lassalle, Ricardo had put out of court the whole mass of middle class special pleading on behalf of self-help by industry, economy, sobriety, saving, and Schulze-Delitzsch co-operation. Accordingly, we find him exhorting the workingmen to let "this gruesome iron law," as he called it, sink unto their minds.

"I can give you and the whole labor world," he said, "an infallible way of escaping, once for all, from delusions and bad

leaders. When anyone talks to you about bettering the condition of the laboring class, put to him before everything else the
question whether he recognizes this law or not; and if he does
not recognize it, you must say at once that this man either
wants to deceive you, or is most pitiably ignorant of the science of political economy. And if now the one who talks to
you of the condition of the laboring man recognizes this law,
ask him further how he is going to change it; and if he cannot
reply to this, quietly turn your back on him. He is either an
empty prattler who wants to deceive you or himself, or wants
to blind you with hollow phrases."

Lassalle then advocated, as the positive result of his economic
conclusions, the establishment of national co-operation in productive associations working with capital advanced by the State,
and of course procured by it from the capitalist class by taxation. The competition of these productive associations must, he
insisted, be as unfettered as that of the private industries with
one another. Under such conditions the supplanting of the taxed
enterprises of private capital by the State subsidised associations
was as certain as the supplanting of the handloom by the power
loom. Our Fabian programme of the extension of the industrial
activity of the County Councils with capital procured by taxation of unearned incomes is simply an adaptation of Lassalle's
proposal to our machinery of local government.

Finally, turning from the history of economics to pure politics, Lassalle pointed out to the workers that they could neither
obtain nor maintain the new conditions until the political power
—that is, the control of the executive—was transferred from the
capitalist class to the laboring class. Therefore he urged the
workers above all things to "constitute themselves an independent political party, and make universal, equal, and direct
suffrage their watchword."

Here then is our present programme—the new politics—complete in all its essentials. To its philosophy we have added
nothing. To its economics we have only added a demonstration
that private property is even worse than Ricardo shewed, inas-

much as the subsistence wage is not guaranteed to every laborer, but only to him who can find employment. John Ruskin, too, has brought us to a fuller consciousness of the fact that the riches and the productive power developed by private property are socially noxious instead of socially useful. To the Lassallian politics we have added only pure detail. Social Democracy, then, as a definite ideal and an intelligible and consistent policy, dates from the year 1862; and Lassalle must be regarded as its founder, though it must not therefore be inferred that he invented socialism, collectivism, political economy, philosophy, State workshops and universal suffrage. Probably Engels and Marx knew more of industrial history than he, and had no less clear an insight to the relation of economics to history. They were "Communists" long before 1862, in the sense the word then bore. We should now call them collectivists. But although it took many hands to build the ship, there can be no doubt that Lassalle was the man who launched it.

Lassalle conducted his agitation with the frankness of a bachelor who believed in himself and had an annuity of £700 a year. The enormous scope of Socialism compelled him to advance it as a universal remedy—a philosopher's stone, and thus to disparage, by implication, the whole middle class pharmacopeia of sobriety, saving, co-operation, and so forth. The routine politicians, helpless without an immediate practical measure to wirepull, or an immediate constituency to jerrymander, could only resent and affect to ignore a departure which they could not understand; which they were bound, on pain of losing their reputation for knowing everything, to pretend to understand; and which began with the work, for which they were unfit, of popularizing a new ideal. The pious people, whose knowledge of philosophy was limited to a suspicion that whoever read Hegel was an atheist, soon found out his godlessness. The amateurs of political meetings, who seek a mild dissipation in cheering and groaning over their doses of platitude, claptrap and flattery, could not stand a man who would explain a thing for four hours at a stretch rather than let them off understanding it, and who told them that he came to inform and instruct them, and by no means to defend himself before them. In short, he offended all the clubs, and societies, and "ists" of one sort and another: his disciples were the nobodies, who made a hero of him. Then the somebodies, large and small, with the curious exception of Bismarck, attacked him with personal calumny, and with such epithets as demagogue, half educated person, and the like. The calumnies he met with an epigram, "The lie is one of the European powers"; but the implication that Social Democracy was an illusion created by illiteracy and ignorance seemed to him specially worth refuting. He made his famous boast that he was equipped with all the culture of his age. Then he made tremendous displays of erudition, after which he would deal with his latest traducer in some such fashion as this. "I declare Professor So and So to be an ignoramus. Now let him call me one; and all Germany will laugh at him." This succeeded because it was true; but it was a dangerous example for future Socialists who were not Lassalles. It was inevitable however that Lassalle should for the moment be an Ishmael in a class the existence of which he threatened. It was inevitable also that other Ishmaels should rally to his banner, pick up a few of his phrases, and start lecturing, ostensibly on behalf of Social Democracy, but really to advance their own persuasion, which might be anything from Free Love to an inconvertible paper currency. In spite of all, Lassalle's success was enormous. In three months he had a thousand enrolled followers; he raised that number afterwards to five thousand; and he actually converted a bishop. The Fabian Society, five years old and not yet 150 strong, takes off its hat to such an agitator. But Lassalle regarded this as a failure. He had expected to enlist 100,000 the first year, an estimate which shews how a very clever man can underrate the density and apathy of his fellow creatures. After two years of terrible exertion, he was forced to take a holiday in Switzerland. There, in a private difficulty, he for the first recorded time was so false to his own principles as to behave like a gentleman. It will be remembered that the poet Shelley, when a boy, did the same thing by marrying a girl who had thrown herself on his protection, although he did not believe in marriage and did not love the girl. All Shelley's misfortunes sprang from that chivalrous but immoral action. And now Lassalle made a similar mistake. A young lady with whom he was in love ran away from her parents' house to his hotel. He did what any conventionally minded gentleman would have done—at once brought her back to her family, who grossly insulted him and proceeded to ill treat her. He threw his principles to the winds and sought the satisfaction of a gentleman from two members of her family. And he got it in its completest form of death in a duel. This was in August 1864.

Now in 1864 in England, the period of Trade Unionism which followed the collapse of Chartism was in full swing. The British workman was very busy with the organization of his trade, and his mind was far from a receptive attitude as to Hegelian conceptions of the State, whilst the constant denunciations of the Unions by the newspapers as flat violations of the laws of political economy had imbued the unlettered mechanic with the most impenetrable indifference to the conclusions of Ricardo. The average age of the Fabian Society at this period was about eight years; and the divorce of the English working class policy from that culture of which Lassalle had boasted might have lasted until their adolescence but for the interposition of another Jew, exiled from Germany, a man no less extraordinary than Lassalle, one who had known him and who claimed to be his master rather than his pupil. Karl Marx saw that Trade Unionism, though it could not solve the great poverty question, was the beginning of the organization of labor. He did not know, as we know, that a violent revolt of the laboring class was impossible and absurd, because he had seen it done, and done, as far as the violent part of it was concerned, with perfect success. It is not possible for any man, or any society, or even any editor to produce by a word or article the supreme emergency of feeling which makes every unit of the masses of a European capital for a moment a revolutionist, but when Fate brings that emergency, as it has more than once during the present century, then the masses sweep out the classes. Unfortunately, the masses do not know what to do next; they find that not only the country, but the organized capitalism of all Western Europe, controlling the military forces thereof, is solid against them; they do not even know how to organize their own labor, and finally, like schoolboys after a barring-out, they have to let the classes return and to endure their vengeance as best they may. But if the masses were educated up to the point of knowing how to manage production for themselves; if in addition to this they were internationally in communication with one another, so that when Paris struck next, Berlin, London and all the great cities would strike simultaneously, what then? The Fabian smile of superior wisdom settles the question now; but if you will deign for a moment to recollect that working class enfranchisement, the constitutional instrument of emancipation, had been harshly denied to the Chartists, that such voting as there was was unprotected by the secrecy of the ballot, that bribery was almost as open as the voting, that Trade Unions were fiercely denounced and persecuted, and that the Reform Bill of 1867 and the Education Act of 1870 were as yet unborn, you will perhaps understand why Karl Marx expected the revolution to be somewhat a rougher job than subsequent events have promised to make it for us.

Now it happened about this time that England had a violent attack of sympathy with the persecuted Poles, and of indignation with Russia, an attack which lasted until her attention was distracted by the necessity of suspending the Habeas Corpus in Ireland. Advantage was taken of this romantic episode to obtain a hearing for a couple of foreign workmen delegates at a Philopolish sympathy meeting. Their speeches, being in French, were immensely received; and Marx, striking whilst the iron was hot, formed the International Association of Working Men, better known as "The International."[1] So little was the labor question understood by the classes, that this harmless and useful international federation of Trade Unions—for it never was anything else—in a few years acquired such a lurid reputation that its foundation for the purpose of assassinating Napoleon III

1. September 28, 1864.

was regarded as a well established fact, and bogus branches of it were started by French police agents at a loss for a job, although the profits of this department of speculative enterprise were rendered hazardous by the possibility of the unlucky agent discovering, when the time came to denounce his dupes, that they too were police agents who had been cheerfully biding their time to denounce him. Meanwhile the real work of the Association flourished. It held annual conferences at various centres—[at Geneva in 1866, Lausanne in 1867, Brussels in 1868, and Bâle in 1869.] The Times devoted [11] columns to the report of the conference at [Brussels]. Numbers of unions sprang up in Germany and France; and the English workers sent generous help to back up foreign strikes. [Thus, in 1870 the iron-moulders of Paris on strike for abolition of piecework, overtime, and Sunday labor, and for fortnightly instead of monthly wages, received £264 from the International.] The voting on the grant was 7045 for to 557 against, the minority being chiefly Scotch. And the International achieved a notable victory during the [London tailors'] strike of 1867 by sending back all the [French tailors] who had been imported by the masters as blacklegs. Meanwhile, it remained very small and ludicrously poor in comparison with the magnitude of its reputation, of its scope, of its actual operations, and of the sums which it transferred. It consisted of two sets of men, quite distinct in character and aim. First, Marx, the president, with such tried fellow communists of his as, for example, Hermann Jung. Second, the president of the English section, George Odger, Trade Unionist and Dilkite Republican, with such followers as Mr Lucraft and Mr George Howell. Their intellectual relation to one another may be compendiously gathered from a collation of Marx's presidential address with that of Odger. Marx, in an elaborate document which might be a chapter from Capital, sets Mr Gladstone's celebrated budget speeches, with their boasts of prosperity advancing by leaps and bounds, beside the most startling items from the report of the Children's Employment Commission of 1863 in proof of the proposition that such prosperity has no hope or interest in it for the wage worker. He also gives a contemporary

scientific estimate of the quantity of nitrogen, carbon and other
comestibles necessary to feed a working man, and proves that the
working man does not get them. Odger simply penned a brief
scrap of conventional rant about despots, without an idea in it
germane to the International. How little his section of the council suspected the ability of the greatest man among them appears in Mr George Howell's article on the International in
the Nineteenth Century for July, 1878, in which he mentions
Marx casually as ["a German doctor."] This early effort of
criticism by the member for Bethnal Green must be classed,
with all due respect, among the things one would rather not
have said. In 1867 Marx published the first part of his great
work entitled Capital; but as he wrote in German, no immediate
effect was produced in England by it. But the cause of labor
was looking up: magazine editors began to regard essays on the
International as good copy; and in 1869 the Fortnightly Review inserted an able but venomous article on Lassalle by Mr
J. M. Ludlow, Chief Registrar of Friendly Societies, and
formerly the best informed and most active spirit in the Christian Socialist movement. In fact the crisis was not unlike that
through which we are at present passing; for we too have had a
great strike with money sent across the sea from worker to
worker, and we too have an article in the Contemporary Review. Then there was the attack of the Government on the
right of public meeting, with plentiful bludgeoning, ending
more gloriously than Trafalgar Square in the overthrow of the
railings of Hyde Park. There was the extension of the franchise
in 1867 as a parallel to that of 1885, and the Education Act of
1870 which still wants a parallel. The kingdom of heaven on
earth seemed nearer than anyone could have supposed possible
ten years earlier, when the Franco-Prussian war broke out, as
wars always will whilst the classes have power to make them
whenever a threatening development of political activity at
home makes it urgently necessary for them to divert the attention of the workers from their own affairs, and swamp the rising
spirit of fraternity in a detestable deluge of military glory. The
International felt bound by its position to meddle in the matter

to the extent of a couple of manifestoes containing certain suggestions as to what the conflicting powers ought to do, and piously explaining that of course Germany would be content with repelling the invader, and would never allow a German soldier to set foot on French soil with hostile intentions. In the light of subsequent events these manifestoes, which were signed by the whole council, can hardly be regarded as successes. Then came the overthrow of the empire, the exit of Napoleon III from French politics; the proclamation of the republic from the balcony of the Hotel de Ville by Gambetta, whose patriotism was powerfully stimulated by the immediate proximity of loaded republican revolvers; and the siege of Paris. The republican government soon found out that surrender to the German army was inevitable; but they did not dare to tell the Parisians so. When the end came, the fools who still believed that a Frenchman could lick any two Germans, and the surrender was either a piece of treachery like the surrender of Metz by Bazaine, or pure cowardice, were as angry as the shrewder spirits who began to see that the resistance, with all its waste of the people's lives, had been prolonged merely to keep up appearances, and that Trochu, the commandant, had been organizing sorties and promising victory with his tongue in his cheek. When an order [came] for the surrender of certain cannon belonging to the National Guards, cannon which had been purchased by subscription among the men themselves, the wives of the Guards, remembering what a hole these same subscriptions had made in the household money, mobbed the soldiers who were sent to carry out the order. General Lecomte, who was in command, ordered his men to fire. They refused, but subsequently thought better of it so far as to shoot *him*. On the same day their example was followed by the soldiers of General Thomas. Instantly the classes, panic stricken, fled helter skelter, government and all, from the city. Those who dared not even run for it shut themselves up in their houses, and persuaded themselves that to venture into the street would mean running the gauntlet of indiscriminate slaughter, pillage and rapine. Here was a new situation. The classes had cleared themselves out,

and the unfortunate Parisians, without having in the least intended it, found themselves with Paris on their hands. They
elected a sort of Paris County Council which they called by the
usual French term—The Commune; and the capitalist classes
throughout Europe are still convinced that a Commune must
mean a Communist government. The Commune was a desperately incapable body. If it had had one tenth part of the business
capacity and public spirit of the late Metropolitan Board of
Works, it might have fortified Paris sufficiently well to have
compelled the Republicans to abandon the mere mad dog theory
of the Commune and to secure a compromise granting the full
measure of Local Self Government which was all that the Parisians demanded. But they were a mere rabble of amateurs. Some
of them were experienced agitators, organizers of irresponsible
secret societies, prison martyrs, barricade heroes and humanitarian conspirators. Most were experienced talkers. The proportion of self-seeking rogues was probably less than in our House
of Commons. But there was nobody with any power of
administration, whether acquired or natural; or if there was, he
had not sufficient force of will to push himself into his due
place. With the enemy at their gates deliberately organizing a
massacre compared to which the St Bartholomew was a mere
street casualty, they wrangled away days and weeks made up
of the most valuable minutes that ever were thrown away.
When Thiers, who had not wasted an hour at Versailles,
whither the Republicans had fled, had completed his arrangements, his troops did not dare to occupy Paris at once, so
inconceivable was it that there was no organized plan of defence. When at last they realized that there was no harder
task before them than to cannonade one barricade after another
and slaughter the wretched defenders like rats in a pit, they fell
to with a bloodthirsty relish. Every member of the Commune
who grasped the situation and who did not care to die for the
mere sake of dying, tried the only avenue of escape from the
trap—the Prussian lines. A few got through; others, repulsed,
returned and died at the barricades; others hid themselves, and,

according to their luck, got away to London or were captured and sent to New Caledonia. Whilst the fighting lasted, the Federals, as the defenders of the Commune were called, exhibited plenty of the one military virtue that a recruiting sergeant never troubles himself about: to wit, courage. The people fought devotedly. Boys of thirteen and women did the sort of things that the Victoria Cross is given for in England. They would not obey orders, would not concert their fighting, would not fight anywhere but in their own street and among their own neighbors, but they stuck to it whilst they had a cartridge left. The regular forces of the Commune, as far as there were any regular forces, fought of course more scientifically, covering the barricades by sharpshooting from the windows, contesting the streets from block to block, and finishing the destruction of the houses as they were forced to abandon them as best they could, though petroleum was even harder to get than ammunition. This did not last long. The Republican troops soon finished the remnant of the fighting Federals with machine guns. The classes ventured into the streets; and the ladies hysterically kissed the boots of the mounted police, their deliverers. The massacre of prisoners went on until even the Tory special correspondents grew restive, when sentences of transportation to New Caledonia were substituted for summary shooting.

The effect of this in England was curious. Napoleon III had made Paris extraordinarily fashionable; and its public buildings and streets were a sort of holiday property of the Englishman abroad, who is usually much gayer than he permits himself to be at home. When it became known that these beautiful new buildings had not only been riddled with shot and shell, but that a parcel of communist wretches had actually deliberately finished them off with petroleum, middle class indignation knew no bounds. As the Republicans had cannonnaded and bombarded Paris quite as ruthlessly as the Germans, there was no denying that the unfortunate city was considerably damaged. All this ruin and demolition was added to that caused by military operations of the Federals, and the desperation of a few

Communards who thought it better to fire the powder magazine than to let the ship fall into the enemy's hands; and the total was represented as the work of deliberate, purposeless, purely envious and destructive incendiarism for incendiarism's sake. The Federal was conceived, not as a soldier, but as a vicious rough prowling in the company of abandoned women, dropping petroleum into dwelling houses until shot down at his hideous work by the honest, respectable forces of law and order. Besides, there was the affair of the hostages. The Commune had held [300] hostages, including an archbishop and a banker. Their lives had been forfeited ten times over by the laws of war; but the Commune did not stoop to the level of those villainous laws; and the hostages were spared. But in the fury and despair of the final massacre, one of their prisons was broken into by men who were almost as merciless as their foes. Almost, but not quite; for out of [300] hostages in the prison they shot only seven; but among the seven were the archbishop and the banker. At the same time another body of the hostages, [forty-eight civilians, gendarmes, and Dominican] monks, were led through the streets from [La Roquette Prison to the Rue Haxo]. The Federals, recognizing in the monk's robe an enemy's uniform, fired on them and killed [them], making a total of [55] killed as against [245] spared.[2] England did not so much mind the archbishop, as he was only a Roman Catholic one; and Protestant Ireland frankly regarded his death as a good job. But there was the banker. If bankers are to be shot by the mob without exemplary punishment, what respectable man is safe? Revolutionary Ireland, on the other hand, did not bewail

2. These figures are conjectural. Authorities vary as to the number of hostages killed and it is not clear which accounts Shaw had read. The numbers given are from Lissagary's *History of the Commune of 1871*, translated by Eleanor Marx and published in England in 1886. Belfort Bax differs slightly from Lissagary in his *Short History of the Commune of Paris*, written in conjunction with Victor Dave and William Morris and published by the Socialist League in 1886. The Archbishop of Paris was executed on May 24 along with five others. The massacre in the street took place on May 26. The banker Jecker had been shot the same morning.—ED.

the banker, but the shooting of a Roman Catholic archbishop was to it a horror, although an English country gentleman would have been more sincerely moved had the Communards shot a fox. On the whole, the effect in these islands was a tremendous surge of anti-proletarian class feeling. Coming on top of the 1869 report of the great Trade Union Royal Commission as to the Manchester and Sheffield outrages, and on the romantic tales of the International, the Commune was too much for England; and the atrocities attending its suppression, instead of exciting disgust and reaction, were accepted as proofs of the pestilential character of the movement against which they were directed.

The first direct evidence of the blow which the working class movement had sustained was the collapse of the International. Marx, knowing that the time had not come for the attempt in Paris to be seconded by simultaneous risings in the other European centres, at once saw that the Commune must fail. But if he could not save the people, he could at least hate and curse their enemies as only a great Jew can. He issued a third manifesto, a fearful document, a withering, scathing, blighting denunciation of the blackguardism and corruption of the fallen Empire and the sordid self-seeking of its Republican successor. He threw off the mask of international Trade Unionism from the International, by forcibly restating the doctrine of the antagonism of the classes and of its final solution by the overthrow of the capitalist class by the working class. He compared the common morality of Paris under the Empire to its morality under the Commune, greatly to the advantage of the latter. He quoted from the Standard and Times some of the most revolting details of the massacre of the vanquished and disarmed by Gallifet and others, about whose antecedents he added a bitter word or two. Finally, he made the best case he could for the Commune as an administrative body; but even he could not say very much for them on this score. This remarkable manifesto, which was published by the steadfastly courageous Mr Truelove of Holhorn, was a touchstone applied to the International. If that body had been veritable Social-Democratic and Marxite, its inmost soul would have rejoiced in every line of the document. But as it was really only a Trade Union Federation in which Marx was but ["a German doctor"], it broke up in disorder and was glad enough to let the manifesto go out with only Marx's and a few other signatures, mostly foreign, in order that it might shift the memory of the International name and the odium of the Commune at once from its own British shoulders to its late foreign associates. This was virtually the end of the International. For a few years it continued to hold congresses; but these were mere discussions as to the merits of Social Democracy and Anarchism, enlivened by the attempts of each party to expel the other for violation of the International constitution, or for betraying it to the police, or what not. A Russian apostle, Bakounine, stood up against the pretensions of Marx, as Marx himself in the early days of the Association stood up against the pretensions of Mazzini; both leaders formed parties; and each denounced the other as a traitor. Bakounine formed a separate organization for which he claimed a place in the International; and of the three orders of which this organization was composed, the highest and holiest were pledged the following comprehensive programme:

"The Association of International Brothers desires a universal revolution at once social, philosophic, economic, and political, so that of the existing order, founded on property, on exploitation, on domination, and on the influence of authority, whether religious, metaphysical, conventionally dogmatic (*bourgeoisement doctrinaire*), or even revolutionary on the Jacobin pattern, there may be left, in Europe at first, and finally in the rest of the world, not one stone on another at the cry of peace to all workers, liberty to all the oppressed, death to masters, exploiters and *tuteurs* of every description. We wish to destroy all States and all Churches, with all their institutions and laws, religious, political, juridical, financial, criminal, academic, economic and social, in order that all these millions of poor human creatures, cheated, enslaved, tormented, and exploited, may, when delivered, from their di-

ꞁecꞁurs and benefactors, official and officious, may breathe at
last in complete social and individual liberty."

In short, the International was now only a debating club
where nonsense was talked and personalities exchanged. It did,
and could do, nothing except give its own members some experience of the futilities and delusions of that particular phase
in revolutionary activity. Finally, after a conference at the
Hague in which Dr G. B. Clark, now the crofters' member
for Caithness and a harmless ornament of the National Liberal
Club, performed the light duties of treasurer, and heroically sustained an overdraft of £30, Marx anticipated Mr Stead's advice
to the Pope by transferring the seat of the International to
America, since when it has not been heard of. We may then
consider ourselves at this point as having reached the close of
a period in working class politics. Just as Chartism vanished
in the reaction after the unsuccessful continental revolts of
1848; so Trade Unionism, which sprang vigorously out of the
impetus given to industry by the gold discoveries, Free Trade
and the Factory Acts, and which culminated in the International, vanished as a revolutionary force in the reaction after
the unsuccessful Parisian revolt of 1871. The next era was the
Fabian era—you see I am coming to it at last. But before quit-
ting the 1848–71 period, I shall mention three things that happened just then.

No 1. In 1871 there was a boy, a member of a pious, respectable and rich middle class family, who had a precocious
habit of reading the Times. He read the accounts from the
special correspondent of the suppression of the Commune; and
he read the leading articles thereupon. Perceiving that the two
were morally incompatible, and being greatly moved by the
sufferings of the people, he cried himself to sleep every night
during the "bloody week" as it was called. Name of the sentimental boy—Ernest Belfort Bax.

No 2. In 1872 a book was published which was then considered by the literary classes a daringly advanced feat of social
and religious speculation. This was "Joshua Davidson" by Mrs

Lynn Linton. One of its hardiest suggestions was that the defenders of the Commune may have been quite as falsely vilified
as the early Christians in the days of their persecution. This passage undoubtedly changed the minds of a good many young
readers whom Marx's manifesto was not likely to reach.

No 3. Mr Charles Bradlaugh, then at open war with the
middle class as a propagandist of atheism and republicanism, was
naturally warmly interested in the success of the French republic. Of Social Democracy he knew nothing. Socialism was
to him the old community founding absurdities of which Mr
Podmore gave us an account in the second lecture of this
course. Consequently Mr Bradlaugh had no idea of what Marx
was driving at; nor could he see any real ground for antagonism between the workers of Paris and the republican over-
throwers of the empire. The proceedings of the Commune were
not calculated to gain over a man of his practical ability and
strong common sense. To him M. Félix Pyat must have appeared, as Mr Hyndman appeared fourteen years later, capable
of nothing except leading poor people into mischief. He was
therefore for the Republic and against the Commune. When he
afterwards collected money for the Federal refugees, they refused his assistance. He and Marx had of course before this had
occasion to form some definite estimate each of the other.
Marx's opinion was that Mr Bradlaugh was an ambitious self-
seeker. Mr Bradlaugh's opinion was that the French police had
received and acted upon certain information which Marx alone
had been in a position to give them, and that, in short, Marx
had given it. Neither opinion is worth anything now except as
an illustration of the radical incompatibility of the two men
and their attitude towards society. Marx's verdict was only a
hostile way of describing characteristics which Mr Bradlaugh
himself probably would not disclaim. And the International was
so beset with police spies that Marx himself could hardly have
ventured to affirm that he had never confided in the wrong
man; and a hostile critic would naturally put the worst construction on such a circumstance. This finishes my three
anecdotes.

Now let us hurry as fast as possible over the great boom of [the early 1870's] when miners smoked pipes with three bowls filled with the rarest Turkish tobaccos, when they fed their dogs on prime beefsteak, quaffed champagne, ordered pianofortes, did not care a rap for politics, and provided Mr W. H. Mallock with an inexhaustible example of the uselessness of throwing away more than a subsistence wage on the British proletarian. The tide turned in 1875, as Mr Giffen has shewn in his valuable address to the British Association at [Manchester] in [1887]; but when the depression began to make itself felt attention was absorbed by the Eastern question and the Russo-Turkish war. Besides, the Tories were in; and the Liberals were explaining that the hard times were the result of unsound Tory finance. Mr Gladstone, in his famous Midlothian speeches, tore their budgets to pieces. Who could wonder that working men were poor when the Chancellor of the Exchequer himself was insolvent? It was just like the Tories to be in debt and at their wits end at the very time that they were chorusing Mr G. H. Macdermott's declaration that they had got the guns, they'd got the men, and they'd got the money too. Evidently the way to set things straight was to kick the Tories out and put in Gladstone and Bright. That was quite as clear as it is now in the parallel—the precisely parallel—case of Gladstone and Morley. The election came in 1880; and the Liberals, going in with a triumphant rush, proceeded after a short breathing space, to bombard Alexandria in the interests of Mr Goschen and the Turkish bondholders at large. Mr Bright, not caring to throw himself away on foreign investments, retired from the cabinet and saved himself up for the benefit of the Irish landlords. Things went ill with the party in other directions. Antijingoism was all very well; but when it came to the British getting handsomely licked in South Africa the contrast between Peace with Honor and War with Dishonor became disagreeable to the national amour propre. Again, although at election time Russia was Holy Russia, and her ruler Alexander the Good, she was now Nihilist ridden Russia, and that ruler was now Alexander the Dismembered and Dead by Dynamite, an event which stimulated the revolutionary imagination afresh. And meanwhile, in spite of Gladstonian finance, the hard times continued harder than ever, and even the decennial boom of the Marxian economic calendar failed to return with its pianofortes and three-bowl pipes. Clearly, there was nothing left for the Liberals but their old trump card of a franchise bill and a dash at Home Rule. But where was Social Democracy all this time?

Well, the election of 1880 had brought forward a candidate who did not go in with a rush. The constituency he wooed was Marylebone: his address was on the "free land" lines of Mr Arthur Arnold, an unexceptionably Whig Liberal, except on foreign policy, for it expressed a strong suspicion of the "holiness" of Russia. At that moment this sufficed to label the would-be member for Marylebone as a Jingo; and he failed to secure the seat. Had the Tories been in the ascendent the result might have been different; for he was an ideal Tory candidate of the new school, generous but ignorant in his notions of the working class, interested in foreign politics as in a game of chance and skill combined, one who on coming up from Cambridge had written his magazine article—on Cavour—and at once had it accepted by the Fortnightly Review, and been added by Mr Greenwood to the list of contributors to the old conservative Pall Mall; therefore a brilliant man, and, as it happened, a rich one, able to make the most of a taking presence and great conversational plausibility. His name was Henry Meares [sic] Hyndman. Like most men of active imagination, he had always been in search of an ideal. He had gone even to the Fiji islands to look for it; but though the voyage gave a certain cannibal flavor to his reminiscences that greatly heightened their conversational effect, it did not lead to the discovery of an ideal. It is safe to assume that the Marylebone fiasco made the real seem more insufficient than ever; and Mr Hyndman would possibly have returned to Fiji had he not by some chance undertaken a shorter voyage to Haverstock Hill, and there met Karl Marx. From that intercourse he came out a finished Marxite Socialist equipped at last with an ideal which he put before the world in his pamphlet entitled "England for All." Meanwhile

Master Belfort Bax, the young gentleman who had cried himself
to sleep during the "bloody week" in 1871, had attained to years
of such discretion as were compatible with the peculiarities of
his temperament. He had spent some years in Germany as student of music and foreign correspondent; had followed his bent
towards history and philosophy far enough to bring himself into
line with the Social-Democratic standpoint, and was an intense
hater of the middle class and its pietism. He had read Das
Kapital and become a Marxite. Accordingly, having made the
acquaintance of Peter Kropotkin, and hearing from him of the
existence of one Hyndman who promised to be the Lassalle of
England, he asked Kropotkin for an introduction; and the
result was a Marxite nucleus for an English socialist party. But
there was not much recruiting to be done by German philosophy and the untranslated Das Kapital. Fortunately, another
book came into the field which opened its readers' eyes sufficiently widely to the fact that our competitive industry based
on private property is one which degrades the masses and robs
them of the fruits of their toil for the benefit of an idle and
pernicious proprietary class. This was Mr Henry George's
Progress and Poverty; and in the course of its large circulation
it began to startle men here and there into revolutionary activity. For instance, there was stationed at Chatham a young officer
who was no common messroom ornament. He had been idle
at school, and had retrieved himself by breaking into the army
by a prodigious feat of application. He had been extravagant in
the army, and had paid his debts by resolutely plunging into
military business as distinguished from military glory by accepting, in India, one of those lucrative but inglorious posts known
technically in the more exclusive walks of Her Majesty's Service as "blokeships." When the Afghan war broke out on the
death of Cavagnari, Mr Henry Hyde Champion put off the
bloke and resumed the soldier. In due time, the wounds of his
country being healed, he returned with his regiment to England.
When the Egyptian war broke out, he naturally desired to avail
himself of the professional opportunities which it offered; but
he was rebuffed and condemned to vegetate at Chatham, where-

upon, like Mr Hyndman after Marylebone, he became convinced that there was something radically wrong with our social
system. Frequent participation in Courts Martial gave him opportunities of studying the quality of mercy as strained through
the classes to the masses. In this temper he read Mr Seymour
Veay's striking pamphlet on the corrupt motives of the
Egyptian war, entitled "Spoiling the Egyptians." Progress and
Poverty finished him. He left the army; came up to London;
selected one of the most discredited publishing businesses he
could find in the realm of heterodox blokedom; and after a
brief apprenticeship to Kegan Paul and Co. went into it in partnership with our fellow Fabian Mr Foulger, and proceeded to
neglect it with a vigor that surpassed all his previous displays
of energy, not because he was idle, but because he joined the
Hyndman-Bax-Marxite nucleus and threw all his force into
the work of propaganda and working class organization. He
took Marx on trust, having no time to read him.

The vogue of Progress and Poverty led to Mr Henry
George's appearance in England as a speaker. One of his converts, an Eton master named James Leigh Joynes—not "old
Joynes," but "young Joynes"—took a trip to Ireland with him,
and was incarcerated for some hours in a country police station
by the coercive myrmidons, not of "bloody Balfour," but of
Buckshot Forster and the Grand Old Man. Mr Joynes wrote
to the Times and published a book containing an account of his
adventures. Eton immediately cast him out; and Mr Joynes, in
the wildness of freedom, read Das Kapital, a feat which came
easily to him, as he was the son of a German mother. At this
time Bax was a member of the Democratic Federation, which
he had joined in June 1882 with an ardent Fenian, formerly an
officer in the British army and subsequently a war correspondent, whose name was C. L. Fitzgerald. In 1883 Bax called on
Mr William Morris, who had refused to join the Federation;
and the Baxic dialectic proved so effectual that Morris changed
his mind; and the upshot was that on Whit Monday 1883, the
Federation received into its ranks Morris, Champion, Joynes,
and R. Q. B. Frost, an old school friend of Champion's, who

had been at Marlboro' with him. Frost was the son of a non-
conformist divine, and had a touch of the pulpit in his manner
as a speaker. He was fanatically in earnest, and soon became a
most active worker. The Federation, now splendidly reinforced,
threw off its old ambiguous character, and issued a definitely
Social-Democratic manifesto, which of course drove away the
mere rhetoricians, amateurs of social reform, and Positivists.
Professor Beesley went, the name of Butler-Johnstone disappeared from the roll; but Miss Helen Taylor held on resolutely.

It now became apparent that the Federation would not at-
tract the Georgite forces. Georgism really revived Christian
Socialism; but how could Christians join the Federation whilst
Mr Bax was declaring that the presence of a Christian clergy-
man in that body was an intolerable anomaly and the rest
seemed in no hurry to contradict him? Accordingly, the Land
Reform Union, now the English Land Restoration League, was
founded to carry out the land taxation scheme of Mr Henry
George, and a paper was started by it under the old title, "The
Christian Socialist."

I have now briefly to introduce an important figure—myself.
I, like Champion and Hyndman, had my fiasco, and had the
lowest opinion of society in consequence. I had come from Ireland to London in 1876; had adopted literature as a profession for
which no expensive plant was required; had written five novels
and a heap of articles, and was the very deadest and completest
failure in the metropolis, not a line of my novels or articles having
ever made its way into print. I was known to a very small circle as
a thinker upon social questions by my having read before a society
of ardent Malthusians a paper advocating the logical outcome
of their doctrine—that is, infanticide. But the reduction of middle class theories to absurdity, a very easy exercise to an Irishman, did not satisfy me. I heard Mr Henry George, and at once
saw that the economic track was the track to be followed up.
I read Progress and Poverty, and went to a meeting of the
Democratic Federation. There I found Mr Hyndman in the
chair; and I saw at once that he had some intellectual basis concerning capital which I did not understand, and that there was a

movement behind his silk hat, his beard, and his plausible de-
livery. Acting on my experience of the best way to provoke
further explanations, I took the first opportunity to rise and
contradict everybody; declare my contempt for the Federation;
and accuse them of drawing a red herring across the track indicated by Mr Henry George. Mr Hyndman replied with
great confidence that I would join them as soon as I found out
what they were at; and I was recommended to read Capital
by our friend Mr Robert Banner, who had been instructed in
Marxism by Andreas Scheu, an Austrian Social Democrat who
in his own country had cut a figure in prison and on the platform in the days of the International, and who was now a voluntary exile, a propagandist of Socialism and bent wood
furniture, a peculiarly eloquent speaker in spite of his Austrian
accent, and the first anti-Hyndmanite. Mr Hyndman had, in
fact, told him that he did not understand the English people.
Well, I read Das Kapital; and I had no sooner done so than I
discovered that very few members of the Federation had done
so. I became a furious Socialist, and attended the Federation
discussions, where I heard various speakers, Dr G. B. Clark,
Miss Helen Taylor, the veteran Mr Hennessey, Mr Joynes, and
the stentorian Captain Tom Lemon, who subsequently devoted
his colossal strength of lung to the more lucrative department
of Sugar Bounty agitation. There was also Mr John E. Williams,
an unskilled laborer and an indefatigable agitator. He had been
educated in the party of Dr Kenealy; and though he denounced
the oppression from which he had himself conspicuously suffered, with great violence and bitterness of speech, yet he kept
out of the quarrels that afterwards arose in a most faithful and
friendly way, and when a martyr was wanted went into prison
without a murmur as a man accustomed to get the kicks whilst
the others got the halfpence. I did not join the Federation,
though I was present at one, or perhaps two, council meetings,
where I witnessed some passages of arms between Mr Hyndman
and a most bloodthirsty Irish desperado, whose very name I
am afraid to mention, and concerning whom Mr Hyndman
would say with great gravity that the moment we began to

march, the provost marshal would settle accounts with this
implacable fire-eater. For remember, we were all Marxites and
insurrectionists. We saw nothing for it but militant organization
and revolt; and when Captain Wilson, the Comprehensionist,
asked Mr Hyndman in Regents Park how many men he would
take the field with, Mr Hyndman said that 20,000 would be
enough—or perhaps it was 200,000; but the exact number is
not statistically important.

One evening I was invited to attend a council meeting of the
Land Reform Union at the house of the Frosts in Woburn
Place; and there I found Frost, of course, Champion, William
Reeves the publisher, Joynes, the Rev Mr Symes of Nottingham, and an unknown gentleman, of about twentyfour, evidently a young man of fashion, clean shaven save for a pointed
moustache, elegantly dressed, with an intellectual head, manners almost as brusque as Champion's, and a curious combination of offhandedness and invincible obstinacy. On making
inquiries concerning this reformer I gathered that he was one
of the early Positivist members of the Federation; that he was
given for the moment to dallying with polite society; and that
his name was Sydney Olivier. At quite an early stage of the proceedings I told the Rev Symes that he was no better than the
chaplain of a pirate ship; and the wrangle on Georgism v. Marxism which ensued lasted into the small hours. I at once joined
the Land Reform Union, and am still a member, unless Mr
Verinder has struck me off for arrears of subscription.

Another picture which I may sketch shortly is that of a
conference on Christian Socialism, at which the Rev H. C.
Shuttleworth, then a Canon, now a Fabian, delivered a tremendously energetic address. He was opposed by the well
known Secularist and Darwinian, Dr Edward Aveling, just then
newly converted to Social Democracy by Miss Eleanor Marx
as a preliminary to their union. She was also there; and I hope
I may be excused for confessing that the daughter of the great
Karl Marx so interested me that I made a speech solely in order
to make an impression on her. Bax also opposed the opener;
and Andreas Scheu, whom I had never seen before, followed on

the same side. Another new face was that of a gentleman whose
manner was so extremely combative that I knew before he
opened his mouth, by the mere glare and twist of his aggressive
eyeglass, that he was going to back up Christianity. This will
hardly be recognized as a portrait of Mr Hubert Bland; but it
was no other. Mr Bland joined the Federation with Mrs Bland:
so did Miss Marx and Dr Aveling. The Federation was now
quite a mine of hope and faith and confidence. Mr Bradlaugh
attacked us strenuously; but you cannot imagine in these days
of sober retrospect and disillusion how absurd, how irrelevant,
we thought him. There was no arguing with a man who was
in the valley whilst we were on the mountain top. Mr Hyndman challenged him to debate in St James's Hall. The hall was
crammed, as much with Hyndmanites as with Bradlaughites.
Anyone can read the verbatim report made by our comrade
Theodore Wright, and can see from it how tremendously effective Mr Bradlaugh was, and how ineffective Mr Hyndman,
from the debating point of view. But to us Mr Bradlaugh was
only stumbling in the dark round a region of light in which
Mr Hyndman was an initiated adept. Mr Bradlaugh's fierce
contempt for his opponent only amused me, though it pained
Stewart Headlam; and at the Hall of Science and South Place
I made outrageously flippant speeches after his lectures—
speeches which earned me a highly uncomplimentary notice in
the National Reformer. The movement now rushed into print.
Justice, financed by William Morris and Edward Carpenter—another recruit of the first quality—was started at twopence weekly,
and continued at a penny. Joynes and Bax bought an unsuccessful shilling magazine called To-Day; and I generously contributed one of my unsuccessful novels, which Joynes accepted
because he could not bear to hurt anyone's feelings, and Bax
submitted to on being told that he could not decently refuse
without at least reading the MS, which he positively declined
to do. Champion, of course, printed both Justice and To-Day.
I offered to report Mr Bradlaugh's lectures at the Hall of Science for Justice; and I contrived, whilst faithfully giving what
he said, to give it an exquisitely ridiculous air. This I considered

perfectly fair; but when Mr Hyndman cut out of one of my reports a really acute remark of Mr Bradlaugh's which I reported appreciatively, and further omitted some polite acknowledgment of the management of a meeting by Mrs Besant, whom I admired with the exasperating chivalry of an Irishman, I retired from the justice staff after writing a letter in which I shewed that Marx's theory of value was incompatible with his theory of exploitation. I mention a trifle like this because it was the cumulative effect of a dozen such trifles which prevented me from entering the Federation, though I stood on the very threshold of it.

One day I saw in a newspaper a phrase which struck me as an inspiration—The Fabian Society. Its first tract, "Why are the Many Poor?", the work of Mr Bland and the secretary Mr F. Keddell made it clear that the society was on the Socialist warpath; and I joined at once. The name suggested the plane of intellectual method and intellectual training which makes the Social Democrat the true aristocrat among politicians. In the course of my guerrilla warfare against middle class ideas I had here and there come across some clever speaker and worker who had struck me as being the sort of person with whom I could get effectively into harness to pull at any reform movement that might turn up. It would be easy to lure them into a Fabian Society, but very hard to get them into a Democratic Federation noted for its cranks, the disquieting celebrity of its individual members, its open intolerance and want of intellectual discipline. So I threw in my lot with the Fabian, and, on my first appearance there, found Mr Bland in the chair, and Mr Rowland Estcourt entertaining the company with masses of statistics. Poor Mr Estcourt was before his time. The psychologic moment for "Facts for Socialists" and "Facts for Londoners" had not yet come. Statistics were voted a bore; and we issued a manifesto in which we declared that we would face civil war rather than another century of such suffering as the last had seen. Then Mrs Wilson directed our attention to the claims of Anarchism with such effect that when we at last resolved to issue a tract entitled "What Socialism is," it was divided into two sections: one, by Mrs Wilson, giving the Anarchist ideal; and the other, by Keddell, giving the Social-Democratic ideal in a form mainly borrowed from Bebel's book on "Woman." It was that tract that finally convinced me that none of us knew what Socialism was. We were all violent reactionaries against the existing system. We had all got tight hold of the cardinal fact that it was dishonest, and that the way to remedy it was to abolish payments of part of the product of labor to idle landlords and capitalists. We believed in educating the whole working class in these opinions until they would fall into the ranks and march irresistibly to victory.

V   Socialism and Human Nature

The British Museum manuscript of this lecture has a note by Shaw—"Read to the meeting of the Fabian Society in Bloomsbury Hall on the 19th September 1890 as the first of a series dealing with Objections to Socialism." The last page bears the date September 11.

The people who object to Socialism on the ground that it is not adapted to the character of Man are not unanimous as to whether Socialists overrate human nature or underrate it. It is clear that to those who regard the expropriation of the landlord and capitalist as an act of unscrupulous plunder, the conversion of the human race to Socialism means its demoralization. When they say to us, "You will never succeed," they mean that human nature is too good to be corrupted by our seditious teachings. We have their austere assurance that until Socialism assumes such a form as to make all collision with the ten commandments impossible, the English nation, founded as it is foursquare on the twentieth chapter of Exodus, will have nothing to do with us. The Fabian Society recognizes this, and has elaborated a perfect method of dodging the decalogue. Nothing can be more honest, more constitutional, more legal, more moral, more just, than the Fabian proposal. It is—and I say it with pride, as one who has had some share in its excogitation—a masterpiece of double dealing. By its means the pious English expropriator can now empty the pockets of the proprietary class without letting his left hand know what his right doeth; and this, as we know, is the feat which reconciles and identifies the highest virtue with the most consummate hypoc-

risy. It lifts us into the Hegelian category in which the contra-
diction between the two lower categories of confiscation and
compensation is solved. I therefore may assume that the socialist
morality is the higher morality; and that the real weight of the
objection to be dealt with is on the side of those who not only
admit the righteousness of our counsels, but habitually exagger-
ate it to the point of a millennial beauty and holiness in order to
give the greater force to their contention that the race cannot
rise to it, the heart of man being deceitful above all things and
desperately wicked. Now I shall smash and ruin that contention
with ease; but yet I shall not attempt to do so by holding a
brief for Man against those who have no very high opinion of
him. The king of Brobdingnag told Gulliver that, as far as he
could make out, our history was "only a heap of conspiracies,
rebellions, murders, massacres, revolutions, banishments: the
very worst effects that avarice, faction, hypocrisy, perfidious-
ness, cruelty, rage, madness, hatred, envy, lust, malice, and ambition, could produce." This statement of the case in terms of
our conventional system of ethics is a perfectly correct one. If
you accept the position that avarice, faction, hatred, envy, lust,
and the rest of them, are absolutely, unconditionally wrong,
then you must admit the king of Brobdingnag's conclusion that
we are about as pernicious a set of insects as ever crawled on the
earth. For my part, I go further than the king of Brobdingnag,
because he quite omitted the worst effects of fraternity, truth,
justice, love, self-sacrifice, duty, religion, and chastity, which,
as far as my observation has gone, do a great deal more harm
than the admittedly objectionable ideals censured by Gulliver's
royal patron, since the virtuous malefactors are praised and encouraged, whereas the vicious ones are punished and made infamous. Another criticism, which touches us more directly, I
also admit. It is that of A. J. Macdonald, the historian of
Utopian Socialism, upon Robert Owen. Speaking of a meeting
at which Owen was recruiting for his community at New Harmony, Macdonald says:—"Owen seems to have forgotten that if
one and all the thousand persons assembled there had possessed
the qualities which he wished them to possess, there would have

been no necessity for his vain exertions to form a community; because there would of necessity have been brotherly love, peace, and plenty." Here again, though I by no means endorse the assumption that it was want of brotherly love that brought New Harmony to grief, I have no intention of evading Macdonald's point by claiming that men are in the least less selfish than he took them to be. I have no objection to place the case for Socialism on the ground that all men are fiercely selfish, and to shew that it works out as the best available system on that ground just as irrefutably as on the hypothesis that all men are naturally fraternal. Indeed it is evident that unless we are prepared to take that ground on occasion, we shall never convert the misanthropic pessimists, who are by no means the least intelligent members of the community. I can confute a pessimist opponent without even denying that selfishness is absolutely detestable, which is an advantage to me; for the last time I hinted at a Fabian meeting that it would be as impossible to form a Socialist State from absolutely unselfish individuals as to build a house with drops of quicksilver, I so offended one of the most fraternal of our comrades, that he denounced me in a public print as a pig incapable of appreciating Beethoven's sonatas; and this, too, without considering that as I earn my bread as a musical critic, such a statement might have cost me my livelihood. Therefore for the moment I refrain from raising the question as to the absolute and unconditional vileness of selfishness, and confine myself to pointing out the utter impossibility of convincing any opponent who is minded to think otherwise, that men will ever act quite unselfishly. The acceptance of the capitalist system by the classes which profit by it proves the contrary. Mind: I do not say that the *existence* of the capitalist system proves the contrary; for the capitalist system was not established consciously and intentionally: mankind stumbled into it by mere force of circumstances; and not one man in a thousand comprehends it fully even now that it has been established for a century. But if we were not wicked enough to deliberately contrive it, we are quite wicked enough to take merciless advantage of it now that social evolution has contrived it for us. The factory owners did not devise the industrial revolution; but when it offered them the opportunity of becoming rich by practising the most devilish inhumanities, they practised them ruthlessly, and had no difficulty in finding workmen-overseers willing to wield the lash for them for a few shillings a day, until they were stopped by force. Where the force is not applied, as in the Bombay cotton mills at the present day, and in the sweaters' dens which are unknown to the inspector, the old villainies are still rife. The shareholders of our Tramway Companies do not consider that the conductors who began work at seven in the morning, and leave off at half past twelve at night, are at all overworked. The landlords of Ireland have devastated it, and are still to the utmost of their crippled power devastating it, without shame and without pity. The horrors of our chemical works, our whitelead, emerald green and match factories, of the Sheffield grinder's wheel and the Cradley Heath nail and chain forges, of the bakeries and "home industries" of London and other towns, have all been exposed again and again without as much as a blush from even the clergymen and members of parliament who look to these horrors for their dividends. Black country or green country, turn where you will, you cannot, if you were the most featherheaded optimist that ever canted, deny the truth of Morris's saying that NO MAN IS GOOD ENOUGH TO BE ANOTHER MAN'S MASTER.

From this point of view, it may be asked why each half of the race has not by this time exterminated the other, like the Kilkenny cats. The reply is, that though a great deal has been done in that direction, yet resistance so far balances encroachment, that men at last give up striving for mastery except when they are backed by artificial or accidental advantages. Given a monopoly, the holder uses it to enslave his fellow. Deprived of it, he finds that it is better to give up the dream of mastery, and make up his mind to live and let live. We see this exemplified in the country gentleman who, fortified by his landed estate, treats his landless laborers worse than he treats his horses and values a laborer's life at about a quarter that of a pheasant's, but has nevertheless to concede the fullest rights of equality to his fellow squires. Again, in the conflict of commercial competition, when the small capitalists succumb, and leave the field to the unconquerably big ones, these latter give up striving, and form a trust. The same selfish considerations which compel the landlords and capitalists to live and let live among themselves would impose the same policy on the whole community if the workers would destroy the monopoly of land and its derivative monopolies of capital and education. This the selfishness of the workers will eventually impel them to do. Now the political formula for the policy of Live and Let Live is Social Democracy. Hence we arrive at Social Democracy just as inevitably by way of what the king of Brobdingnag would call our evil passions as by way of our fraternal impulses. The same forces that made Squire Western the social equal of Sir Isaac Newton and Handel can make the ploughman equal to Squire Western without the intervention of a single fraternal impulse on either side. Social Democracy is thus pessimism-proof. In fact, we can offer the pessimist certainty where we can only offer the optimist hope.

But for my part, I set little store by pessimism and less by optimism. If all dogs were constantly chained, there would be a great prevalence of the opinion that all dogs were fierce brutes, only fit to be shot. Living, as I do, among chained men, I am not surprised to find the same opinion rife as regards mankind. And just as the ferocity of the chained dog makes people afraid to let him loose; so the ferocity of the chained man makes us similarly dubious as to the wisdom of unchaining him. Five years ago I was asked to give my own opinion on the point in the form of a lecture. Whilst I was puzzling my brains as to what string I should hang my ideas on, I came across a book which contained a classification of human depravity by no less an authority on the subject than the Roman Catholic Church. The name of the book was "The Crown of Jesus: A complete Catholic Manual of Devotion, Doctrine, and Instruction." From it I learned that there were, roughly speaking, twentysix sins open to me if I chose to embark on a career of vice. Many of them I had already committed. Seven were classified as deadly; six were sins against the Holy Ghost; four cried to heaven for vengeance; and the rest were described as "noteworthy ways of incurring guilt by causing others to sin." It was encouraging to find that oppression of the poor and defrauding laborers of their wage were among the four which cry to heaven for vengeance; but the moral is undoubtedly that of the fable in which the laborer cries to Jupiter to take his cart out of the rut for him, and is told to put his own shoulder to the wheel. As the nine noteworthy ways of incurring guilt by causing others to sin included Praise or Flattery, Concealment, Partaking and Silence, I could not but feel some concern as to what might be in store for our newspaper editors and professors of political economy, who must certainly be damned fathoms deep if my manual of devotion is to be believed. The book was not without consolation for both poor and rich; for it included fasting in a list of three eminent good works, which will perhaps please those who have nothing to eat, and who are British enough to make a virtue of necessity; whilst the four last things to be remembered are Death, Judgment, Hell, and Heaven, which may cheer the rich, as they are certainly the last things they ever do remember.

However, these niceties need not concern us here: we shall find the seven deadly sins enough for us this evening. The question for us to consider is whether, assuming the seven to represent propensities in man which are ineradicable, they will be more mischievous under Socialism than under private Capitalism. If so, then it may well be that human nature is not good enough for Socialism. If not, it may well be—and this is what I shall contend—that the present system is not good enough for human nature. First then, what are the seven deadly sins? They are 1, Arrogance; 2, Covetousness; 3, Lust; 4, Anger; 5, Gluttony; 6, Envy; and 7, Sloth. Now I, having, as already hinted, been at one time or another guilty of the whole seven, sometimes to my own hurt and that of others, but sometimes also to my own benefit and that of others, am by no means satisfied with this sweeping dismissal of them as "deadly sins." I perceive plainly that morals are not to be learnt by culling flowers of rhetoric in "The Garden of Jesus." These seven deadly sins do not describe the ineradicable propensities in human nature, but only certain modes of exercising them. Exactly the same propensities, exercised in another way, might be described as the seven blessed virtues. This is no mere dialectical splitting of hairs; it is a distinction recognized in everyday life. If a man has a propensity to having his own way, why does he call it Firmness whilst his wife calls it Obstinacy? Why is Mr Stanley applauded in England as a heroic example of the imperial instincts of his race, and cursed by many Africans as a pirate and filibustering marauder? Why I am told on one hand that Mr Sidney Webb is an able and earnest reformer, and on the other that he is a seditious scoundrel? Why do the economic essays and the Ibsenist criticisms which win me flattering encomiums from The Star, move the St James's Gazette to denounce me as "a Trafalgar Square casual," and Justice ("the organ of the Social Democracy") to call me a pig? The answer is obvious. A propensity is a vice from the point of view of the persons whom it injures or offends, and a virtue from the point of view of those whom it benefits and encourages. When I am brought to my final account, and accused of the seven deadly sins, I shall be at no loss for a defence. In imagination I can see the devil, as general prosecutor, making sure of me as I stand in the dock to answer for my life. And I assure you I shall not call upon the hills to cover me. "I accuse this man," the devil will say, "of all the seven deadly sins: to wit, Pride, Covetousness, Lust, Wrath, Gluttony, Envy, and Sloth." To which I will indignantly retort, "What! are my actions to be thus foully distorted in the mirror of this filthy fiend's mind? Is my manliness and self-respect to be stigmatized as arrogance, my prudent thrift as covetousness, my natural affections as lust, my righteous indignation—for, like St Paul, I have sometimes said to myself that I did right to be angry—as wrath, my genial and neighborly conviviality as gluttony, my honest emulation as envy, and my easygoing humility and contentment as sloth? If so, there is no justice in heaven." I think that would settle the seven deadly sins. But it would not settle my case. It would simply force the devil to give up his attempt to have me judged by my conformity to a series of conventional conceptions of absolutely fit conduct, and come down at once to the real question of how much harm I had done. Probably he would not suffer on the whole by this change of base. It is true that he would lose a great many vicious men who had done more good than harm; but then think of all the virtuous men he would catch because they had done much more harm than good. Observe, mankind have foreseen this for many centuries as plainly as I foresee it now. I am no novelty hawker or paradox monger, whatever the *good* people present may think. The world found out long ago that hell is paved, not with bad intentions, but with good ones.

We are now in a position to deal with the opponent who asks us whether Socialism will eradicate vice. Vice being merely an injurious exercise of exactly the same propensities that form the virtues when beneficially exercised, it is evident that vice cannot be eradicated without eradicating virtue also, since they both grow upon the same stalk. The true question at issue then is, "Will the conditions of life under Socialism compare unfavorably with present conditions in point of encouraging the beneficial exercise of our propensities, and checking the injurious exercise of them?" The point is a vital one; for we now see that there is no need to alter a man's nature in order to turn him from a scoundrel into a saint. Human nature is only the raw material which Society manufactures into the finished rascal or the finished fellowman, as the case may be, according to the direction in which it applies the pressure of self-interest. I shall have no difficulty in proving that our system of leaving the industry of the country to take its chance in the hands of competing private proprietors places a premium on sordid and unscrupulous rascality, and starves out the wider social instincts as if they were criminal. Our typical successful man is an odious person, vulgar, thick-skinned, pleased by the contrast between his own riches and the poverty of others, unable to see any reason why men should not be degraded into flunkeys

In his kitchen, or women poisoned by phosphorus and white-lead in his factory, so long as his pride and his purse are swelled. Need I add that he is religious, charitable, patriotic, and full to the neck of ideals—respectability, true womanliness, true manliness, duty, virtue, chastity, subdual of the lower nature by the higher, self-sacrifice, abstinence, the constitution, the family, law and order, punctuality, honesty, a good name: he has the whole rogue's rosary at his fingers' ends. How do we contrive to make such a monster as this out of anything so innocent as a man? For if you converse with these blackguards, you will find them no such fiends as you might expect, but potentially decent fellows enough, who have found that the line of least resistance has led them to unintended enormities, and whose attempt to disguise those enormities from themselves by the clumsy but well meant hypocrisies of idealism shews that they have plenty of good in them if only our social arrangements gave it a chance. Consider for a moment these seven deadly sins of ours: Arrogance, Covetousness, Lust, Wrath, Gluttony, Envy, and Sloth. We have seen that they are only sins when the propensities they represent are indulged to the harm of somebody. That is, they are social acts: a man cannot be envious or angry all to himself: he must envy someone—be wroth with someone. Even sloth and gluttony, which at first sight seem self-regarding, are socially objectionable only when the culprit attempts to do less and take more than his fair share. All these sins then have their victims. The natural cure for them is the resistance of the victims—the same cure that makes a child understand that it cannot have everything its own way. The spoiled child is the one which never encounters this salutary resistance; and a man can be spoiled by exactly the same deprivation. The king who forbids his minister to mention the word Impossible to him is a spoiled man; and the lady with a habit of reading in bed, who rings for her maid at five o'clock in the morning to pick up the book when it slips over on to the floor, is a spoiled woman. It is no more their fault that they are spoiled than it is the child's. Make the minister the king's equal and the king will be roundly told not to talk like a fool when he makes his petulant objec-

tions to the word Impossible. Make the maid the equal of the
Duchess and she will meet the request to pick up the book with
an emphatically expressed determination to see the Duchess
elsewhere first, with some additional remarks on inconsiderate
and lazy people which will be much harder to bear than the
alternative exertion of getting out of bed and picking up the
book when it slips over on to the floor, is a spoiled woman. It is
ister may speak his mind more freely than formerly to the
king—one cannot imagine the Prince of Wales giving himself
the airs of Louis XIV with Lord Salisbury—yet the maid, and
the class which she represents—that is to say, the great bulk of
the population—must submit without a murmur to be arrogantly
insulted, covetously exploited, lustfully prostituted, and wrath-
fully coerced, by the slothful and gluttonous, until they themselves are consumed with wrath and envy, and take refuge in
dull apathy, or in drunken recklessness, or in the hope that by
pinching and scraping they may themselves rise to be idlers
and oppressors, as the Bishops and "grand old men" so earnestly
exhort them to do.

The great London landlord, with a thousand or two a day
for doing nothing, rolls past the laborer who cannot with his
utmost toil make a thousand pounds in fifty years, and who is
yet three times as rich as women of his own class who work
sixteen hours a day. Imagine the frame of mind of the moralist
who, though in full view of this, says to the Socialist, "You
will never get rid of these contrasts until you have got rid of
the sins of Arrogance and Covetousness." As if the landlord
had made himself rich by his arrogance and the laborer had
made himself poor by his covetousness. Again, we pretend to
so abhor lust that we can hardly think it quite decent even to
preach against it. We then offer a pretty woman a position
either behind the refreshment bar at a railway station for fourteen hours a day, or in some other place where her good looks
will attract custom and make profit for us, assuring her at the
same time that it would be the lowest infamy for her to use
her good looks to make profits for herself. As to the man who

would live on her earnings in the event of her taking such a
step, no words can express our loathing for him, though if he
owned the refreshment bar or was a manufacturer employing
women at wages which they could not live on without resorting
to prostitution occasionally to bring them up to bare subsistence
level, he would be a highly respected member of society. Here
then we have a second contrast brought about by our economic
arrangements: to wit, on the one hand a female proletariat so
ill paid and contemptuously treated that it matters little to them
whether they sell themselves for one purpose to a brutal employer or for another to a drunken libertine, and on the other
the whole male sex, headed by a contingent of gentlemen with
a growing reluctance to marry before they are thirtyfive, and
seldom without a sovereign or two to spare. Evidently the one
condition necessary for giving Lust its very widest scope is
the reduction of women to mere commodities at prices ranging
downward to two or three farthings an hour for the dullest
sorts of drudgery. As to Anger, what likelihood is there of that
being bridled in a community where the great majority of the
workers are under the thumb of a master who can turn any one
of them into the street an unemployed man with perhaps
months of starvation for himself and his family before him?
And so on through all the weeds in the garden.

Here then is a pretty soil for the seven deadly sins to take
root in and multiply seventy times seven. Armed by the State
with bludgeon and bayonet, shot and shell, prison and gallows,
starvation and disgrace, they stamp out the resistance that would,
if set free, cure them in a day. They enslave the very wills of
their victims by setting up their own power as the sole earthly
reward of merit. When the smug apostles of competitive scoundrelism declare that the poor are made poor by their vices, the
poor themselves half believe it, even though when Mr. Charles
Booth goes down among them to count heads he finds in every
five hundred East Enders only four scamps to every hundred
of the miserably poor. And these very poor are the people who
must purge society of its deadly sins by simply refusing to put

up any longer with the Arrogance, the Covetousness, the Lust, the Anger, the Gluttony, the Envy, and the Sloth of their present masters.

Once shew them the way to an independent equality with the aggressors, and you will have shewn the way to a clean sweep of the seven deadly sins from the non-criminal world. This is why every advance towards equality improves conduct and character. Until perfect equality is reached, wickedness cannot be diminished to its irreducible minimum. But perfect equality is the consummation of Social Democracy. How then can the replacement by Social Democracy of a system under which idle and useless persons receive incomes four thousand, six thousand, nay, ten thousand times as great as the precarious earnings of the hardest worked classes in the country—how is that going to make men worse instead of better?

In laying before the Fabian Society on a previous occasion an analysis of the economic development of the Private Property system, I had to point out the extravagant bedevilment of the national industry which is produced by the enormous inequality inevitably resulting from that system. I shewed that whilst masses of the people are rotting, morally and physically, for want of sufficient bread, efficient teaching, and wholesome dwellings, yet capital automatically flows away from the production of these things to that of plush, velveteen, laces, race-horses, yachts, carriages, hothouse flowers, canvas backed ducks, turtles, and December strawberries; and that men can earn more as flunkeys, jockeys and gamekeepers than as bakers, school-masters and plumbers. Tonight I have had to shew that in-equality depraves human nature as inevitably as it wastes wealth. It enables—it encourages—it actually forces men to indulge their propensities to the point at which they become vices and sins, instead of keeping them, as they would be kept in a com-munity of equals, within the limits of harmless enjoyment. To such an extent has this gone that the people who are incapable of comprehending the relation of the parts of society to the whole, have come to the conclusion that enjoyment must al-ways lead to bestiality, and that the only safety lies in renunciation. Hence our dismal Puritanism, our conception of Sunday as a day on which it is wrong to do anything pleasant, and our cant about the beauty of self-sacrifice. Hence, too, our danger that Fabianism, with its numerous recruits from the middle class, may taint Socialism with the ideal of self-sacrifice. The message of Socialism at present is one of rebellion, of implacable self-assertion, of resolute refusal to be unhappy in any avoidable fashion on any terms. So far from idealizing fraternity, we shew the working class that they must utterly refuse to fraternise with those who deny them the rights of social equals, that they must place 'the destruction of arbitrary privilege before all other ends, and that the objection that such conduct is selfish must have no weight with them against it. Further, we shew the workers that that supreme gift will never come by way of gift —that it must be taken, and that too by the strong hand. The man who hates servitude with starvation, but can tolerate it with eighteen shillings a week, will never be free. If, in Hamlet's phrase, we are "pigeon livered, and lack gall to make oppression bitter," Fabianism will come to mean nothing but an excuse for not fighting. I am afraid some of our recently acquired middle class vogue is due to an impression that we have found out a way of making socialism itself an excuse for exhorting the working class not to do anything rash. If we take to using that phrase in any other sense than one generally uses the other ancient formula, "Dont nail his ear to the pump," we shall stay in Bloomsbury Hall, and the capitalists in parliament, to the end of our lives. We want that capitalist parliament to pass measures which will give the working class the control of the whole co-ercive force of police and soldiery which are the sole bulwark of Private Property today. They will pass those measures only when they are convinced that otherwise a worse thing will be-fall them; and nothing can convince them of that except the determination of the workers to resort to force if parliament fails. I do not mean, as I have sufficiently explained in previous papers, that the workers are to fight, in the manner laid down by middle class novelists, at barricades under the leadership of a hero in a red sash; nor do I deny that if they would anticipate

Payment of Members by a general subscription to a Parliamentary Candidates fund, that proof of their determination
might save them much further trouble; but if they do not want
to be kept waiting fifty years for a change they will have either
to pay or force their masters' hands.

What I have just said may serve as a sample of the sort of
language which is sure to be denounced as dangerous, likely to
be misunderstood by ignorant men, provocative of class hatred,
and so on and so forth. If I add that our politicians at present
seem to me to be a phalanx of fools who have bought their
seats in parliament as they would buy a house in Prince's Gate,
led by a few unscrupulous aristocrats on the Tory side, and a
gang of hypocritical plutocrats on the other, with certain
cowardly timeservers in the philanthropic, learned, and popular
line to act as go-betweens in the incidental work of humbugging
the Radicals, I shall be told that my language is in bad taste. But
I do not see how a man is to be a candid Social Democrat with
the approbation of the middle class. He cannot stir up the
people mightily against inequality and all its bitter fruits if he
is also to win golden opinions for his moderation by finding
polite excuses for the ignoble ruck of place hunters who have
as much intention of abolishing inequality as a pirate has of
scuttling his own ship. Therefore pray understand that in spite
of my smashing proof that society under Social Democracy
will be to society under monopoly and competition as Heaven
to Sodom and Gomorrah, yet the respectability of today will
never admit it; and the thoroughgoing Fabian propagandist will
soon find his lately earned character for moderation and ability
slipping away from him as completely as if he were an avowed
emissary from the kingdom of darkness. For, indeed, to the
Powers that be, Socialism is the veritable Wrath to Come.
Therefore I conclude by recommending you to the approbation of your own consciences, and the gratitude of a posterity
which will be remote in proportion to your shrinking from the
bad opinion of all your respectable friends in this generation.

VI   Bureaucracy and Jobbery

The Annual Report of the Fabian Society for the year 1890 records that "In the autumn a course of 15 papers by members on Common Objections to Socialism," was arranged for seven evenings, and proved on the whole attractive and successful." Shaw spoke twice in this series. The following lecture, originally titled by Shaw, "Bureaucracy and Jobbery as Objections to Socialism," was given in Bloomsbury Hall on December 5, 1890.

It is pretty well understood by this time that a good deal of jobbery goes on in government departments. The theme is a favorite one with writers on social subjects, because it is very easy and very popular. It has mighty wars for its advertisements, wholesale carnage for its results, and laisser-faire, always acceptable to the comfortable classes, for its moral. The present generation may not remember the burst of indignation provoked by the exposure of the callous indifference and unscrupulous greed with which redtape and jobbery between them managed to wreck or slay more British soldiers in the Crimean war than the Russians did. But perhaps some of us may have read Dickens's imaginary conversation with Dr Pangloss, in which he states the grievances of the soldiers, only to be received at each point with the stereotyped official assurance that the arrangements and materials were the best that could be procured, and that the government was satisfied that everything had been done that was possible to secure the comfort and safety of Her Majesty's troops. After the Crimean war came the great civil war in America; and of this some remarkable particulars have been preserved for us by the late Professor Stanley Jevons.[1] On surveying that Titanic struggle or that squalid carnival of murder, whichever you please to call it—Jevons saw one central fact standing out like a great bloodred banner above the smoke and dust of battle. That fact was that the Federal government, in the throes of the conflict, once sold a gunboat to a speculator for a mere song, and three days later bought it back from him for an enormous sum. The figures given by Jevons in the essay in which he has immortalized this transaction will convince the most rabid Collectivist that the speculator did unquestionably come out considerably ahead of the State in point of dollars; and I regret to have to add that in the all-important point of morals he does not seem to have been at any appreciable disadvantage, as there is but too much reason to suspect that the whole affair was what is usually called "a put-up job." The Jevonian eye saw here no mere passing quarrel of north with south, but the eternal conflict between private enterprise and Socialism; and there could be no doubt whatever as to which had got the better of it on this occasion. Private enterprise was first and the State nowhere;

1. The following passage is deleted in the typescript: "Jevons was not a man of large and sympathetic imagination; and mathematics and university life did not improve him in this respect: we at last find his extraordinarily active mind busying itself exclusively on details, and losing all sense of their proportion to the wholes of which they were parts. Thus we have him coming out on the social question with a proposal, not for the Nationalization of the Land or the Socialization of Industry, much less for the abolition of the family and the internationalization of the State, the Church, and private property, but simply for an improvement in library cataloguing, the particulars of which startling reform he elaborates with a feverish energy and prodigality of labor that make Fabian Essays seem in comparison a quite lazy and superficial production. Far be it from me to disparage Jevons on this account; for if Fabians do not regard the defects of our library catalogues as being so pressing an evil on the whole as private property in land, yet we may cheerfully admit that Jevons knew more about cataloguing than Henry George does—although I shall not be surprised if some ardent member of the English Land Restoration League rises in the discussion to repudiate this statement as an insidious attack on the principles of Land Nationalization."—Ed.

and accordingly we are hardly surprised to find Jevons presently offering a fresh contribution to the social problem in the shape of an exhaustive argument proving that a parcels post could not be established successfully by the State in this country. And the proof is so complete and solidly founded on facts that no Socialist has ever shaken it in the least: any question that may have arisen as to its validity is due, not to any logical refutation, but solely to the accident that a parcels post has been established since on grounds of mere expediency, and is preferred by the public to the alternatives provided by private enterprise.

After the American war, the next huge advertisement provided by the State for the principle of laisser-faire was the Franco-Prussian war, into which the French entered with a ministerial guarantee that their troops were armed with the best rifle in the world, and that everything was ready down to the last button on Private Pitou's gaiters. The rifle, though it did its duty effectually by a considerable number of Germans, did not, on the whole, come up to European expectation; and it turned out that though the gaiter buttons were ready hardly anything else was; and France came tremendously to grief in consequence. The Russo-Turkish war could do little for the Manchester School, as nobody for a moment expected any sort of honesty or competence from Russian or Turkish officialdom. Besides, Russia and Turkey are a long way off; very few of us have ever been in either country; and the result is that the death of a few thousand Turks or Muscovites from rotten food and marches through the snow in brown paper boots causes us less concern than the death of twenty Frenchmen or Germans, or of one Englishman. Consequently, between the exposure and downfall of the French Empire and the exposure and downfall of the Metropolitan Board of Works we have only one first class object lesson in laisser-faire, the bombardment of Alexandria, and its sequel, the Soudanese war. At Alexandria, though no expense was spared in the provision of shells, they wasted the taxpayers' money in several instances by not going off, one highly expensive projectile in particular, which had been considerately fired into a hospital, disappointing the patients by merely knocking over a portion of the building, and then lying there, an inert mass, amid the greatest expectancy on the part of the bedridden spectators. Another took several months to explode; and it is questionable whether it would have gone off even then had not a British workman who was silver-mounting it as a coal scuttle for presentation to the Prince of Wales, incautiously poured some water into it and stirred it up with a file. One can still recall the sense of wonderful good fortune that thrilled through the country when we realized that it was not the Prince of Wales, but only a mere workman, that was killed. Such incidents as these appeal to the popular imagination more forcibly even than Mr Herbert Spencer's facts and figures in The Coming Slavery. In the Soudanese war, there were swords that broke and bayonets that bent, cartridges that jammed, consignments of boots adapted exclusively to the left foot, and finally a railway, which never reached the Soudan at all, but at once attained the status of an historical relic, in which character it is now much appreciated by visitors to Plumstead. Thus we see how it is the unhappy fate of governments that they cannot blunder and job with the unostentatious modesty of the private speculator. The scale on which they work is so vast, the consequences so tragic, the episodes which rend the veil of secrecy so dramatic, that they are always found out in the most glaring manner. And as their rival, Private Enterprise, runs all the newspapers, and the social essays and treatises on political economy are mostly written by members of the class that profits by private enterprise, our wretched official departments get their misdeeds rubbed into the public mind most remorselessly by the Press. Consequently, the moment the Collectivist proposes State action, the average reader of the Daily News at once puts down his foot. "Oh no: we have had enough of that. We know what State management means. Redtape, jobbery, peculation, bribery, the highest prices for the worst quality of goods, bungling, delay, complaints met with official insolence or Treasury Bench equivocation, and an insufferable dead level of official routine like a blight upon all the activity of the country."

Now nothing can be greener than to attempt to meet this objection by any attempt to deny that government departments have been guilty of all these sins over and over again, or to attempt to inspire any hope that they would not, under similar conditions, be guilty of them all tomorrow. Fortunately that is not the point at issue. The alternative before us does not lie between State management and perfection, but between State management and private speculation. Therefore it is necessary to inquire whether the private speculator, throwing stones at the State, does not himself live in a glass house. Jevons's gunboat, for instance: that was a good story: no doubt it was a rare game to cheat the public by buying up their stores cheap and selling it to them again dear. But it is to be observed that it was private enterprise that patriotically took advantage of its country's need in war time to cheat it, and that if the government had had the organized industry of the country at its command for the production of gunboats and stores and munitions of war, as would be the case in a Socialized State, the job could not have happened; so that the gunboat incident is a clear illustration of the evils, not of Collectivism, but of the present system. Since then, this very business of buying up stores of what the nation most urgently needs, and compelling them to buy it back again at an exorbitant price, has become the recognized sphere of the Napoleons of commerce in times of peace as well as of war. It is to private enterprise that we owe our cotton corners, our copper corners, our wheat corners; and it is the society founded on private enterprise that bows down before the Secretans and the Steenstrands who flourish by this sort of gambling, and holds it up to our young men as the true philosopher's stone—the only genuine transmuter of metals and maker of millionaires. Now if Mr Steenstrand had been a public official in a department charged with the socialized cotton industry, he could not have made a cotton corner; and if he could he would have been cashiered and

probably imprisoned, instead of having his portrait published
in the papers as one of our leading men. It is nothing to the
point that if he had been a minister of agriculture under the
old French monarchy, he might have jobbed and robbed, fore-
stalled and regrated, with impunity: we are not now under the
régime of the Regent Orleans, under whose auspices the laisser-
faire school was very excusably conceived; and Socialism does
not countenance any proposal for a return to that *régime*.
Neither are the public indemnified for the enormous rise in the
price of copper caused by the copper corner because that rise
fell just far enough short of what M Denfert-Rochereau was
playing for to drive that unfortunate gentleman to shoot himself. Nor has the loss inflicted on the country by Mr Steenstrand's successful cotton corner been in the least reimbursed to
us by the fact that Mr Steenstrand tried again and overreached
himself; although no doubt it was gratifying to perceive, by the
remarkable change of tone with which the press received the
result of his second attempt, how greatly the moral sense of the
community had been elevated in the interval between the two.
However, a condition of public feeling which rewards a man
when he succeeds in cheating the nation, and condemns him
when he fails, is hardly any security for the spread of honest
dealing. The fact is that this Private Enterprise, which arrogates
to itself all the good qualities and imputes to Public Enterprise
all the bad ones, is in itself a certain guarantee of dishonesty,
and has already, by the operation of unnatural selection, placed
the wealth, the morals, the religion, the art, the education, and
the so-called "public opinion" of the great commercial and
manufacturing centres of England in the hands of persons who,
though capital fellows from the standpoint of their private
acquaintances, must be described from the point of view of
public interest as a crew of sanctimonious rascals as sordid and
hypocritical as ever drove a socially disposed man to despair
of the future of the race. Yet, they are only what Private Enterprise and Competition have made them: every individual
blackguard of them would probably be a useful and harmless
citizen of a socialized State.

Coming now to the examples of State armies marching to battle in brown paper boots and the like, and waiving the merely personal point that I happen to be a native of a country where private enterprise has left a considerable section of its industrial army without any boots at all, I must insist on the fact that the brown paper boots have usually been supplied by contractors to whose dishonest establishments the State has been driven simply because it has not socialized the industry of Northampton. When bayonets bend and swords break, the English manufacturer of such things, in a burst of patriotism, traces them to a German firm, and asks why the contract was not given to an English house. He then buys up from the government all their discarded Enfield and Snider rifles for a mere song, and sells them to the Zulus, or to any other barbarous race which happens to require them for the purpose of shooting English soldiers, and is too poor to order the latest thing in liquefied gas and smokeless and noiseless magazine rifles. Having thus established his claim to the gratitude of the fatherland, he perhaps gets preferred to the German firm, and obtains a contract for the next relay of bayonets. But the quality of what are called "regulation weapons" does not necessarily improve: the old complaints recur. People ask indignantly whether it is not perfectly easy to test the weapons; and the official reply always is that they have all been tested, and are unquestionably first rate. The truth generally is that the contractor supplies weapons capable of standing the test whilst there is plenty of time to test and, if necessary, reject them. But when they are suddenly wanted for active service, and the government must take what they get or go without, the contractor may safely calculate that if the bayonets break down under the test, the government will stop testing them rather than leave the troops without arms, or articles that look like arms. The moral is that in emergencies —and a war always is an emergency—it is useless to keep the testing in the hands of the State if the manufacture is left in the hands of the sweater. On the whole the argument—"The State is not to be trusted: ergo, the private contractor IS to be trusted"—will not hold water. If Socialism in these affairs is the devil, Unsocialism is the deep sea. When the Liberty and Property Defence League point mockingly to that railway at Plumstead that never got to the Soudan, I sardonically direct their attention to the locomotives buried in the sands of Panama, and to the thousands of abandoned and burst-up enterprises, from bogus gold mines, real coal mines that turned out anthracite instead of bituminous, bankrupt Great Eastern steamships, unsuccessful Edinburgh Exhibitions, insolvent banks only saved from collapse by State aid, and monster theatres closed all the year round, down to crossings deserted by their sweepers and cobbler's cellars invaded by the brokers. And when I am taunted with the bribes taken by the officials of the Metropolitan Board of Works, and have Mr Herbert Spencer's Man and the State flung in my teeth, I produce Mr Spencer's own essays on The Morals of Trade, as well as a certain instructive series of articles on the same subject lately published in the Pall Mall Gazette, in order to shew that private enterprise is honeycombed with channels for bribes, tips, and every conceivable species of blackmail to a degree which must excite the envy even of the officials at Woolwich Arsenal. The notion that the private employee is purified and made incorruptible by his freedom from the State taint, whilst the public official is stamped with fraud, collusion and simony as his buttons are stamped with V.R., is, to say the least, the index of a refreshing *naïveté* in the mind that harbors it.

All this is so very obvious that it may well be doubted whether it touches the real objection which men entertain to State industry. Granted that a private speculator is quite as corrupt as a State official, the question remains as to which of the two is the most effectually bound by his own interest to please the public. For instance, is not the officer who goes into the open market, and selects his sword and revolver from the stocks of private tradesmen competing for his custom, likely to be better armed than the trooper who has to take the regulation weapons served out to him, whether he likes them or not? Let us see. At present, when the officer is a good judge of weapons, which he is less likely to be than an official expert with no interest in cheating him, no doubt he often comes out better armed than the trooper. But if he were limited to the amount spent on the trooper, which is the only fair basis of comparison, he would most certainly get worse value for the money. He would have to buy readymade weapons; and readymade articles are "regulation" articles just as much when they are sold in armorer's shops in Pall Mall as when they are issued by departments. And since, in addition to the cost of production of the weapons, he would have to pay for cost of retail distribution and ground rent a sum far exceeding what the State would incur, it is absolutely impossible for him to get the same value in weapons for the same money as his troopers unless there is *much more* swindling and jobbery in the State arsenal than in the private trade. If this is the case even under the present system, how much greater would the advantage of the State be if it were organized on a Collectivist basis. A Social-Democratic Arsenal could supply weapons as a Social-Democratic bakery could supply bread, for their cost of production alone, without charging a farthing for rent. Against such prices the most honest and obliging private shopkeeper must compete in vain, provided the State was not intolerably dishonest and disobliging.

But that is just exactly what many people fear that States will always be; and it is to that point that I now propose to address myself for a moment. As to the origin of the tradition that State officials are by nature insolent and inefficient, I need add nothing to what we have already said in the Fabian Essay on the Transition to Social Democracy. The old fashioned Civil servant was (and is) a snob, a Jack-in-office, a nincompoop, and a nuisance, not because he drew his salary from the Treasury instead of from a shopman's till, but because he gained and held his position by privilege, and was practically irresponsible. The introduction of the system of open competitive examination, though it is but an instalment of reform, has already made an immense difference, the elderly civil servant being now as obsolete as the snuffers which were once indispensable to every genteel pair of candlesticks; whilst their successors are polite and efficient, often joining the Fabian Society and rendering notable services to the Collectivist movement in and out of office hours. Still, it is not necessary to rest our case on an assumption that our Fabian civil servants may be taken as representative types of the State official of the future. It is sufficient to bring out the point that the education and capacity of State officials is now more severely tested in all departments than in the corresponding grades of privately organized labor. As to the great question of civility, there can be no dispute about the fact that the influentially connected civil servant of yore felt it due to himself to be insolently haughty to the lawyer's clerks who brought routine business to him, just as he felt it to be due to himself to wear a silk or beaver hat. But even in the palmiest days of the service as a relieving institution for younger sons and a preserve for gentlemen, can we believe that the average Englishman (who is a poor laborer, remember) ever suffered from a public official a tithe of the bullying and insult which he had and still has to put up with daily from his employer and his employers' slave drivers. If the haughtiest official in Somerset House is impertinent to a laborer, the laborer can ask him who he is a 'torking to; can remind him that he is the servant of the public; tell him that he ought to go to school and learn manners; threaten to report him; and otherwise despitefully use him and persecute him. If he is in the right, he can do this not only with considerable effect, but with absolute impunity, as far as a laborer can do anything with impunity. What laborer dare utter a word of this to his master, or to a foreman or overseer, even in reply to oaths and foul abuse? If he did he would go home to his wife and children an unemployed man. We all remember the middle class gentleman in Dickens's novel who was so disgusted because a government clerk told him to shut the door after him, as he was letting in a devil of a draught. An England in which no greater indignities than that were to be feared would be a paradise to the vast majority of the population. Perhaps Mr Oakeshott will tell us whether the modern civil servant addresses the public in this fashion. Judging from what I have seen of official insolence—and I have seen all that there is to be seen of it as far as it affects the middle class—I have no hesitation in saying that it is really class insolence and not State insolence. The official is insolent just so far as his office implies social superiority. The policeman who shoves, cuffs, kicks, and swears at the homeless wanderers of the streets, is active and intelligent, civil and obliging, to a prosperous solicitor; and the under secretary who is curt and impatient with that solicitor is obsequious to a cabinet minister or a peer. In a Social-Democratic State, where everybody would be an official, or an ex-official, or a future official, or the relative or at all events the unquestionable equal of an official, it is hardly conceivable that it would not be pleasanter to deal at a municipal store than it is at present to encounter the cringing, insincere, mercenary attentions of the private shopwalker. Even now it is far pleasanter to me to buy a dozen stamps from the officialesses of the postal service than to make a purchase in Shoolbred's, Maple's, or Marshall and Snelgrove's. It is true that the officialesses are much more independent in their attitude than the counter hands of the private shops. That is exactly why I prefer to transact business with them. The worst of all bad manners are servile manners.

The question of jobbery is usually treated as if it turned upon the corrupt nature of Man and of the State, especially the State. But it really turns upon the opposition of public and private interests under the present system. So long as the County Council can do nothing with a site except sell or lease it to a private speculator, so long will it be worth that speculator's while to bribe anybody and everybody whose official report or whose vote can help him to a good bargain at the expense of the public. Again, so long as the School Board has to resort to private contractors to get its schools built, building firms will try to jerrybuild our public schools and bribe the supervising officials. But when the County Council and School Board use the sites themselves and do their own work, where can the job come in? There must be two parties to a job. It may be that the propensity to jobbery will remain so strong in public departments that the County Council may secretly bribe itself just as some inveterate gamblers relieve the tedium of solitude by tossing matches between their right and left hands; but however exciting the game may be, they leave off no poorer than they began. On the same ground the man who believes that municipal bodies will always job can console himself with the reflection that the jobbery of a Social-Democratic municipality can hurt nobody, though it may amuse the town councillors. For example, at the present moment the Ecclesiastical Commissioners are trying to get the better of the County Council over a piece of land at Lambeth; and it may very possibly be better for the Council to submit than to refuse the deal. In other words, the Church is trying to make money at the expense of the State. If the land at Lambeth were collective property, this indecorous spectacle would be impossible. There might under such circumstances be a fierce conflict on the Council as to whether a particular site should be used for an Archbishop's palace or a powder magazine; and the canvassing for votes might go to all possible lengths of persuasion, backed by menaces of foreign invasion on the one side and perdition on the other; but here could be no motive for pecuniary bribery unless the Church and the Army held landed property separately from the municipal or common property. In the case of building schools there would be no sort of sense in a public building department bribing a public education department to give it a job. One might as well object to the organization of the Fabian Society on the ground that no express precautions have been taken against the possibility of the Literature Committee bribing the Finance Committee to induce the General Executive to allow it to issue a tract.

I shall take two more instances, both dealing with interests which Social Democracy would not reconcile. Only a limited number of people can live on Richmond Terrace; and as Richmond Terrace is unquestionably a specially desirable dwelling place for those who appreciate a beautiful view, people would be willing to bribe the County Council to let them have the houses there to live in rather than those in Gower St. But this is precisely what it is proposed that they shall do. Rent is just such a bribe. No secrecy is possible in so familiar a transaction: the public will know that a rent is paid, just as they know now

that it is paid to the private landlord. The disappointed appli-
cants will insist on knowing not only that the successful one
is paying more than they are willing to pay, but exactly how
much more, and on having their compensation in the appropriation of the rent as revenue for public use. The second instance
is the simplest of all forms of public corruption. Suppose a
measure were before the County Council in which the pious
sections of the community were spiritually interested. Suppose
that the division were likely to be a close one; and that Rev
Fleming Williams were to offer John Burns a ten pound note
(or its Social Democratic equivalent) for his vote in the matter.
Or suppose that on the London School Board, when the question of having a little theatre attached to every school for the
children to get up plays in is ripe for discussion, our friend
Stewart Headlam were to sound the Rev Joseph Diggle, and
the no less Rev John Coxhead, as to whether, in the phrase of
the gentleman in *Great Expectations*, they would have the con-
descension to allow themselves to be bought off. Now it is quite
clear that the present system provides no safeguard against
corruption of this sort: on the contrary, it places a premium
on it, not by openly declaring that it is a man's business to be
rich first and honest afterwards, but by accepting a good income
as a certificate of character, which is of course only a hypocritical way of doing the same thing.

The middle class had better abandon their academic discussions as to whether man is the creature of circumstances, and
whether equality is possible or not. The fact that no disparity of
taste or ability need be a bar to perfect social equality stands
proved today by facts. Foxhunting squires, successful tradesmen, cardinal archbishops, engineers, men of science, soldiers,
surgeons, sculptors, statesmen, genteel nonentities and jejune
university undergraduates associate on terms of perfect social
equality, although the differences of character and capacity between them are wide enough to positively caricature the diversi-
ties which are pointed to everyday by complacent middle class
persons as obvious and conclusive refutations of all schemes for
securing equal social rights to all members of society. The

other discussion—that about man being the creature of circumstances—arises out of the same confusion of thought. Every man's character is so far predetermined that the most exact similarity of circumstances will not make any two men altogether alike. Gentlemen's sons who go from neighboring country houses to the same public school, and thence to the same college in the same university, come out of it all with very different characters, although similarity of environment can hardly be more complete in our society. The same thing is true of laborers' sons who go from a slum tenement to the same board school, and thence into the same trade. But if the two laborers be compared with the two gentlemen, it will be found that there is a stock of ideas and habits common to the two gentlemen and another quite different stock common to the two laborers. Now it is evident that if the two gentlemen differ in natural character, any stock of ideas and habits peculiar to their class which they hold in common must be due not to character but to circumstances. The same is true of the two laborers. But it is the difference between these two common stocks that constitutes the whole difference between the laborer and the gentleman. Consequently social reformers are perfectly justified in assuming, with Owen, that the differences between the rich and poor classes are altogether created by circumstances and have nothing to do with those natural differences which are alluded to in the proverb "You cannot make a silk purse out of a sow's ear."

Let us go a little deeper into this question of circumstances. The peerage has its percentage of louts and blackguards; and so has the proletariat. But in order to scientifically compare one class with another, we must calculate not only the percentage of louts and blackguards in each, but also take into account the pressure of temptation towards loutishness and blackguardism produced by the circumstances of each class. For example, an officer in the army, when in London, is much cleaner in personal habits than a sweep. Give the sweep a thousand a year, and send the officer on active service, and you may easily find your officer not only in urgent want of a bath and even a fine toothed comb, but willing to sacrifice a chance of both for an hour's sleep, whilst your sweep will be shining with soap and starched linen.

We must, too, if our discussions are to have any reality, give up wrangling as to whether grey is white or black, men absolutely virtuous or absolutely vicious. An engineer does not discuss whether a girder is absolutely trustworthy or untrustworthy: he ascertains the strain under which it will break and guarantees it as trustworthy under a less strain and treacherous under a greater one. The sociologist, dealing with the normal man, has to decide, not whether the normal man is absolutely honest or dishonest, but under what strain his honesty will break down. The ideal man who would die rather than steal a pin may be treated as non-existent or morbid: the normal man is clearly less Quixotic. Where then does the normal man draw the line? Can you trust him with a pound—or with ten pounds, or fifty, or a thousand, or a hundred thousand, or a million? Evidently that depends on his circumstances. If I lose a purse with ten sovereigns in it, my chance of getting it back depends not only on how honest the man who picks it up is, but also on whether he is a banker or a dock laborer. If the giving up of ten sovereigns would impose more privation on a dock laborer than the giving up of a thousand pounds would on a banker (which may very easily be the case) then the dock laborer who keeps my purse may be a hundred times as honest a man as the banker who restores it to me.

A little reflection will convince any person with adequate social experience that even in the well-to-do section of the middle class a man who is no more than ordinarily honest will have reason to plume himself enormously if he resists a legal chance of making £50 at the expense of a neighbor. Private buying and selling is not very common among such people; but horses and grand pianofortes occasionally change hands among them without the intervention of a dealer; and on such occasions let the purchaser beware; for the man who would be incapable of passing off a broken umbrella or a damaged hat on you as sound and whole for the sake of a few shillings will leave it altogether to you to find out whether the horse he wants to sell you is vicious or the piano rickety. Not that horses and grand pianos have subtle depraving influences from which hats and umbrellas are free, but simply because their prices often run into three figures. Every man has his price except the martyr; and even the martyr probably has his price on every point save one. It would no doubt be quite possible to find a teetotaller who would be burnt alive rather than drink a glass of whiskey; but it would be very unsafe to infer from his constancy on this point that he would resist with equal fortitude a temptation to make a bet or to outwit a railway company. So that the man who has one or even two points of honor on which he is incorruptible has his price on an hundred other points on which he is comparatively indifferent; and on each point his resistance becomes weaker as the price offered gets higher. As public statistical proof of which we have the significant fact that every additional penny on the Income Tax produces less revenue than the penny before it. The Englishman who confesses to a thousand a year when we want to tax him sixpence in the pound will only confess to eight hundred if we put on another penny or so. In short, we are honest according to our means; and the old Greek precept, "First make an independent income; and then practise virtue" is as authoritative today as ever.

Let us now take the case of one of our munificent and public spirited captains of industry—some great manufacturer or merchant prince who began life with a pound a week or so, and is ending it as representative of his town in parliament, with his statue in the park he has presented to the people, and his name engraven in the foundation stone of the Institute or Public Library or Art Gallery or Almshouse or what not that he has built and endowed. We will suppose that he pays wages to two thousand "hands." Out of the labor of everyone of the two thousand he makes a profit: otherwise he would not employ him (or her). Every penny added to the wage reduces this profit: every penny struck off increases it. Now suppose you take this man into the house of a poor widow, not in his em-

ployment, and shew him her wasted fingers and her pinched
cheeks and her half starved but still perhaps miserably neat
and uncomplaining children. He is touched; and when he learns
that half a crown a week would make all the difference between
grinding anxiety and humble contentment in that household, he
naturally makes a little calculation. Six-pound-ten a year: that is
what the widow wants. It means to him less than a hundred
pounds capital, even if it were to go on forever, which it will
not. It is a deserving case; and he longs to do a good action. He
promises the half crown a week and retires, pleased with himself and clothed with the gratitude of the widow and the father-
less as with a shining garment. Next day his workmen, being
in need of an extra penny much as the widow was of an extra half
crown, ask for an increase of wage to that modest extent. Without a moment's hesitation he resists their demand tooth and
nail. A penny a week for two thousand men— £8-6-8 a week
— £433-6-8 a year—capital value at five per cent nearly £9,000!
And no public credit for it either—only a defeat by the Trade
Union! No: fifty pounds to a hospital if you like, five hundred
for "restoring" a church, even five thousand towards a Technical Institute with Art School and Library attached, and the
parliamentary seat secure for ever; but no advance in wages;
for any or all of these benefactions would be cheaper than a
penny rise-in labor. Nay, now that he thinks of it, since there
would be all this heavy loss by a penny rise, would there not
be as great a gain by a penny reduction and twice as great
a one by a twopenny one. Apart from merely selfish considerations, look at it from the public point of view. Twopence a
week is no real loss to the workman: it is only a little beer
the less for him—a positive gain to him and to the town in sobriety; whilst to the employer the two thousand twopences per
annum multiplied by fiftytwo mean hospitals, parks, statues, art
schools, museums, all sorts of public benefits, not the least
among them being "a lofty standard of civic worth." Is it to
be wondered at under these circumstances that the parks,
statues, Institutes &c, which are the glory of provincial England,
are for the most part as much monuments of remorseless sweat-

ing as the pyramids of Egypt, and that such advances in comfort as our factory operatives have made since the horrors of the white slavery of the first half of the century are due to Trade Unionism, Co-operation, and above all to Factory Legislation (i.e. State Socialism) and not to voluntary concessions on the part of the masters?

The moral of all this eludes us the moment we begin to exclaim at the capitalists as rascals. The case I have cited above is a fairly typical one; and it is not the case of a rascal, but the case of a reasonably goodnatured and public spirited man. If you or I were to act as generously in his place we should give ourselves a good deal of credit for it. Yet we see that even inside the narrow limits within which commercial competition leaves him any choice between doing his best and his worst in the way of wages, the pressure on him to do his worst is overwhelming. If, as you openhandedly throw an extra sixpence from your modest purse for quarter of an hour's work to a cabby, you feel contemptuous towards my typical millionaire who is fiercely wrangling over a penny with a poor factory girl, remember that to imitate your generosity would cost him over two hundred thousand a year, representing a capital of between four and five millions. If ever you embark in a business which compels you to take two thousand cabs every day for nine hours, you will not, believe me, tip the cabman sixpence every quarter of an hour. On the contrary, you will pay them the bare legal fare, and vote for the parliamentary or municipal candidate who promises to try and get it reduced.

How then are you to turn our captain of industry from sweater-cum-philanthropist into a good citizen? Only by putting an end to the opposition between his interests and those of the community. Make him head of a public department, with no direct pecuniary interest whatever in reducing or increasing wages, or in anything but securing his position, promotion and pension by the force of his talent as an organizer and administrator, and you will effect his conversion without elevating his natural moral character one jot. And, as the experience of our public departments shews, you will, as one of the com-

munity employing him, secure for yourself and your fellow
citizens the benefit of his ability at a salary which is insignificant
compared to the profits which he now expects for securing the
benefit of other people's ability entirely to himself.

I should overload this essay were I to give illustrations of
all the ways in which the competitive system offers to immoral
conduct inducements which normal virtue cannot withstand—
and do not forget that social systems must be based on the
normal, though romances may be based on the heroic. For instance, since, with the supply of the munitions of war in the
hands of one set of capitalists whilst those of peace are the business of another, and with the profits of the drink traffic going
to the drink trade whilst its huge cost in disorder, sickness and
crime falls on the whole community, our system practically
offers overwhelming bribes to irresponsible speculators to involve us in wars and encourage us in our drunkenness. But the
illustrations already given will [suffice].[2]

2. The last sentence of the manuscript is incomplete. It is not clear
whether Shaw meant to add others.—Ed.

VII   Capital and Wages

This essay was originally titled by Shaw "Technical Socialism." There are, however, two Shaw manuscripts in the British Museum that bear such a title. The first, not reprinted here, was apparently written in 1888–1891. Shaw's diary for August 3, 1891, contains the entry, "Began book on Technical Socialism for Sutton and Garner." This may be a reference to the chapter below. In 1931 Shaw listed "Technical Socialism (MS)" as one of the titles he was considering publishing in the volume Essays in Fabian Socialism *in the Constable Standard Edition. It is likely Shaw had in mind this second essay, whose style is less mathematical than the first. However, he did not finally include it.*

There are three practicable ways of providing for the production of commodities and exchange of services in civilized communities. These three are—

PRIVATE PROPERTY,
COLLECTIVISM,
COMMUNISM

The first is a non-socialist system. The other two are socialist.

In all modern States the three are in operation side by side, but as Collectivism and Communism are purposely restricted to those departments of industry in which the Private Property system is practically impossible, the predominating and characteristic method of organizing the industry of the world is at present non-socialist.

As the method of producing and distributing wealth has irresistibly influenced custom, morality, the forms of law and

religion, and indeed all social institutions, being only less fundamental than human nature itself, it is important that the three
systems should be known and understood as working arrangements, quite apart from their abstract principles. Whoever
masters the subject in this way will perceive that discussions
as to whether Private Property in the abstract is better or worse
than Socialism are as idle as discussions as to whether black in
the abstract is better or worse than white. The applicability
of either system depends on the nature of the commodity or
service to which it is proposed to apply it, on the industrial
and moral development of the community—in short, on diverse
factors which vary in all possible manners. There is no inconsistency of principle in our present arrangement of Private
Enterprise in the medical profession, Collectivism in our postal
service, and Communism in our London bridges. If the student,
as the outcome of his study, concludes that it would be well to
effect such an extension of Collectivism as would make it the
predominant and characteristic system in this country, then he
may conveniently call himself a Socialist. But there is no universally applicable abstract principle of Socialism or Individualism by subscribing to which men can claim to be Socialists or
Individualists without troubling themselves about economic
science or practical industry.

PRIVATE PROPERTY

II

When a man claims the right to do what he likes with his own,
he is making the strongest possible assertion of the right of
private property. To do what one likes with a thing is the essence of owning it. But society only grants that right within
the limits of custom and morality, which are constantly chang-
ing with the growth of public conscience and the shifting of the
balance of political power. No man may cut throats because he
may do as he likes with his own knife, nor may he contribute
more than his share to the smoke of London on the ground that
a man may burn what he likes with the chimney of his own

factory. A glandered horse or a ton of fireworks may be private property; but the owner may not keep them where he pleases. In short, everything that a citizen possesses is held by him on conditions dictated by the community; and every new act of Parliament, every change in fashion, every invention which supersedes established modes of action by new ones, changes those conditions by forbidding that which was formerly permitted, licensing that which was formerly forbidden, making valuable property useless and waste property valuable, destroying vested interests on the one hand and creating or reviving them on the other. Land Acts, acts for the regulation of labor, Employers' Liability Acts, Sanitary Acts, commercial treaties, the enactment or repeal of articles of the criminal laws defining or punishing crime all restrict or enlarge the privileges of private proprietors and actually transfer property from one proprietor to another or to the public. The value of property, especially of industrial plant, is altered by them as effectually as by the introduction or disappearance of crinolines, the replacement of nankeen, moleskin, and corduroys by tweeds and meltons, the desertion of the high roads and country inns by travellers on the invention of the railway, or their partial return on the invention of the bicycle.

The private proprietor is also subject to the direct expropriation of a percentage of his income annually for public purposes by the hands of the collector of rates and taxes. There is no constitutional guarantee that this percentage may not be raised to the highest practicable limits even to the extent of reducing the income of a millionaire to that of a man of moderate means.

If we compare the cases of two men of equal social standing and income, one of them a resident clerk in a Government department, depending on public conveyances for his travelling, and the other a private man of business keeping his own horse and carriage, so that his house, his office, and his carriage are his own, we find that the clerk, instead of being hampered by his comparative propertylessness, is actually as well served as the man of business and has less than half his responsibilities or worries. When a man has the use of anything, and has no reason to fear that any attempt will be made to deprive him of it, it is no advantage to him to own it as well: it is rather a burden. The chief economic advantage of civilization is the facility it affords for procuring the use of things without incurring the cost of private ownership of them. Clubs, public washhouses and baths, street lamps and pavements, railways, theatres and circulating libraries are among the more obvious and familiar examples of things which are not the private property of those who use them.

There are things which are made for the private use of individuals, and others which are made only for the use of masses of people. A watch is only useful when privately appropriated; and Big Ben, which to a private person in a private house would be a monstrosity not worth the cost of its maintenance, is only useful as a public clock. A man living by the riverside would willingly exchange the exclusive use of an Atlantic liner for that of a canoe. No modification of the legal ownership of such things can affect the physical conditions of their use. If a watch or canoe were by legislative enactment made the joint property of the nation, they still could not be used by more than one person at a time. If a Cunarder were similarly transferred from its joint proprietors to a single owner, it would still have to be used by some two thousand persons at a time if it were to be worth while to use it at all.

There are things which are made to be consumed, others which are worn out by use, others which are none the worse for use, but which wear out independently of it, and others which do not wear out at all. A loaf is made to be immediately consumed. Tools, machines, carriages, clothes, houses wear out with use. Pictures and statues, all objects which are used by simply looking at them, wear out independently of their use; for the Venus of Milo does not wear out any faster in the Louvre, where she is used by many thousands of persons every year than she did when she was hidden in the soil of [Melos]. Land does not wear out at all. The loam on agricultural land may be exhausted temporarily; but land in its fundamental capacity as space or standing room can be neither made nor consumed. Air, and the light and heat of the sun are like land in this respect; but they cannot, like land, be appropriated.

The cases of bread and land illustrate certain conditions of human life: to wit, that the things which men must consume must be replaceable by them and that those which they must use and cannot replace must be imperishable. Obviously, these are the only conditions on which men could have lived otherwise than as wild animals live. Now the consumption of a thing is the most complete possible private appropriation of it. The right of private property in a loaf cannot go further than the right to eat it. And it is necessary that such a right should exist for every man eternally, provided he replaces (i.e. pays for) the loaf when he has consumed it. Thus the extreme right of private property—the right to destroy—can always be granted when it is necessary because it can always be bridled by the obligation to replace. But in the case of land, which Man must use, but which he cannot either consume nor replace, there are no such reasons for granting rights of private property: it is neither necessary nor equitable that it should be appropriated by any-one, whilst it is both necessary and equitable that its use should be shared by everyone, and equitable that it should be shared equally. Therefore we find in this country that landowners are not in law landed private proprietors, but only tenants of the Crown. The taxation of landed property, and the conditions under which it may be bought and sold, or inherited, differ from those which affect bread, clothes, and what is called generally "personal property."

Between the two extremes of food and land, there are many degrees of appropriation. At one end of the scale, use and ex-clusive ownership are virtually the same thing: at the other they are differentiated and entirely dissociated. At one end of the scale, therefore, we find that the commodities must be bought outright by the user, since he buys them for the purpose of wholly consuming them. As we proceed towards the other end we find him more and more substituting hire for purchase until he reaches a point at the opposite extreme where he can-not purchase at all, but can only hire the use of them for stipulated periods. At intermediate points we find [commodities] purchased by one man and hired by another according to his circumstances. For example, the omnibuses which ply in the main streets of our towns may suffice for all his ordinary needs in the way of conveyance. The omnibus, however, will not turn out of its course to deposit him in a bye street: if he desires that accommodation he must take a cab. If he has to make a large number of calls every day, as physicians in general practice have, he must, to save time, drive to all of them. He then finds that public cabs cost more than a private vehicle and horse, either hired by the year from the stable keeper, or purchased outright. In every town the omnibus, the cab, the livery vehicle, and the private carriage are in use side by side, just as the private houses, flats, furnished lodgings, hotels and restaurants flourish together. The same picture dealer who sells a work of art to one customer for several hundred pounds lets another look at his pictures for a shilling taken at the turnstile. As social organization advances, the proportion of cases in which the individual privately and separately owns what he uses diminishes by the mere gravitation of greater economy and convenience, the tendency being to reduce the privacy of property to the minimum.

Here again we find that there is no abstract principle that can be "attacked" or "upheld." No man has any absolute right to do what he pleases with anything, whether it is his own or not. The degree of control which he desires and is granted over the things he uses varies over the whole range of commodities from a power of life and death in the case of a cow or goose, to the mere right to share the use equally with his fellow citizens under police regulation, as in the case of a bridge or a street. Its physical, legal, and social conditions vary from commodity to commodity, and, in the case of the same commodity, even from one set of circumstances to another, proprietary rights being one thing in a period of peace and plenty and quite another in a beleaguered city or on a raftful of castaways. It therefore proves as idle to discuss Private Property in the abstract as we found it to discuss Socialism or Communism or Individualism in the same way.

THE STRENGTH OF THE PRIVATE PROPERTY SYSTEM

III

A Private Property system of social organization is not, then, a
system based on recognition of Private Property in the abstract,
since there is no such thing. It is a system based on private property in land, to the extent of allowing the owner a practically
unconditional power of excluding all other persons from the
use of it. This, as we have seen, is in flat defiance of the physical
conditions of the case. At certain stages of social development,
however, it is unavoidable. In England today it is the established
system, in spite of the legal position of the landowner as a mere
tenant of the Crown; for the Crown does not exercise its powers on behalf of the community against the landowners; and
the practical result is that land can be appropriated as completely as food can, except that when it is sold a lawyer must
be paid to conduct the transaction, and when the owner dies
intestate it passes to his eldest son instead of being divided between his widow and all his children. And the taxation on the
succession is actually lighter than in the case of personal property. These peculiarities in the conditions of land appropriation
are the survivals from a social order in which the landlord, as
feudatory and local representative of the Crown, was not permitted to sell it at his pleasure or to hand his estate down otherwise than in its integrity to the male member of his family who,
as the oldest, and therefore presumably the wisest and strongest,
was likely to be the fittest to take up his functions upon his
death. But however historically interesting they are on this
account, they are so far from being any set-off against the privileges conferred by this form of property on the proprietors
at the expense of the community, that insofar as they increase
those privileges by exemption from full taxation, they are generally felt to be a nuisance both by the landowners themselves
and the rest of the community. A landlord owning a populous
district may drive the inhabitants away and turn it into a
sheeprun or deer forest: he may refuse to allow a place of wor-

ship to be erected on it by any denomination to which he does
not himself belong: he may, in short, disregard every consideration
except his own pecuniary interest and personal caprices in
dictating the conditions on which he will permit his land to be
used. His rights over the land could go no further if he had
made it with his own hands. Private property is thus found to
be most complete practically where in theory there is not and
should not be any such thing.

The reason for this is not that men are wantonly perverse, or
even that they have not thought out the subject. Savages do
not use bows and arrows [instead of] rifles as a matter of preference, but as a matter of necessity, because the production of
rifles is only possible when the arts have progressed far beyond
the savage stage. The North American Indian quite appreciated
the superiority of firearms and took to their use the moment
civilized races offered them to him in exchange for furs; but
until the offer was made he had to put up with his bow. In the
same way, the choice between private property and administration of land, and public property and administration is, in the
earlier stages of civilization, Hobson's choice: everybody can
demonstrate the superiority of Land Nationalization; but nobody can nationalize the land. The necessary political machinery does not exist; and consequently the treatises on the
subject are of no more avail than a set of volumes of specifica-
tions from the Patent Office would be to the Fuegians.

Land is the universal requisite. It is wanted for everything—
for food, fuel, wood and metal; for standing, sitting and sleep-
ing; for the accommodation of the poet, the mathematician and
the philosopher no less than for that of the ploughman and
the blacksmith. You may use land for farms and produce tur-
nips, or for factories and produce steamengines: the mode of
using land varies; but nothing can be done without it. Therefore
a community cannot exist unless the land is in constant cultivation, since the products of such cultivation are the necessaries of
life. And the more vigorously, intelligently, and economically
it is cultivated, the better will the community live.

Now it is an ascertained fact that if a man be given a piece

of land as his private property, he will, for his own sake, cultivate it with all the vigor, intelligence, and economy of which he
is capable in order to enrich himself. Consequently, if every
person in the community has a piece of land, and every acre
worth cultivating has a private proprietor, the first social necessity, that of providing for the cultivation of the land, is provided for. It is true that the provision is a rough and ready one;
and we shall see that it must eventually lead to unbearable evils
[and is] suited only to comparatively scattered populations and
primitive forms of cultivation, and, as such, is only deliberately
and consentaneously chosen by advanced communities as a
method of colonizing new countries. But if the student, before
allowing himself to be led into indignant denunciation by a survey of its obvious imperfections and impossibility as a permanent institution, will check himself for a moment, and ask
himself what alternative to it is available, he will perceive that
the alternative was no more practicable for the nineteenth century English community than for the backwoodsmen of North
America or the squatters of Australia. For this alternative plainly
is the holding of the land in joint stock by the whole population,
each adult being a shareholder having a vote in the election of
the directors appointed to administer the common property.

Now it is clear that something more than mere dissatisfaction
with the results of private property in land is needed to make
this alternative practicable. A high development of social organization and public spirit, and a completely democratic political constitution are primary requisites; and these are never
attained in civilized communities until the evils of private property have reached such a pitch that men lose all hope of satisfying themselves by seeking their interests separately and
selfishly. The difficulties of Land Nationalization do not appear
very formidable to those who see in the landlord nothing but a
rent collector; and some eminent writers on the subject have
represented this essentially revolutionary measure as being a
mere affair of sending the tax collector to collect for the public
treasury the rents now collected by the landlord for his private
use. This is much as if the tenants of a house with a damp

basement were to propose to remove the lowest storey and leave the rest of the house alone. Landlordism is the basis of our civilization; and to remove it without replacing it would be to bring the whole fabric down about our ears. This general statement, however, is like most general statements: it is useless until its content is known in practical detail.

The commonest knowledge of the world will make it plain to the student that modern society as we know it is dependent for its existence not on the bare existence of land alone, but on capital, not on labor alone, but on technical education in the widest sense. To maintain civilization means to maintain capital and education: that is, to renew them constantly at great cost as fast as the rusting and wearing of metal, the rotting of wood, the decay of buildings, and the aging and decease of generations of men destroy them. To progress in civilization means something more than this: it means to add to the store of capital and to extend and improve education. And there is no possibility of a return to more primitive methods with our present population; for we are too thick upon the ground in England to subsist without the aid of capital. In modern communities, then, provision for the cultivation of the land involves provision for education and capital; and any system which makes this provision, however wastefully and perversely, must hold its own of necessity against all proposals which omit it. It can readily be shewn that at present our private proprietors of land keep up the supply of capital and education for us; and that it is their proprietary rights alone which enable them to do so.

All capital, in the first instance, is nothing but spare subsistence. It is the superfluous part of a man's income—that which he is content not to consume, or can easily be persuaded to forego for the present for the sake of some future advantage. Thus capital has been called "the reward of abstinence"; and though the phrase has fallen into general ridicule through its absurd and hypocritical implication that the quantity of capital saved by any person is in direct proportion to their powers of virtuous self-denial, yet if we substitute "result" for "reward," and strip the word "abstinence" of its moral implication, we can accept the definition as practically true. Capital, then, is the result of abstinence. If a man wants a flour mill, he must save the cost of building it and fitting it up out of his income. If he wishes to maintain it, he must not spend on his immediate personal satisfaction all that it brings him in, but must set aside a certain sum annually to make good the wear and tear of the millstones and machinery. If he desires to enlarge the mill, to put in additional pairs of stones, to substitute steam power for water power, or to introduce the steel roller system method of grinding, he must abstain from consuming the cost of these things in personal expenditure. The accumulation and maintenance of capital is possible in no other way. Abstinence is the inevitable condition.

Now abstinence in the abstract has no moral character whatever. When it is spoken of as a virtue, what is meant by it is abstinence from excess, an abstemious eater, for example, not meaning a man who does not eat at all, but one who does not eat more than is good for him. The abstinence of the miser who destroys his health by denying himself sufficient food is a vicious folly, not a virtue. A father who denies an ailing child extra nourishment in order to have the more money to leave it at his death excites abhorrence instead of admiration. In short, he who starves the present need to provide for the future is every whit as great a fool as he who sacrifices the future in order to surfeit the present. The future can only be reached through the present; and indeed it is a sort of provision for the future, and by no means an ignoble one, to lay up for it a stock of memories of happiness and generosity in the past. The old man who has become rich lives in his past no less than the old man who has become poor; and if the one looks back bitterly on a mean and sordid career, and the other on a happy and generous one, then, though neither can be said to have hit the golden mean in providing for his future, yet the poor man's provision is better than the rich man's. There are men who squander great riches without gaining even present happiness, self-respect, or the affection of others; and of such a one it may justly be said that he had better have been a curmudgeon than a ne'er-do-weel, since the curmudgeon at least has money if he has no pleasant memories; whilst the ne'er-do-weel loses everything except remorse. But neither the curmudgeon or the ne'er-do-weel can be said to have thriven in the world; and there is no more foolish misuse of language than to speak of thrift as if it consisted in the saving of money any more than in the spending of it. Until the student clears his mind of that unscientific canting, he will never comprehend the true conditions of social welfare. The thrifty man is he who is able to give the present and the future their due, no less and no more. He should abstain from nothing that is good for him to have, and indulge in nothing that he is likely to be the worse for. There is no absolute virtue in abstinence any more than there is absolute vice in consumption.

However, it is not without a reason that popular preaching traditionally runs so much more on abstinence than on indulgence. The claims of the present need no reminding among people who are fairly free and happy: they assert themselves through the appetites with a persistence and urgency which ensures that they shall not be forgotten, whereas the claims of the future have no such safeguard. In times like the present, when the dread of poverty so oppresses large sections of society that men dare not think of happiness as a thing they can afford, life becomes so unhealthily ugly and joyless that it is for the moment more important to urge the importance of to-day than of tomorrow. But when things are in a normal condition the preacher will always feel justified in leaving today to take care of itself.

In foresight and abstinence, as in other things, one man is very like another. There are spendthrifts and misers, just as there are giants and dwarfs; but the average of prudence holds as good in individual cases as the average of any other quality. The difficulty of recognizing this fact arises from the extreme inequality of the distribution of wealth under our system. If, as is very commonly done, a man's abstinence be estimated by the quantity of money he saves, without any reference to the circumstances under which he has saved it, the most ludicrous conclusions can be drawn. To take a moderate example, first let us suppose that two men, belonging to the same class, and with equal families, but having respectively £800 and £1,000 a year, are both equally self-indulgent and equally abstemious. Suppose that they both indulge themselves to the extent of spending £800 a year. At that rate one of them will have £200 saved at the end of the first year, £406 at the end of the second, £618-3-7⅕ at the end of the third (assuming that he puts his savings out prudently at three per cent) and so on, whilst the other will save nothing at all. Here both men are equally abstinent, yet one becomes richer and richer, whilst the other remains as he was. The same thing might happen even if the man who saves were less abstinent than his fellow; for he could clearly afford to spend £900 a year as against the other's £800, and yet grow richer. Again, a third man, more abstinent than either of these, and so contenting himself with an expenditure of £500 a year, would come to speedy ruin if his income happened to be only £250, which it might easily be under existing circumstances without his being a whit less industrious than his richer [fellows]. But the Private Property system tends to produce far greater inequalities than these. If we compare the great ground landlord with an income of a thousand a day with the laborer earning half a crown a day—and this is well inside the extreme of difference at both ends—we have one man eight thousand times as rich as another. Here the rich man, by exercising the same degree of abstinence as the poor man who saves nothing, can save £999-17-6 a day. Or, to put it in a more probable way, he can indulge himself by consuming eight hundred times as much as the laborer (i.e. living at the rate of £36,500 a year) and yet save £900 a day, or £328,500 a year. To call this huge accumulation the reward of abstinence, and to imply at the same time that the propertyless condition of the laborer is the punishment of self-indulgence is a folly so gross that it could not be believed possible if it were not so frequently and publicly committed.

Evidently the difficulty of abstinence—and in its difficulty lies

its virtue—depends on the extent of consumption which pre-
cedes it. If a man is hungry it is hard to abstain from a mutton
chop. When he has eaten it, it is not so hard for him to abstain
from a second, actually pleasanter to abstain from a third than
to eat it, whilst the consumption of further ones would pass
rapidly from discomfort to torture, and finally to impossibility.
The first mouthfuls of a meal whet the appetite; but it soon begins to be appeased, after which point every mouthful taken
makes it easier to abstain from another one. In the same way,
every pound of income makes it easier after a certain point to
save the next pound, if there is another left, until, when the
spender has purchased everything that he cares for, he finds that
no further immediate expenditure which he can devise brings
him any enjoyment, at which point the rest of his money saves
itself, as it were. But most men are induced to save before the
point of complete satiety is reached by the offer of interest for
the use of their money. The rate of interest which will induce a
man to abstain from consuming any part of his income is an
index of the pain the abstinence causes him. A trifling consideration will induce a rich man to abstain from a second bottle of
wine: no commercial consideration whatever would induce a
man dying of thirst in the desert to abstain from a cup of water.
Hence we have people who would rather leave portions of their
money out at three or two-and-a-half per cent than spend it,
alongside of others who "turn up their noses" at offers of five
per cent. The professional economist often finds the views of
the members of the Bankers' Institute far more moderate on the
subject of interest than those of the working men to whom he
lectures in the north of England; but this does not mean that the
working classes are less abstemious, but that they are less sati-
ated. The banker has consumed so much that his appetites are
appeased: the workman has consumed so little that his appetites
are only whetted. The banker can abstain from consuming another hundred pounds with less sense of privation than the
saving of a shilling costs to a laborer: consequently the fact that
the banker saves and the laborer does not, proves nothing as to
their relative comparative powers of self-denial. The difference

in sacrifice is so enormous that the fact of the poor saving anything at all would be unaccountable but for the terrible penalty of utter destitution under pain of which they must strive to make some provision for their old age. When a man of property spends his whole income, on the other hand, his penalty is, not that he becomes any poorer, but simply that he does not necessarily become any richer. Thus, whilst abstinence is easy and even agreeable for the rich, their incentive to practise it is comparatively weak; and on the other hand whilst it is painful and indeed for the most part intolerable for the poor, the incentive to it is comparatively strong. This is why the prosperous members of our manufacturing populations in the north are induced to save by a rate of interest much less in excess of rich fund-holders' rates than might be expected from the difference of immediate personal self-denial demanded.

The student will now see that there is nothing in the facts around him which really contradicts the statement that, for public purposes, one individual may be considered about as capable of abstinence as another, just as for the purposes of the builder a door which will admit a man six feet high without stooping will amply accommodate men of five feet eight in height, or a theatre floor which slopes enough to enable them to see easily over one another's heads, will suffice for all ordinary persons. It will be seen presently that this, so far from being an argument against inequality of distribution of wealth, is in fact its sole justification, and that consequently those who flatter the rich or seek to apologize for their privileges by attributing special virtues to them, not only bring the discredit of timeserving and hypocrisy on the science of political economy, but shew that they do not understand the scientific ground of that inequality.

If a country depends on the voluntary abstinences of its inhabitants for the accumulation of its capital, as it does under the Private Property system, the equal distribution of wealth will prevent all accumulation of capital until the country is so rich that each person's share amounts to more than he greatly cares to spend. Now such abundance is impossible unless labor is aided by capital: so that equality is impossible without capital, and capital is impossible with equality. For experience shews that men cannot be induced to save until they have spent more than the income which an equal division of purchasing power would leave them. Out of the £6,000,000 which have been accumulated in this country during the last fifty years, hardly £200,000,000 has been saved out of incomes at all approximating to an equal quota of the national income, which the best available estimates put at between thirty and forty pounds per head per annum. Out of this deadlock there is only one way so long as the accumulation of capital is left to the pleasure of individuals. That way is to give the mass of the population, in return for arduous toil, just enough of its product to enable them to live very abstemiously from week to week, and to throw the entire surplus into the hands of a minority who are thereby enriched to such a point that they surfeit themselves with all that money can procure and yet have enough left to give their sons the most complete educational equipment available, and to save large sums for investment as industrial capital. Any system which will effect this unequal distribution, and either reconcile the laboring majority to it or compel them to submit to it, is, so far, a stable, progressive, and practicable system, and will stand its ground in spite of all demonstrations of its abstract injustice. The Private Property system, because it has fulfilled these requirements, has held its own from the break-up of the feudal system to the present time, and will stand impregnable until its provision for the maintenance and accumulation of capital and educated directors and organizers of industry is replaced by some better provision. It cannot be executed for its crimes, and dispensed with, as we dispense with a murderer: it must be supplanted, or else borne with. We shall see that the process of supplantation has already begun; and in the nature of things it is probable that persons now living will see the Private Property system, which is now being edged politely out of a park here, a telegraph office there, a gas works, waterworks or tramway line in the other place, and that too, with excuses and liberal compensation and profuse apology, driven from street to street and from field to field until its relics are [met] with a hostility as open as the nineteenth century has shewn towards the remnants of the feudal system. But its strength will lie to the end in its command of capital and of higher education. No system which does not supersede it in those departments can prevail against it.

THE WORKING OF THE PRIVATE PROPERTY SYSTEM

IV

In order to establish the Private Property system in a new country, it is only necessary to allow all immigrants to select and "pre-empt" as much vacant land as they are likely to be able to cultivate; to allow them to treat it in all respects as if it were their private property; and to provide an armed force sufficiently strong to protect them in the enjoyment of that privilege and to enforce all contracts for the exchange of services or the like that may arise between them and the rest of the community. In old countries where the land is already held by feudatories of the Crown, or persons who have acquired their estates from them by foreclosure of mortgages or direct purchase, it is sufficient to give the existing holders all the privileges of private proprietors, and to enforce contracts as aforesaid. Hence the Private Property system is often spoken of as the Free Contract system; and a declaration in favor of freedom of contract is understood as a declaration in favor of the Private Property system. The term "free" applied to contracts which landless men are forced by necessity and law to enter at a heavy disadvantage is often made the subject of bitter irony; but its apparent unsuitableness is explained away by its origin. Formerly the Government meddled with many sorts of contracts, particularly those between shopkeeper and customer, and between employer and laborer, lender and borrower. Instead of allowing the parties to bargain freely with one another, the seller trying to sell or lend as dearly as possible, and the other trying to buy or borrow as cheaply as possible, the authorities attempted to fix prices, wages, and rates of interest by law, as a check upon the avarice of tradesmen and moneylenders, and on the ambition of laborers. When the Private Property system was fully developed, however, it was found that the competition of shopkeepers for customers, of laborers for employment, and of capitalists for investments, automatically regulated these matters in the way best suited to the working of the system, so that when the law interfered in a contract, even with the best intentions, it frequently did more harm than good to the interests of the private proprietors, who, having the control of legislation in their own hands, accordingly repealed most of the laws, and so established what they called "freedom of contract." The fulfillment of contracts was still enforced by law; but the terms of them were no longer dictated by the law. There are, of course, exceptions. For instance, the terms of contracts for hiring cabs and railway travelling are fixed by law; and the terms charged by school proprietors are indirectly regulated by the subjection of schools charging less than certain fees to governmental inspection. But in the main the old system of legal interference with contracts has disappeared: Statutes of Laborers, bread assizes, laws of settlement, bounties and protective duties have been swept away on grounds which will be found set forth by Adam Smith in his Wealth of Nations; and the normal assumption now is that the individual exacts for his goods or his labor as much as he can induce anybody to give him. Competition is a sufficient check on all extortion except that which we have seen to be fundamental in the Private Property system, that is, the extortion from the masses of the riches out of which the proprietary class saves capital and educates the *classe dirigeante*. Thus it is that the Private Free Contract system is sometimes called the Free Competition system. And since Free Contract and Free Competition are vital parts of a system providing capital by the enrichment of a special class, who thereby become the capitalists of the nation, the system is also called the Capitalist system. Finally, since the control of the nation's capital practically means the control of the nation itself, the domination of the capitalist class has earned for the system the name of Capitalism. Since, however, it is not in the capitalist's interest to call attention to his privileges, but rather to the "freedom" of the system under which he enjoys them, the terms Free Contract and Free Competition are employed chiefly by the advocates of the system, whilst The Capitalist System and Capitalism are the favorite terms of its enemies. The Private Property System is the least used term, precisely because it is the most impartial. But all five mean objectively the same thing.

The working of the system is simple enough whilst there is plenty of vacant land, and every man is either a landholder or can become one if he chooses. They produce from their own land and exchange the products, or else sell their labor for no less than they could make as direct cultivators of the soil. The landholders thus find that hired labor is as dear to them as their own, since the laborer, having the alternative of working for himself on land of his own, will demand the full equivalent of what his labor produces on anyone else's land. Hence labor is dear, large families are counted advantageous because of the value of the children's labor, and capital, as it can only be acquired by those who are willing to add the full labor it costs to that which they have to do for their daily bread, accumulates very slowly, and is invested chiefly in implements of which the want is immediate and pressing, and the return not too remote. Civilization of the most developed modern type cannot begin until the privations entailed by the accumulation of huge masses of capital becomes vicarious by being imposed upon a class economically enslaved: that is, which is compelled to bear the whole burden of labor without receiving more of the product than is necessary to maintain its own efficiency. With Freedom of Contract, such a class could never arise whilst there was vacant land of any value available. But since the quantity of valuable land available is limited, the natural increase of population finally creates a landless class or proletariat, which has no alternative but to sell its labor to the landed proprietors. Before this point is reached the hire of labor has been merely an exchange of equivalent services, by which neither party profits at the other's expense. The farmer, for instance, exchanges services with the blacksmith, not because he is able to get any more than he gives by the transaction, but simply because he wants his horses shoed and does not know how to shoe them, whilst the blacksmith wants farm produce and does not know how to grow it. But neither of them can make any pecuniary profit out of the transaction: the farmer could not sell the horseshoes for a farthing more than he gave the blacksmith for them, nor could the blacksmith induce anyone to give him more for the farm produce than it could be bought direct from the farmer for; so that such exchanges only take place for the immediate use of the parties, and not for resale at an enhanced price.

When proletarian labor enters the market, this state of things is altered. The proletarian comes to the farmer whose horses are all shoed, or the blacksmith whose larder is completely stocked—in short, to the landed proprietor who is provided with everything that he cares to work for, and who therefore is not willing to enter upon any further exchange of services, not that all his desires are satisfied, but that he has had his fill of work. Consequently he will add nothing further to his possessions unless he can get it for nothing. The proletarian, who must get at productive land or else starve, must therefore approach the landed proprietor with a proposal to work on his land and claim less in return than his labor adds to the product, thereby producing not only what he himself consumes, but something to boot for the landed proprietor as well. This proposal is of course very acceptable to the landed proprietor; and so the system of wages and profits comes into use.

It is evident that the proletarian's interest in this transaction is to make the bargain as favorable to himself as possible by giving up no more out of the product of his labor than is needed to tempt his employer to consent to the arrangement, whilst it is the employer's interest to allow the proletarian as little and make him work as hard as possible. Hence there will be a haggling between them, the laborer taking advantage of every increase in the productivity of the land (due, for example, to a good harvest or the like) to claim a higher wage, and the proprietor trying at every depression in trade or fall in prices to throw the loss on the laborer. The terms they make with one another will vary according to circumstances in the following manner.

As it is the increase of population that produces proletarian labor, there will, at its first appearance in a country colonized from the beginning on the Free Contract system, be fewer proletarians than proprietors. If, at this stage, a proletarian were to offer a very large share of the product of his labor as profit to a proprietor, he would soon be offered better terms by some rival proprietor; and this competition among proprietors for the surplus labor of the proletariat would raise wages nearly, though never quite, up to the full equivalent of value of the product of the labor. Taking this as the highest possible point for wages to reach, it is evident that it would be maintained until the demand on the part of the proprietors for proletarian labor ceased in consequence of every proprietor having as many laborers at work on his property as could extract more than their wage from it by their labor. Therefore, when the increase of population brings fresh proletarians into the field, it is not worth the employers' while to take them on at the old terms.

It does not follow, however, that a landed proprietor who cannot profitably employ more men at a given wage on his land is equally unable to find room for them at a less wage. A tract of land may yield a variety of commodities, some of them much less profitable than others: that is, fetching a much lower price in proportion to the labor they cost. It may produce both prime wheat and inferior wheat, gold, silver and lead, oak and deal, milk and mineral water, or, in manufactures, not only the main products of the factory, but bye products of inferior value which would not be worth collecting and preparing for sale unless the required labor could be had very cheaply. Now a crop of prime wheat can be raised from a good fertile farm, or a ton of prime coal from a rich mine, with less labor than inferior qualities from poor farms and mines, and yet the better quality will always fetch the higher price in the market. Naturally then, the fertile farms and rich mines will be the first to be appropriated; and it is upon them that proletarian labor will get its first and, considered as a fraction of its product, its highest wage. And the first check to employment at that wage will come when all the prime land is fully stocked with laborers. At this point the fresh relays of proletarians will be met, not with an unconditional refusal of employment, but with an offer of employment at lower wages, since their labor may still be used for the production of articles of inferior value—for growing barley instead of wheat, cutting down larches instead of oaks, breeding swine instead of horses, and utilizing bye products instead of main products. Obviously they must accept the lower terms or else starve.

This is the first step downward in the condition of the proletariat caused by "the diminishing return to land." Later on, when the second level of wage industry is fully occupied, a second descent to the third level will be necessary; and the process will be continued with the increase of population until the minimum wage is reached, this minimum being the bare subsistence of the laborer. If at any step in the descent a laborer presents himself who is weaker, slower, stupider, less practised than the average man of his class, he must take a step downward even before the descent takes place in the productivity of industry in general, because, though he is not employed in producing an inferior class of goods, yet, through his individual deficiency, he produces less of them in his day's work. Thus in an industry which demanded labor of such a character that two men could produce as much at it as three women, a woman could only obtain employment by consenting to take two thirds of a man's wage; and this is why women and half-skilled workmen receive smaller wages than the most skillful and productive workers in the same industry. In this way workers of all grades of strength and skill find employment at proportionately varied rates of wage on each level of cultivation.

It must not be supposed that the result of this process is the maintenance of high wages on fertile land simultaneously with low ones on inferior land. The moment a fresh relay of proletarians finds itself forced to accept lower wages, the wages of all the rest must fall too, since there cannot be two prices for labor in the same market. A landed proprietor who gives his laborer thirty shillings a week (say) only does so because he cannot get him for less owing to the competition of other employers for labor at that price. But the moment the demand for laborers at thirty shillings is satisfied, the next proletarian who comes into the market must take the step down, and consent to work for (say) twentyeight shillings. But the moment a man is to be had for twentyeight shillings, our landed proprietor will, in the exercise of his freedom of contract, immediately take him on at that rate and discharge the man who asks thirty. The discharged man is thereby placed in the position of the man who has replaced him: he cannot get employed unless he, too, consents to take twentyeight shillings. As soon as this becomes obvious, all the proletarians who are demanding thirty shillings will save themselves from discharge and replacement by accepting twentyeight shillings instead of thirty. Thus the descent from level to level of cultivation means not merely a reduction of wages for those who are driven to work on that level, but for the whole body of laborers. No employer will give a farthing more than the lowest wage he can get an efficient laborer for, no matter how large his profits may be. Just as the richest millionaire in England pays no more for a loaf of the best bread than the baker's poorest customer, so the proprietor of the richest mine or the most fertile farm in the country pays no more to his ploughmen or pitmen than the proprietor of farms and mines which are only just barely worth cultivating or working. As the cheapest loaf fixes the price of all the other loaves of equal quality, the cheapest laborer fixes the price of all other laborers of equal efficiency; and thus the necessity of the latest comer becomes the necessity of all the rest. Hence it is that the tendency of wages to fall to the bare cost of the laborers' subsistence is a general tendency affecting the whole body of labor, and has been described by Socialists, notably by Ferdinand Lassalle, as "the Iron Law of Wages."

This depreciation of the price of labor is entirely independent of any variations in the value of the products of labor. If the methods of mining and agriculture production and the prices of products were to be fixed immutably for a thousand years, the increase of population would steadily drive down wages shilling by shilling uniformly and obviously. But as a matter of fact both the methods and the prices vary considerably; and it is the effect of fluctuation brought about by these variations on wages that disguises the uniform action of the Iron Law, and often makes it seem to be flagrantly contradicted by facts. Now these variations, especially in methods of production, are inseparable from the constantly accelerating accumulation of capital produced by the operation of the Iron Law. Every step downward in wages is a step upward in profits for the proprietors, since in their case there is no levelling down. Their land is as efficiently and completely cultivated as before, though they give less of the product to the laborers and have consequently more left for themselves. Thus enriched, they can, if they are so disposed, save capital to the full extent of their gain without abstaining from any comfort to which they are accustomed. And as successive descents in cultivation make them richer and richer at the expense of the proletariat, they will be able to save with less and less self-denial until at last such a state of things will be reached as we now have in England, where agricultural laborers work for eleven shillings a week, and the rich can save so easily that in spite of extravagant living, a rate of less than 3 per cent safe interest on fresh savings suffices to keep capital accumulating at the rate of two hundred million pounds per annum.

Now the effect of the accumulation of capital on wages is first to raise and then to depress them, the subsequent loss being greater than the initial gain. Its effects on the spending money of the capitalist are of course the reverse: that is to say, he loses at first, gains afterwards, and finds his final gain greater than his initial loss. Take, for example, such simple examples of the introduction of capital as the substitution of ploughing for digging, of roads and bridges for packhorses and ferries, and of a railway for the road. Whilst the plough is being made the cultivation must go on as usual; whilst the road is being levelled and the bridge built the packhorses and the ferry must be as active as ever; and whilst the railway is being constructed traffic must still be carried on by horse traction on the ordinary roads. Consequently, in addition to the wages paid to the usual staff of laborers out of the product of their own labor, a second set of wages must be paid to the plough makers, road makers, bridge makers, or railway makers, as the case may be, and these cannot be paid out of the product of their own labor, which is as yet unproductive. Therefore this extra wages bill must also be paid out of the produce of the productive laborers' toil; but as it is paid out of that part of it which is first taken by the proprietor and then saved by him as capital, it is said to be "paid out of capital."

Here, since all the labor is done by the two bodies of proletarians, one at the expense of the other, the function performed by the proprietor-capitalist seems at first sight to be merely that of robbing Peter to pay Paul. And in truth the capitalist who bases any pretence of superior self-denial or public spirit on his part in the process deserves no better retort, since the whole advantage of the private property system consists in its enabling him to save capital without any exceptional moral qualities whatsoever—nay, by mere dint of his more selfish instincts. His proper defence is that the accumulation of capital is necessary to progress, and that without the enriched proprietor there could be no such accumulation. His function, in fact, is to levy a tax on the labor of many Peters, and having consumed his fill of the sum so raised, devote what remains to the support of a few Pauls whilst they are laboring unproductively (for the moment) in preparing ploughs, roads, bridges &c, to replace his slow, cumbrous, wasteful spades, packhorses, ferryboats, and waggons. The poor Peters would never individually abstain from consuming the full product of their labor in order that the Pauls might be paid to create capital; but if a landed proprietor is allowed to compel all the Peters to yield him up enough of their product to make him a comparatively rich man, then he will be able without privation to set aside the money for the Pauls in order to enrich himself later on.

Meanwhile, one of the effects of this accumulation of capital is to make the proprietary class,—now become also the capitalist class—require the services of additional laborers, and so to offer higher wages to tempt them away from other employment. But just as we saw that the arrival of a body of proletarians in the labor market offering to work for lower wages lowered wages in general; so exactly does the arrival of a body of capitalists offering higher wages raise wages in general, since no laborer will work for lower wages with one master when he is free to contract for higher with another. Consequently the effect of the accumulation of capital on wages begins by running counter to that of the Iron Law.

This initial tendency of capital to raise wages is kept within sober bounds in the early stages of cultivation by the fact that the first applications of capital are comparatively simple and obvious; their results are easily foreseen; they are intended for the immediate use of the facilitation of the business carried on by the capitalist himself; and they are necessarily limited in amount to the savings of individual proprietors who would not now be considered rich men. But when civilization becomes fully developed, and thousands of rich proprietors club their capitals together in joint stock to speculate on the needs and fancies of millions of people, capital begins to lavish itself in the most extravagant projects. To illustrate this, let us compare the investments of a miller who puts by a little money to enable him to discard his water wheel for a steam engine, and of a joint-stock company formed for the purpose of trying a service of penny steamboats on the Thames. The miller's investment is not a speculative one at all: he knows beforehand with sufficient exactitude what the engine will do for him, and therefore how much it is worth his while to spend on introducing it. The steamboat company have no guarantee whatever that any boat of theirs will ever attract passengers enough to pay the cost of the journey. On the other hand the miller's expectations, though certain, are limited: he knows too well how much flour he can sell and how much grain the engine will grind for him to indulge any wild dream of enriching himself beyond the dreams of avarice. Besides which, as the whole risk of trying the engine falls on him, and is a serious one for him, he is particularly cautious to do it as cheaply as possible. The steamboat company divides the risk between a number of shareholders and enables each of them to please himself with visions of crowded boats following one another up and down the Thames at intervals of a couple of minutes, and bringing in enormous dividends. In the case of a new invention, these exaggerated hopes of public patronage are intensified by wild imaginings as to the potentialities of the invention itself. The invention of the railway and of the electric light produced manias in which vast quantities of capital were squandered; and the introduction of joint-stock enterprise with limited liability, of new developments of banking and insurance, of conspiring to control market prices by "cornering" copper, wheat, salt, cotton and other commodities have all produced fevers of speculation in which men have gambled with their capital at the most reckless odds. In such moments they will madly overestimate the quantity of wages it is worth their while to pay; and whilst they are ordering machinery, and building and buying and engineering in all directions, wages spring up for the moment from the level to which the Iron Law has brought them; and for the moment prosperity and hope prevail over poverty and despair. Thus we see that the richer the capitalist class gets and the more the risks of investing capital become subdivided, the more reckless and wasteful it becomes in its projects, and the more sudden and violent are the fluctuations it produces in the labor market.

We have now to consider the effect on wages of the failure or successful accomplishment of capitalistic enterprise. In the case of failure the laborers employed on the bankrupt or abandoned enterprise are discharged and thrown back into the labor market to obtain employment in productive work by accepting employment on some lower level of cultivation than that already occupied, and so bringing down wages in general by the operation of the Iron Law. In the case of success, their discharge will follow the completion of the enterprise with equal certainty; but the effect on wages will be different. For the failure left the land no more productive than before, whereas the success has increased its productivity, since, other things being equal, a country well provided with roads, harbors, bridges, mills &c, will yield much more in a given time to a given expenditure of labor than a country without these conveniences. When a landed proprietor brings capital to the aid of his laborers, it enables him to obtain the same product as before with much less labor, so that, if wages do not rise, he can at once increase his profit by discharging a number of his laborers, thereby saving their wages, but also, of course, throwing them on the labor market unemployed where they depress the general level of wages. Labor saving machinery in factories, for instance, some-times has this effect so obviously and immediately that its in-troduction has often been fiercely resented by the proletariat on that account. Yet it is found that up to a certain point the pro-letariat gains absolutely by the introduction of capital, and that proletarian wages are highest in the countries where there is most capital.

The reason for this becomes obvious when we realize the sit-uation of the landed proprietor who has just brought capital to bear on the cultivation of his land. It is true that he is, as we have seen, in a position to obtain the same product and to give less of it away in wages by discharging all the hands whose labor is saved by the capital. But why should he not pursue the alternative course of retaining all his laborers and enjoying an enormously increased product? Nay, since the effect of many developments of capital is to enable a given area of land to pro-vide work for a much greater number of laborers, so that, for example, a cotton factory built several stories high and crammed with machinery, occupying only [a few] square yards of land, can accommodate as many workers as [many] acres of agricul-tural land, why should not the landed proprietor use his capital to double, treble, or quadruple the number of laborers employed on his land? What though the demand for more laborers raises wages: it is more profitable to pay twentyfive shillings a week to a man whose labor produces thirty, than sixteen to a man whose labor produces only twenty. Again, though the increase of the output reduces the market value of the things produced, it is more profitable to sell 1,000 articles at a penny apiece with a profit of a farthing on each, than 150 articles at sixpence with a profit of three halfpence on each. So far, this is what has taken place in the history of civilization. The savings of the rich, invested in labor saving machinery, have increased their demand for labor and so raised the wages of the proletariat absolutely. The increase in production caused by capital has overtaken the Iron Law and caused wages to rise absolutely with an increasing population. But the underlying action of the Iron Law is seen in the fact that wages, considered as the laborer's share of the product of his labor, fall steadily with the increase of population in spite of the absolute rise. In the illustration just given of the laborer getting sixteen shillings and producing twenty being superseded by the laborer getting twentyfive shillings and producing thirty, we may regard the transaction in two ways, either as a rise of wages from sixteen shillings to twentyfive, or a fall of wages from four fifths of the product to five sixths.[1]

If the student will now apply this economic process to increases in the efficiency of labor caused by improvements in the personal condition of the laborer through better food, technical and general education, or the like, he will find that these also have exactly the same tendency to raise wages absolutely as the investment of capital has, in spite of the fall in relative wages produced by the increase of population. It should be noted, however, that the two lines of improvement act and react on one another. An ingenious mechanic, technically trained, will invent a machine to do something that has hitherto been done by skilled hand labor. The skilled workers in this department are accordingly at once superseded by the machine and thrown on the labor market as virtually unskilled men. But the tendency of the machine is to employ more men than it threw out, and so compensate this, not necessarily to the individual sufferers,

---

1. Shaw is wrong: five sixths is, of course, greater than four fifths. Since his figures in his comparison are, however, arbitrary, he might have avoided the difficulty simply by having the week's labor in the second case produce (say) thirty-two shillings worth of goods instead of thirty. In such a case there would be a rise in wages absolutely along with a fall in the proportion of the produce which goes to the laborer.—Ed.

but to the proletariat as a whole. On the other hand, the introduction of machines into any department of industry often
raises the standard of skill and intelligence required from the
workers in it. For instance, driving a locomotive engine is a
much more difficult matter than driving a waggon cart. This
leads in turn to a constant effort to make a locomotive as automatic in its action as possible; but the advance in mechanics
which makes one machine more automatic produces new machines which are only practicable if handled with higher developments of skill in their application.

On the whole, then, it may be taken that all improvements in
production, whether due to machinery, technical education, or
what not, benefit the proletariat workers by counteracting the
Iron Law, and even raising absolute wages in spite of it; whilst
they benefit the proprietors by increasing their profits. In short,
all classes are interested finally in the improvement of the efficiency of industry, and of the capacity of the working class.
And yet, as the improvement in the condition of the working
class depends on their maintaining their own immediate efficiency as workers, they have to spend more on themselves and
their industrial equipment as they advance, so that the increase
in wages cannot be depended upon to lead to any substantial
improvement in their powers of saving. But this is provided for
by the relatively much greater increase in the riches of the proprietors, who therefore continue to discharge their function of
saving capital in spite of the enormous enlargement of the opportunities for spending which distinguish highly civilized
communities from primitive ones.

All this improvement depends on the maintenance of a rate of
increase of production which outstrips the increase of population, in other words, an increase of productive power per head
of the population, so that each laborer, no matter to what plane
of industry he has been driven by the law of diminishing return
from land which operates concurrently with the law of increase
of efficiency in cultivating it, is producing more upon that plane
than he did formerly. The saturation of the best sort of land
with labor may drive the next contingent of proletarians to

accept employment on inferior land; but if simultaneously with this the introduction of capitalistic cultivation increases the output from both sorts impartially to such a degree that the inferior land now produces more than the superior land used to (though not, of course, more than it now does) then both wages and profits will rise instead of falling. Hence it is that economists speak of a diminishing return from land and an increasing return from capital. The two factors must be set off one against the other. If the result shews a net increase in the rate of production per head of the population, wages will be tending upward. If the contrary, they will be falling. During this century the movement has been all one way, production having trebled whilst the population only doubled. But whilst industry as a whole increases in fertility, this or that particular trade may decay, either because the things it supplies are no longer valued owing to a change in the habits of the nation, or because some other mode of supplying them has arisen. Men may give up carrying arms and lanterns as policemen and gas lamps in the streets are introduced; matches take the place of tinderboxes; snuffers disappear with the disuse of tallow candles; the trade in alcoholic drinks shrinks with the spread of temperance; vegetarianism, steam locomotion and electric traction threaten the trade of the cattle dealer and horse breeder; and so on. As a result, the capital and labor which has been specialized for these trades (for after a certain age it is almost as impossible for a man to change his occupation as for a machine to change its use) has its productivity greatly diminished, in which case we see wages falling in that trade until no man will set his boy to learn it, and no capitalist will invest in it, so that it presently disappears or at least narrows itself to the reduced demand for its products. And we shall see later on that all trades proceed, not by a steady increase of productivity, but by alternate expansions and contractions, much as the tide comes in. So that there is no lack of opportunity for observing the action of net diminishing return in special cases, though on the whole the return is increasing.

It only remains to remind the student briefly of the way,

already familiar to him in his experience of the world, in which in course of time landed proprietors cease to deal personally with the proletariat and become mere pensioners on the product of their land without, perhaps, ever in their lives paying it a visit.

VIII   The Simple Truth about Socialism

The internal evidence suggests that Shaw began this selection with the intention of making it the first chapter of a book and then began to adapt his material to serve as a Fabian lecture. The last page of the typed manuscript bears the date "9th December 1910" in Shaw's hand. Fabian News *for December 1910 announced that a lecture by Shaw originally scheduled at Memorial Hall, Farringdon Street, for December 2 had been postponed till December 9 because of the election. The general title of the series was "Some Open Questions of Socialism." Shaw's lecture was announced simply as "Equality."*

There are some subjects about which you will learn the truth more accurately from the first man you meet in the street than from people who have made a lifelong and accurate study of it. Socialism is one of them, provided the first man you meet in the street does not happen to wear a red tie or be a member of a Socialist society.

Ask, then, the first comer what Socialism is. He will tell you that it is a state of society in which the entire income of the country is divided between all the people in exactly equal shares, without regard to their industry, their character, or any other consideration except the consideration that they are living human beings. And he will be precisely right. That is Socialism and nothing else is Socialism. It is true that this simple end may involve complicated means; and that these means may include some or all of the various things which the Socialist societies declare to be their objects, and which they habitually confuse with the end they are meant to secure. It is at all events clear that you could not establish Socialism and leave everything else, or indeed one may almost say anything else, just as it is. But the means are not the end; and the means have no sense out of view of the end.

It is true, of course, that considerable reconstruction of our political and industrial machinery is involved by Socialism as defined above, almost all our present machinery being contrived to achieve and make stable just the opposite state of things. It is true also that as all Socialists today are working at this reconstruction, they commonly say that the reconstruction is Socialism. But those Communists who are also great men, like William Morris, never make this mistake. They know that their end is equality. Most honest Unsocialists, not having this end in view, regard the reconstructions with horror as insane and ruinous mischief-making. And they are quite right, reasonably speaking. The miseries and infamies of our civilization are the price of inequality; and the only opponents of Socialism who are really formidable intellectually are not those who foolishly and ignorantly deny the existence of these horrors and infamies, but those who, like Austin and Macaulay and the early Victorian Whigs generally, look them in the face and say that terrible as they are, inequality is worth them.

Nevertheless the unconscious struggle is always towards equilibrium; and this is why we make so steadily for Socialism in our politics though the Socialists are in a minority, and a really resolute and convinced stand could still effect the very easy operation known as turning the clock back.

Let me begin by summarizing my whole argument.[1] Political science, once called political economy, has established one thing beyond all dispute; and that is, that there is no way of distributing wealth conscientiously—that is, according to a definite conception or ideal of what each person either deserves, or, if payment according to merit be impracticable (as it is), what

1. The canceled opening sentence of this paragraph originally read: "As the number of people who read more than the first chapter of a book like this is very small (I confess that I have not yet finished Wealth of Nations or even Munera Pulveris) I shall begin . . . ."—Ed.

each person should have in order to obtain the best social results —except the simple and direct plan of pooling the entire income of the country in the hands of some conscientious agency which will give to each man what he ought to have. This is what we do with the King, with our judges and generals and Secretaries of State, our soldiers and sailors and civil servants, and our children in the matter of pocket money. And please note that the civil list is the same for a good king as for a bad one; and that all the judges and all the generals, good, bad, and indifferent, alike get the same salary.

This practical solution has not been reached without exhaustive discussion and hazardous and terrible experiment. The struggle for personal liberty of which the English revolution of the XVII century, the American Declaration of Independence, and the French Revolution were the leading incidents, involved so strong a reaction against government of all kinds that there arose an intense desire to discover some automatic scheme by which wealth should distribute itself fairly and wholesomely without the intervention of the State. Under the influence of this desire political economy ceased to be a science and became a vehement propaganda of Industrial Anarchism, or, as it was called, laisser-faire, the theory of which was that if every man were left to make as much money as he could for himself in his own way, subject only to the laws restraining crude violence and direct fraud, then wealth would spontaneously distribute itself in proportion to the industry, sobriety, and, generally, the virtue of the citizens, the good men becoming rich and the bad men poor without any interference by the State. Like most wildly unpractical short cuts to Utopia, this error soon became popular; and it still enjoys some credit, and even works well as a practical scheme in communities where there is plenty of land available for settlers, and where life is still essentially village life, though even there it totally fails to grapple with the fact that poverty, idleness, and drunkenness are not any the less mischievous because the individuals with whom they begin happen to be bad characters and are therefore considered to deserve them. But in the more advanced stages of social evolution with which

we in Western Europe are alone concerned, laisser-faire is hopelessly discredited as the most disastrous failure of all the many
experiments that have been made in anarchy. It has been proved
beyond all question that under any private property system
whatever—and only under a private property system is laisser-
faire possible—it not only does not produce the results it promised, but absolutely must produce the exactly opposite result of
automatically distributing wealth in so wicked a manner that
not even the worst buccaneers known to history would deliberately effect so mischievous and manifestly unjust a distribution
of their plunder as that which made the XIX century one of the
blackest pages of human history.

In spite of this appalling experience, human laziness, which is
at its worst when the work to be done is political and therefore
severe intellectual work, still clings to the delusion that anarchy
is possible if only a right basis for it can be found. There are
men who say that laisser-faire has never been tried—that if the
land were nationalized, or rent nationalized by the single tax, or
the means of production, distribution and exchange made common property, or all men brought to conviction of sin and faith
in salvation by the blood of Christ, or all resistance to evil discontinued, then without further interference the clock would
go by perpetual motion, and go right. The reader must either
take my word for it that the clock would do nothing of the
sort, or else read the demonstrations I have already given of this
point in the pamphlets of the Fabian Society and elsewhere,
none of which I propose to repeat here. Nothing human in the
higher sense will grow or even live continually and certainly
except by human design and human activity working hard, purposely and tirelessly, to maintain and develop it. Whether we
conclude that Tom, Dick and Harry should have six-and-eight-
pence apiece, or that Tom should have fifteen shillings and Dick
and Harry half a crown apiece, we can give effect to our conclusion by no other way than by cutting off the three from all
money except what we choose to give them, and then giving it
to them in the desired proportion. No matter what system of

property or no property you begin with, the right division will not happen spontaneously.

The next fact to be grasped is that money is fortunately one of the things that can be distributed equally. You cannot distribute character equally between individuals, nor honor, nor general ability, nor specific talent, nor stature, nor wit, nor wisdom. But you can give one man half a crown and his next door neighbor two-and-sixpence with absolute precision. There is as much variety of character and ability among private soldiers and upper division civil servants as exists in the world. But all the units of these groups get the same pay.

It may be assumed without argument that nobody but a lunatic can believe that difference of character or ability could be measured by difference in money. No doubt people do foolishly and thoughtlessly talk sometimes as if the fact that the income of an English royal princess is much smaller than the allowance of an American billionaire's daughter, is due to the princess's inferiority in merit or beauty or industry or the like. That kind of nonsense can be silenced quickly enough. Ask the man who talks it to put down on paper the relative incomes he would allow to the Archbishop of Canterbury, Johnson the Prizefighter, Peary of the North Pole, the Astronomer Royal, Mr Paul Cinquevalli, Professor Karl Pearson, King George V, the late King Chulalongkorn, the Kaiser, Mr Roosevelt, Mr Sidney Webb, Mrs Humphrey Ward, Miss Corelli, Mrs Pankhurst, General Roberts, General Booth, Mr Gilbert Chesterton, and the Living Skeleton. I purposely pick out instances of such conspicuous and ascertained talent or peculiarity that the task of pricing them in money, if it be really possible, ought to be exceptionally easy. If money is really a practicable common denominator for all the virtues of human faculty and character, it must be possible to replace each of these famous names by a numerator; and since the talents vary the numerators must vary correspondingly. I offer the task to anyone who believes in the arithmetic of Unsocialism. For my part I cannot imagine how to begin. It is like asking how many minutes of a beautiful sunset are worth a pint of whelks. No doubt the Jevonian calculus could be applied even to that problem by ascertaining how much money a commonplace man would pay for each; but that would not help; for the Jevonian calculus measures, not the total utility of sunsets and whelks, but only the utility of the last minute of the sunset and the last whelk in the pint. No doubt some rough test might be applied. All the illustrious individuals in question might be starved to the point of cannibalism, and then a meal for one person placed before them, to be disposed of by him best able to capture it by his unaided strength and cunning. Probably by the time Johnson had disposed of the victor in the contest between Mr Roosevelt and the royal Chulalongkorn he would find that Miss Corelli had eaten the meal whilst Mrs Humphrey Ward and Mrs Pankhurst were arguing about it, and then find himself compelled either to die of hunger or to eat Mr Chesterton. I apologize for the frivolity of the illustration; but I declare most solemnly that I cannot think of any way of finding out the best man or woman which would be a whit less ridiculous. If any one else can, let them do so. Until they do I shall remain obstinate in the belief that the notion of making the distribution of wealth correspond to the difference of character and talent between individuals is quite the wildest, maddest, most unpractical, unbusinesslike, insane crotchet ever promulgated in or out of a mad-house.

It follows therefore that in the distribution of wealth we must apportion the shares solely with a view to producing the best social results, without regard to individual peculiarities. Now I defy anybody who has arrived at this point to escape the conclusion that the only shares that can be justified from the modern democratic, or the ancient Christian, or the practical commonsense point of view are equal shares. Just as the Church must assume that all souls are equally precious, and that we are consequently all equal before God, or else reduce religion to absurdity—just as the Sheriff must assume that twelve men of different sorts and sizes are the peers of the prisoner at the bar, who may differ from every one of them in height, weight, faculty and character—just as the vote of the silliest small shopkeeper that ever voted. for keeping the rates down must be counted for as much as the vote of the most enlightened Fabian; just so will it be found a practical and inevitable necessity to assume that every man's and woman's money needs are equal on pain of tearing society to pieces as it is torn today.

But I cannot carry this point, as I did the other, by bludgeoning you with the manifest absurdities and impossibilities in which your dissent would land you. Not only is it possible to distribute income unequally as between classes, but no nation has ever yet distributed it in any other way, intentionally or unintentionally. It is true that inequality, even of income, is so repugnant, suspicious, and in many respects obviously mischievous that it may be doubted whether any of the social schemes based on it could ever have been imposed on mankind by the utmost cunning of priests and princes if it were not for the natural phenomenon of economic rent, which makes inequality a necessary consequence of private property and carries it to lengths undreamt of by any priest or any prince. Even with such powerful help from what was practically a hidden and unknown cause, inequality between closely associated individuals has never been possible: what can be and has been done is to divide society into castes or classes and to set up a custom of regarding different levels of income as proper to different classes. Thus we pay judges more than policemen and majors more than privates; but we do not pay one judge more than another, one policeman more than another, one major more than another, one soldier more than another, though no two judges are alike, no two policemen alike and so forth.

There is a solid reason for such inequalities in all societies which, like our own, are based on Idolatry. It is absolutely necessary, if you are to have an ordered society at all, that Bill Jones, who may possibly be a more muscular man than Jack Smith, should nevertheless obey Jack Smith even when he has not the least notion of what Jack Smith is driving at. To induce him to do it, you must somehow contrive to make him idolize Jack Smith: that is, to regard him as a superior with mysterious and altogether super muscular powers. If Jack wears corduroys and lives in the same alley with no more money than Bill, this idolization cannot be produced. Bill is hard to please: you cannot even induce him to marry without first persuading him that a woman is an angel and has no legs and no stomach, a deceit which often leads to serious disappointment when the angel is brought home and unwrapped. Nature, for good reasons, helps the fraud in the case of the woman by the illusions of love; but Nature has no interest at all in passing off Jack Smith on Bill Jones as an [idol]. If that is to be done, you must put a crown or a tiara on Jack's head; prevent him from ever doing— or at least letting anyone see him doing—anything that Bill does; give him much more money and quite different clothes, besides lodging him in a much finer house and surrounding him with minor idols to set the example of worshipping him. Thus you get a whole hierarchy of idols, from kings to beadles, from Lord Chancellors to police constables, from field marshals to corporals, from dukes to barons and so forth. And you get something more: you presently get a real difference behind the manufactured one. When Bill has been hewing wood and drawing water in poor circumstances for a few years; and Jack has been kinging it under very prosperous circumstances for the same period, Jack will be a better man than Bill, not only in Bill's fancy, but in fact.

But it must be remembered that this superiority depends on the idol actually doing the superior work. When an artificial aristocracy is created by idolization it will work with all the appearance of a natural and inevitable system as long as the aristocrats not only wear their trappings and keep up the observances which set their daily lives and habits apart from those of ordinary folk, but also do the work which the idolization system was invented to provide for, and without which it has no sense. But once let them evade the work whilst retaining the privileges, and they will become an idle class, and, as such, an inferior class; for no mortal power can maintain the idler at a higher level than the worker. The idol who does not earn his worship is an impostor and a robber; and it is found in practice that whereas an aristocracy which really governs can maintain

its supremacy even when its members are in their personal conduct what we should call infernal scoundrels, aristocracies of
the most charming ladies and gentlemen imaginable who do not
govern, finally collapse and are trampled out with every circumstance of violence and insult by the mob. By the mob I
mean the unidolized.

The question for the political scientist, in other words for
the Fabian, is whether it is possible to devise any system of constitutional checks or safeguards by which the system of government by idolized aristocracy can be secured against this danger.
And when I say idolized aristocracy, I include its latest form,
which is an idolized bureaucracy of experts. Socialism without
experts is as impossible as ship-building without experts or
dentistry without experts. In so far as we have already done
without experts, we have done without Socialism; and all the
fears expressed that Socialism will produce a huge increase of
officialism are quite well grounded: under Socialism we shall all
be officials, actually or potentially.

Let us consider for a moment the proposals of the Minority
Report in this connection. These proposals are the most valuable
we have yet made; and for years to come our main business will
be to induce the country to accept them. And yet Herbert
Spencer must have turned in his grave when they were first
conceived. Just consider what they mean. They mean that every
man or woman shall be a ticket-of-leave man or woman. We
shall be regimented and inscribed: we shall have our papers
like travellers in Russia: the police will have impressions of our
thumbs as if we were murderers or burglars: if by shaving or
letting our beards grow or the like we make ourselves unlike our
official photographs, heaven knows what trouble we shall be
into. We shall be serfs of the bureaucracy as completely as
Gurth was the serf of Cedric the Saxon. We are to be drilled
like soldiers if the bureaucrats cannot find us a job; and if they
find us one, and we do not choose to take it, they are to haul
us off to a penal colony and flog us as prisoners are flogged
today if it pleases them to allege that that is the right way to
deal with refractory laborers. No such total abrogation of per-

sonal liberty has been proposed for white men since Liberalism
was invented. What are the safeguards against the abuse of this
appalling extension of bureaucratic power? In the Minority
Report, absolutely none. It is left an open question whether we
seriously believe that democracy and representative government will be a sufficient protection, or are taking it as a
matter of course that the new methods will be accompanied
by constitutional guarantees of some sort, or, worst of all,
are assuming that all the new officials, the masters of the Labor
Exchanges and the new style Relieving Officers and the rest,
will be Sidney Webbs with an enthusiastic staff of gifted
Colegates and Clifford Sharps and so forth. I submit that if
there is anything certain on earth it is that when the generation
of men and women who sit at the feet of the Committee for
the Prevention of Destitution have passed away, and the principles of the Minority Report are as completely forgotten as the
principles of Free Trade—and I can hardly put the case more
strongly than that—the relations between the laborers and the
new officials will be exactly like those now existing between
officers in the army and the rank and file: that is, relations of
pure despotism in which it will depend altogether on the character of the official whether he is a kindly master or a tyrant of
the most detestable sort.

Nearly twentyfive years ago, in my paper on The Impossibilities of Anarchism, I had to point out that the aversion of
many men to any sort of official despotism was so strong that
they would exultantly exchange a comparatively comfortable
state of slavery for a comparatively wretched state of freedom.
It is not so with all men: the slavery of the soldier is pleasanter
to some than the responsibilities of freedom; but in the South
of Europe Socialism has no chance unless it is called Anarchism;
and even in France the Syndicalists conciliate a mass of Anarchist sentiment by preaching the policy of holding aloof from
official politics, and depending on parliaments threatened by
powerful labor organizations rather than on parliaments in
which labor is directly represented. In Germany State Socialism

is still a term of reproach. In spite of the Fabian logic which proves that all Socialism must be State Socialism, and that Socialism means nothing else politically but the substitution of the State for the private adventurer, the instinct of the people still demands a State that is not *the* State: a government face to face with which they can feel free as they never can with the States of today. It is useless to put this demand off with chopped logic: we shall never persuade the people to trust such governments as we know with the enormous powers which Socialism must confer on the State. They are all class governments; and as long as classes exist, governments always will be class governments. Adult suffrage does not help the matter at all: the more we extend the suffrage in England the more firmly does the plutocracy establish itself. America is abandoned to plutocracy: England and France have nothing to oppose to it except the relics of the feudal system and the Napoleonic despotism.

I now invite your attention to my own personal case. As it happens, I am already what everybody will be under Socialism: a man carrying papers which may be demanded from me by every policeman I meet, failing to produce which I can be severely punished. I am numbered, ticketed, photographed, registered, licensed like a ticket-of-leave man. Yet I cannot pretend that all this has caused me the slightest inconvenience: on the contrary, it has fortified my position and enabled me to identify myself once or twice when a free man would have been at a loss to prove that he was himself. I have been asked for my papers once, under quite exceptional circumstances, in England, and never in France. The demand has not offended or inconvenienced me any more than the demand made for my railway ticket at King's Cross a few hours ago, or the demand for a cheque with my endorsement on it when I require money at a bank. But if these demands were made by persons who regarded me as inferior to themselves, or who, by being richer and more cultivated, actually were superior to me, and were determined to make me feel it, I should feel every such demand as a humiliation, and finally lose my self-respect if I habitually submitted. I am therefore of opinion that equality is necessary to make bureaucracy tolerable.

But if the Minority Report were superseded by a plan dispensing with all officialism, the arguments for equality would still be overwhelming. I shall proceed to marshal those which are quite independent of any particular administrative scheme, and are inherent in the very nature of society.

If a respectable Englishman heard a street corner orator preach as the golden rule of civic duty that we must all resolve to cut our neighbor's throat sooner than allow him to have sixpence a day more than we have, the respectable Englishman would probably believe that he had at last discovered the lowest depth of crudity in social theory and malice in its application to which the human mind and character could descend. But if any respectable Englishman will think and work his way carefully through all the theories and all the formulas, from Christianity and Feudal Toryism to Darwinism and Anarchism, he will come out, as I have done, with the conviction that no stable civilization is possible without the rigid maintenance of equality of income for every individual in the state, and that no assassin, no incendiary, no blasphemer, no libertine can strike so deadly a blow at his country as the man who persuades it to allow him or anybody else the extra sixpence on any pretext whatever. Unless every person who wants sixpence more is inexorably confronted with the condition that it can only be gained by devising such an increase in production as will enable everyone else to have it too, the granting of it will be the beginning of the decline and fall of that state as inevitably as it was the beginning of the decline and fall of Rome and Spain, or any of the other civilizations which have decayed or perished on our present principles.

Let us first take the economic reason for this doctrine. Political economy as an art of life means the satisfaction of the nation's needs in the order of their importance. A nation is in this respect like an individual. If a naked and destitute individual, who is starving, and who receives a shilling to relieve him, spends that shilling on a bottle of scent, he is clearly an insanely bad economist. If he receives a thousand pounds, and proceeds to buy a first rate motor car and a grand piano before he has bought a suit of clothes and taken a house, he will not improve his reputation in this respect. No doubt his folly will be very agreeable to the motor car manufacturers and the piano makers; but it will be disastrous to himself and his family, if he has one. The instance may appear extravagant; but as a matter of fact people are acting in that way every day. People insist on keeping horses when they cannot afford bicycles; they take country houses with parks when even a semi-detached villa is beyond their means; they put bad wine on their table instead of good cider or beer; they give expensive suppers at fashionable restaurants whilst their children are left at home half fed; they prize brandy above books, vanity above health, and, generally, show above substance, beginning their expenditure at the wrong end and holding to the precept of the Frenchman who said "Give me the luxuries of life and I can do without its necessities."

We have all noticed and condemned this unthrift on the part of our neighbours. But it has hardly yet occurred to us that a nation can sin against economy in exactly the same way. If a nation begins to build elaborate and costly stables for racehorses, with the most perfect ventilation, warming, and sanitation that money can buy, whilst thousands of its children are dying for want of the commonest necessaries and decencies of bare life, then that nation is behaving as thriftlessly, as heartlessly, as foolishly as the stupidest collier that ever bought cutlets for his bull pup and left his wife and children hungry. A gentleman leaving his son without a tutor or his daughters without a governess in order that he may have a footman on the box of his carriage is hardly considered a good parent; but what of the nation that employs large bodies of men and women as valets, ladies' maids, jockeys, gamekeepers, jewellers, and modistes, when it has not enough builders, plumbers, bakers, greengrocers, tailors, dressmakers, weavers and spinners to supply the first needs of its citizens! What sort of political economy does such folly call itself? And what final prospect is there for nations which persist in such a policy?

Take another department of thrift: the division of income between production for immediate consumption and production of means for cheaper and better production in future; or, to put it in the compendious popular terms, the division between spending and saving. There can be no question among sane people that spending comes before saving. It is true that we have heard bishops advise men with starving families to spend their wages not on bread, but on shares in projected railways in South America; but that is because bishops are apt, like other people, to think that what is good for a bishop is good for everybody. A laborer paid as laborers are today should not only be excused for not saving, but punished for saving; and as to the rich people who incite him to the crime of starving his already stinted household in order to save the said rich people's rates in his old age, it is difficult to say what ought to be done to them to mark our sense of their detestable thoughtlessness and selfishness. No doctrine can be more clearly sound, both economically and ethically than the doctrine that spending comes before saving, and that until the fullest welfare of the present is achieved the future must be left to its contemporaries in the days when it, too, shall have become present. And as a matter of fact the sense of this is so obviously a part of good sense, that the miser has always been more despised than the prodigal. The dead Knight's motto: "What I spent I had; what I saved I lost; what I gave I have," is instinctively felt to be a nobler lesson than the exhortations to people with too little to be content with less, and to put by for a rainy day whilst the rain is actually coming in through the holes in their children's boots. Indeed the notion that it is meritorious or even commonly decent to secure the dinner you expect to eat twenty years hence before you have secured your dinner for today is so grotesquely absurd that it is difficult for the people who have actually preached it to admit even to themselves that they have been guilty of such idiotic folly when it is stated for them, not in their own familiar cant phrases, but in its raw reality as a practical economic counsel.

But here again, what is silly for the individual is equally silly for the nation. Imagine a country with black spots all over its map denoting slums in which the vital statistics reveal a frightful death rate and fever rate, in which it is difficult to say whether the dirt, drink, and violence, or rebellion and despair, or the submission of patient and miserable drudgery are the more hopeless—imagine, I ask you, callously leaving these centres of social infection to stew in their own poisonous juice, and sending hundreds of millions of money abroad to exploit diamond mines in South Africa, and to provide electric light, railways and hotels for South America, not to mention building a cathedral in Khartoum and motor omnibuses for Persia and China. That is what we are doing at present; and we esteem our Foreign Secretaries in proportion to their success in facilitating such operations, and revile our Home Secretaries and Local Government Board Presidents in proportion to their activity in retaining for slum reform some of the money that might otherwise be exported. But though this is a gross example that proclaims our folly to the ends of the earth, it is really a small matter compared to our practice of the same unthrift at home. It is better to clear a British slum than to build a Christian cathedral in a Mahometan country; but it is better to build a cathedral even in Khartoum than to build another Ritz Hotel for people who celebrate the importation of the American Twenty Million Baby into this unhappy country. And much more plausible enterprises than Ritz Hotels have been undertaken out of their turn. The underground railway is a useful thing; but it should never have been made whilst there was a child over ground in London going hungry for want of the money it cost. Man shall not live by bread alone; but he cannot live without bread; so bread has to come first, even though the things that come later be higher things. We must serve Mammon diligently and intelligently before we can serve God, as anyone may prove by trying to substitute prayers for meals.

And here let me say a word in defence of Judas Iscariot. I

doubt whether the general prejudice against Judas is really founded on his betrayal of Jesus: most Christians betray Christ every day of their lives without turning a hair or exciting the smallest disapprobation. They sell him for much less than thirty pieces of silver, and instead of hanging themselves afterwards they hang anybody who blows them up for it. What we really dislike is Judas's protest against spending money in very dispensable luxuries whilst the slums of Jerusalem were a disgrace to the municipality. The retort of Jesus was an act of kindness to Mary and, like so many of the sayings of Jesus, an amusing repartee. It was also practical, because selling the ointment and giving the price in alms to the poor would have done no more good than the operations of the Charity Organization Society do today; but none the less Judas was right in revolting against the spectacle of a woman's toilet table being furnished with gold and alabaster whilst other people's dinner tables were not yet furnished with bread and butter.

Now it will hardly be disputed that the needs of the individual must be determined by his own tastes within such general limits as the law may prescribe. The law may decide that clothes are part of his needs, and may compel him to wear them, though he may happen to be an apostle of nakedness. It may in some cases compel him to wear a dress of which the shape, color, cut, and material are prescribed down to the last button; and it may forbid others to copy and wear that dress. The Pope, the monarch, the bishop, the parson, the soldier and sailor and police officer, the barrister and the university student, all wear prescribed costumes, some of them unbecoming to the point of being ridiculous; and there is the unofficial tyranny of society which makes the frock coat and tall hat, the black evening suit with white shirt front, as compulsory upon thousands of us as if there were sumptuary laws on the statute book to enforce their use. No man or woman in a city has any large freedom as to dress; and uniformed officers have no freedom at all. Still, the unofficial person has a certain limited choice of color and material. The State orders you to dress; but it leaves the majority of us to do as we please (if our neighbours will let us) when these two conditions are complied with. Also, it insists on our eating, and will even feed us forcibly if we refuse. And to some of us it prescribes a diet: the soldier, for instance, has his ration. But here again the majority can choose their diet within limits. Cannibalism is ruled out; but most of us can be vegetarians and teetotallers or meat eaters and winebibbers, as we please. And when we pass from the satisfaction of the needs of mere animal existence to the specifically human needs, our freedom is limited only by our means. We do not force a bicycle on a youth who wants a gramophone or a camera. We do not say to the man who wants a motor car: no, you must have a harp and hymnbook instead. No compulsion either of law or of public opinion is felt by the man who spends the price of a library on a racing stable, the price of an aeroplane on a picture. The officer who is not allowed to appear on parade in pepper and salt trousers or even to wear a beard, has so large a choice in his amusements and hobbies and sports and tastes and so forth that his sense of freedom is practically unlimited.

Now the line of progress certainly does not lie in limiting this freedom: on the contrary, we want more scope for individual initiation and variation. The impulse to attack and punish a man who acts differently from his neighbors is the impulse of a street Arab; whilst an interest in novelty—a disposition to tolerate and discuss every innovation hopefully and to wait and see what will happen before condemning it—is the mark of the highly evolved citizen. Grotesque as it is to hear the opponents of Socialism objecting that it would end in all our lives being reduced to a dead level and every detail of our lives prescribed to us and regulated for us by the government when, as a matter of fact, everyone of these objectors is levelled and prescribed for and regulated, dressed and fed and classed and placed and sent to church by an unofficial tyranny which inflicts ostracism and ruin ruthlessly for every defiance of convention, yet there is at the back of their nonsense a fact that must be faced; and that is, not, as they fear, that a Socialist government would interfere with them as their employers and clients now interfere with them, but that it could not do so even if it tried. To keep a whole modern nation under military discipline might or might not be a bad thing: the reason we do not discuss it is that it is impossible. It is not that people would not stand it: we know now that people will stand anything that is practicable; and the reason we are not all as enslaved as any felon in prison is that no government that has ever been devized is capable of so enslaving us. It is very questionable indeed whether any despotism that ever existed was able to interfere with the personal affairs of its subjects half so much or so oppressively as the democratic republics of France, Switzerland and the United States do at this day. We boast that our own limited monarchy is really freer and works out more democratically in practice than these republics; and there is a good deal to be said for this contention. If anyone were to assume in a debate with me that the subjects of Henry VIII were much less free than the subjects of a modern Liberal Cabinet, I should challenge the assumption at once. The simplest test of individual freedom is the proportion of the individual's income which the State either confiscates or dictates the spending of without regard to the individual's wishes. Speaking for myself I can find nothing in history to justify me in believing that Henry VIII would have interfered with me in this way to anything like the extent to which the Chancellor of the Exchequer, the President of the Boards of Education, Trade, and Local Government, the London County Council, and the Corporation of the City of Westminster do at present. It may be that the result of their interference is that I have a better life of it than I should have under Tudor conditions; but that is another affair: a soldier may have a better life of it than a tramp, but he is not so free politically.

Now my point is not that Henry VIII loved liberty more than Mr Asquith or Mr Balfour—though that, too, might be argued with some plausibility; for the absolute responsibility which Henry VIII and Elizabeth had to face must have sharpened their consciences to an extent unknown in these times when every statesman can throw all the blame on the electorate. At the risk of doing Henry an injustice I shall take it for granted that he exercised just as much power as he could grasp, and that he would have paid as little heed to the feelings and rights of every yeoman in England as he did to those of Katharine of Aragon if he could have laid his hands on them as effectually. My point is that his hands were not large enough, and that in proportion as a government is physically able to interfere with the lives of its subjects it must employ so great a number of civilians to do its thinking and acting that it perforce becomes more and more a representative and democratic government, no matter what its forms and its theories may be. The contrary notion, and all the terrors of "the coming slavery" and the like that are founded on it, are partly relics of the vulgar notion that a king or highly placed person has nothing to do but tyrannize, and that despotism is consequently easy and indeed automatic, and partly a romantic illusion produced by the reaction of our snobbery on the art of the historian, who represents the cruelties of Nero as a political tyranny, whereas they were really the incidents of an anarchy produced by making a despot of an incapable young debauchee. Nero was popular with the people: his despotism reached them only in the shape of splendid entertainments. His government was so unrepresentative, so undemocratic, that it was no government at all: the moment the people immediately about Nero had the sense to tell him that if he did not cut his throat they would save him the trouble, he had to obey like the meanest gladiator. To attain real power he should have made himself the keystone of an oligarchy. To attain extensive power that oligarchy would have had to make itself the keystone of a democracy. Let me put this evolutionary process in blunter terms. An assassin may be feared and dreaded, but he can enjoy neither power nor safety. To escape from this position he associates other assassins with him and becomes a brigand. To make brigandage pay, it is soon necessary to resort to blackmail, and protect travellers who pay for protection. Thus the brigands, with the worst possible intentions, find themselves transformed into a police force. At last they become regular policemen as poachers become gamekeepers. At which point their power reaches its maximum. Hence the paradox that Democracy represents the extreme of possible State Tyranny.

If we take it, then, that Democracy is far more able to interfere with the ordinary private man than Autocracy or Oligarchy, how does the comparison stand between Capitalistic Democracy and Social Democracy? Here in the Fabian Society we have no difficulty in answering that question. The Society was built up largely by the independence of men who were in the direct service of the State. In the beginning were Pease and Podmore and Bland. A little later came Webb, Olivier, and Shaw. At that time, as at present, no considerate chairman at a Socialist meeting ever asked a speaker to declare his name publicly. Yet we six did and said and wore what we liked to an extent that would have cost most private employees their livelihood. Podmore, Webb, and Olivier were civil servants. Pease was a stockbroker who was not dependent on stockbroking. Bland and I enjoyed the glorious freedom of being nothing: we were waiting for an opportunity of breaking into the profession of literature. As to what we wore I may say that I have seen Mrs Bland on a doorstep with a needle and thread, trying to establish some sort of connection between the sleeve and shoulder of a chestnut colored velveteen jacket on the person of Olivier so that he might enter the drawingroom with no more than the usual portion of his shirt visible. My tailor, when it became known that he was my tailor, had to change his name. On the other hand, Bland always dressed like a company director, which no clerk in the Society dared do. There can be no doubt at all that there is only one man so free as the man in public employment, and that is the man in no employment at all. Later on, as municipal trade widened, instances of this were visible in all directions. A municipal engineer was as comfortable on £400 a year as a joint stock company engineer on £1000, because he could dress unpretentiously; ride third class; live in Kentish Town; and do or omit to do, believe or disbelieve, pretty well as he pleased, provided he did his work and stuck to his post, whereas his privately employed colleagues were dressing and dining and entertaining and paying club subscriptions and pew rents on rigidly prescribed lines: in short, being intimidated into all sorts of reluctant compulsory expenditure from which the public employee is free.

Now the difference between capitalistic democracy and Social Democracy is that public employment will be, not indeed universal, but universally available as an alternative to every person who is dissatisfied with private employment; so that the private employee will be as free as the public one. Consequently I think we are justified in assuming that in capitalistic democracy we have the maximum of practically possible coercion of the individual in the matter of personal habits and expenditure, and that as we change to Social Democracy—if we do—such coercion will become less and less effective and particular.

What is the moral of all this for my present purpose? Just this: that the only way in which a Socialist State can keep production in its proper economical order, necessaries first and luxuries last, and prevent saving from setting in before spending is complete, is not by dictating to individuals how they shall spend their money, but by equalizing purchasing power as between individuals: that is, by equalizing income. Once allow any class to have more purchasing power than another and it is idle to pretend that any personal coercion that could possibly be exercised by a Socialist government could keep production and expenditure in their proper orders. No municipality keeping a bread shop could force a man to buy bread enough for two because some other man who had not money enough to buy the extra loaf would be the better for it. Indeed the whole point of giving one man more money than another is just that the due social order of production should be dislocated in his favor. Maintain that order and the man who has a thousand a year more than his neighbors may just as well throw it into the river or build a free library or a King Edward Memorial with it; for he cannot find anything to buy in the market that he has not already his fill of. Even as it is, our multimillionaires are compelled to give enormous sums away because, in spite of all the extravagances of fashion, there is nothing in the market to buy that they cannot consume to satiety before their incomes are exhausted.

Consequently, if production were restored to its proper economic order the only privilege the millionaire would enjoy would be freedom to idle whilst others worked. Let us examine this privilege for a moment.

When a certain sequence of events occurs so commonly in our experience as to be practically invariable, we end by assuming that one follows from the other either logically or necessarily. In our society there are two events that occur in this way. The first is giving a man an independent income. The second is his ceasing to work for the community's living. We have come to regard these as we regard the disappearance of darkness on the rising of the sun, or the hanging of a man convicted of murder. That is, we assume that it is both logical, justifiable, and even necessary. It is therefore expedient to wake up public opinion to the fact that it is neither logical nor justifiable any more than it is necessary. When the Twenty Million Baby grows up, it will be just as much bound in honor to do its share of civil service as it would be if it were a German baby to do its share of military service. The fact that it will not be so bound by any as yet existing law is clearly an omission in the law and not a recognition of the right of any individual to be a parasite, millions or no millions. The law omits many things: some of the most abominable crimes an individual can commit are still not punishable by law; and parasitism is probably by far the most mischievous of them, if not the most sensational. It would be classed as a punishable offence today with vagrancy and theft if it were not that the parasites not only use their wealth to corrupt the government but actually become the government and openly run the country in the interests of parasitism. It may be asked how the practice of tolerating idleness in the rich ever grew up if it had no basis in any sort of utility. The answer is that it had. There was a custom once of exempting people who could read from the penalties of crime. It is so recent that its name "benefit of clergy" is still quite familiar to us. It was really a class privilege; and it lingered as such to the days when gentlemen duelists indicted for manslaughter pled their clergy and got off scot free. But in earlier days it must have been a powerful incentive to education: indeed the appalling illiteracy of our rich classes today almost tempts us to propose a revival of it. But when the spread of education to the commercial class made it a means by which a cloth merchant could run a Colonel in the Guards through as safely as the Colonel could run him through, it was restricted and finally abolished. At present it would be an absurdity in its original form, because, as everybody is now taught to read, an exemption from a penalty to all who could read would mean the abolition of the penalty. The State no longer desires to bribe individuals to learn to read: it compels them to.

Precisely analogous to the benefit of clergy is the benefit of capital. Just as the State once said to the individual: "If you learn to read we shall not hang you when you commit murder," so it still says to him: "We shall not hang you for idling if you save capital." This is quite well understood: every measure that is directed against capitalist idling is objected to on the ground that it will discourage saving. And such arguments are bound to prevail in every community where there is too much spending and too little saving, and where the State is still so rudimentary a social organ that it cannot take the work of saving into its own hands. As in the case of benefit of clergy the exemption soon became a class privilege. As such it is still kept up among us in spite of the fact that we not only save £200,000,000 a year which is urgently wanted for expenditure on pressing present needs, but recklessly export a great deal of it to remote countries.

That this benefit of capital will go the way of benefit of clergy and be sternly abolished can be doubted by those only who doubt whether human nature has sufficient virtue to weather the point at which all previous civilizations have been wrecked by it. These sceptics may be right: indeed I shall presently shew that one of the most powerful arguments against our existing system is that it fails to produce as much political virtue as we need; but if we assume that we are inevitably going to the dogs there is no use in studying social questions or making political proposals at all: we had better say at once "Let us eat and drink; for tomorrow we die." I shall proceed on the assumption that the situation can still be saved.

Suppose then that we abolish the benefit of capital, and compel every person to produce what they consume, whether they are millionaires or proletarians. This will mean that the millionaire may as well invest his entire unearned income at compound interest, deriving no personal benefit from it except that which he shares with all the rest in the lightening of the daily task or the increase of its reward by the improvements affected by his and other people's capital. In a sense he would be an enormously rich man if his shares still stood in his name and the dividends were still paid to him and not taxed to extinction as unearned income. But if he had to work like the rest he would inevitably be compelled by his circumstances to live much as they did. The habits which distinguish our idle rich today are possible only because there are enough idle rich to make it profitable to organize special industries and services for the gratification of idle habits in a carefully segregated idle society. If we did away with these habits, and with the segregation, and consequently with the insanity which segregation involves (for please do not forget that if people are deprived of work and rigidly confined to one another's society they go mad; and no agreement on their part to give fine names to their madness can make them sane), the fashionable ways of our smart sets would soon go out of fashion and finally become impracticable. Anyone conversant with our existing society must be aware that the working rich, by which I mean those members of our plutocracy who accept social duties, whether as statesmen, soldiers, or landlords assuming feudal responsibilities, are quite distinct in mind and social habit from the idle rich, whose money comes to them without effort as a bank credit, and who do not know what social responsibility means. William Morris, a rich man who worked hard all his life, and, like Ruskin, accepted social responsibility in the fullest sense, called these people "damned thieves"; and they deserve no civiller term. They are disgusting people, degrading everything they meddle with, insulting everybody they address (especially when they mean to be charming), and setting every conceivable sort of bad example to the masses who are dazzled by their expenditure. And, like all parasites, they are themselves surrounded by parasites who acquire all their vices without their independence. Compared with the working rich, they present themselves almost as a different species.

Now the working rich very often echo the complaint of the Irishman in the bottomless sedan chair. "But for the honor and glory of it, I might as well have walked," he said. The difference between the life of a common soldier or sailor and that of Napoleon or Nelson almost vanishes when contrasted with the difference between the life of a petty tradesman in Camberwell and an idle millionaire on the Riviera. The millionaire is always surprised at the simple life of a king, who, without at all meaning to live like a well-to-do busy alderman, finds himself doing so because his life is dominated by the exigencies of his business. If all our idle rich people could be worked as hard as the king (and one would really like to hear from them why they should be more privileged than the king) they would get common sense in its strictest meaning; and their characteristic follies and vices would drop from them with the habits of life which their duties would make impracticable. But they too would then begin to ask themselves what use it was to be rich if they had to work as hard as poor men.

We have to consider, in guessing the answer to this question, that a society in which even the richest man would be obliged to do his share of the world's work would also be a society in which every man would have that share organized and provided for him, and based on his own needs. The destitute person of today, unemployed because somebody else does not want anything from him, would no longer exist. In other words, whatever else the millionaire may be able to buy, he will not be able to buy men, women, and children. He may have to clean his own boots in spite of all his millions if the tradition still lingers

that there is anything derogatory to human dignity in cleaning
another person's boots. Certainly, if the bootblack still exists, the
millionaire will have to be as civil to him as a doctor is to his
solicitor or a captain to a chaplain. The class of private servants,
that is, of persons who will sell for wages all claim to have their
dignity or their convenience considered, will disappear everywhere as completely as it has already disappeared in some of
our factory towns. Now without slaves you cannot have masters. Without economic dependence on and legal subjection to
the head of the household you cannot have patriarchs or
matriarchs. If you take an idle rich man, and not only compel
him to do his share of work, but place the position of master
and patriarch out of his reach, you destroy the value of his
riches to himself personally. If he employs them to surround
himself with retainers, they are so independent that he must
address them respectfully and court them as persons on whom
he himself is dependent: a relation infinitely less comfortable
than that of free fellow workers and social equals. Even at
present the servant question is becoming so irksome that many
rich people are wretchedly afraid of their own domestics; and
the gardener is more master in the garden and the chauffeur in
the garage than the owner. The old-fashioned country house
may still be patriarchal enough to remain in working order; but
the domestic life of the modern idle rich is breaking up more
and more into hotel life, which is now regarded and even systematically used as a refuge from the worries of housekeeping
instead of as a makeshift in the absence of home comforts. And
if satisfactory menial service is so hard to obtain with masses of
unemployed in the streets and the idle rich richer than they
have ever been before, or, let us hope, will ever be again, what
would it be like when the richest man could not find a single
human creature at the beck and call of his money, nor himself
escape from the universal obligation to earn his own living?
Granted that the earning would be so simplified that his leisure
would still be abundant (and here I must remind you that this is
not a necessary consequence, as economy in production may be

taken out in higher products as well as in shorter hours of
labor), is it not likely that the individual incentive—I will not
say to amass riches, for the power to do that on any serious
scale would vanish with the present system of capitalistic exploitation—but even to retain inheritances from the old regime,
would be reduced to negligibility.

In short, if you are really going to emancipate labor and make
everybody do his share of work, compulsory equality of income
would be no hardship: on the contrary, it would relieve the
rich man from an invidious position which would carry no
compensating advantage. And the State would have to undertake the duty of saving. There is no difficulty in this: every
municipal electric lighting enterprise now has its reserve fund,
and has to scrap obsolete machines and instal the newest ones,
just as any private enterprise does. And democratic public
capitalism has conspicuous advantages over private. It does not
send capital abroad when it is wanted badly at home; and it
does not ruin hosts of unfortunate widows and orphans. It has
no interest in saving when it ought to spend, or in dislocating
the proper economic order in production. And if it attempted
to court popularity by spending where it ought to save, and
letting its industrial machinery depreciate to enable it to lavish
entertainments on voters in the low old Roman fashion, it would
very soon have to announce a reduction in dividend which
would bring the voters sharply to their senses, even if they
could be conceived as stooping momentarily to the level of the
debauched proletariat which applauded Nero's chariot races and
gladiator fights.

Strong as the economic argument for equality is to those who
have learnt to appreciate the overwhelming importance of
getting the economic basis of society right, and the hopelessness
of getting anything else right whilst that remains wrong, most
people will be more affected by a statement of the secondary
than of the primary results of economic inequality. We suffer
so continually from economic anxiety that we come to hate the
subject; and the Fabians who try to broach it often find them-

selves in the position of a doctor whose patient meets him by
exclaiming "For heaven's sake dont begin talking about my
health: I'm sick of the subject."

Let us then pass from the production and distribution of wealth
to the production and distribution of public opinion. Let us
assume, to begin with, that we are committed to democracy,
and that future extensions of the franchise can only enlarge and
intensify it.

At present the working classes have a huge majority of votes
in America and most of Europe. Yet government is not democratic: it is oligarchic. It is true that the oligarchy is open to
the talents and the long purses. What is more, no politically
sane person can wish to break down this oligarchy as long as
the alternatives to rich men and cultivated men are poor men
and ignorant men. Burke shocks some of us by his remark about
the hoofs of the swinish multitude; but must we not admit that
the only creatures concerned who have much to resent in the
comparison are the swine? Everyone who has taken any practical part in public affairs must have observed that poor men,
even when they have been elected as representatives of the
most millennially magnificent conceptions of the future of society, are lamed and made reactionary, the moment they come
to solid business, by the penuriousness of their ideas. I have
known men who were in favor of the socialization of all the
means of production, distribution, and exchange, indignantly
resisting a proposal to substitute a supply of clean towels for a
single roller towel in a lavatory used by nearly a hundred men.
Poor men of the middle class were tried as members of parliament by Cromwell; and he had to pack them back to their
chapels. Poor men of the laboring class were tried in the French
Revolution; and they had to be hammered back into their slums
by the cannons of Napoleon. A small example of the same thing
occurred only the other day at Tonypandy. For the most part
the multitude knows so well that it cannot govern that it never
wants to, and never tries to unless it is organized by agitators;
and even then, though it may cheer the phrases in which the
agitators declare that it shall govern, it confines itself to cheer-

ing and rioting and fighting. Professor Gilbert Murray told the Fabian Society in a remarkable paper which he has since reprinted as a preface to his translation of The Bacchae, how the Greeks revolted against democracy with a disgust as bitter as that in which Marat revolted against aristocracy. I myself, when I want to use a motor car in Switzerland, and find that the Swiss farmer is determined that Swiss Government shall tolerate nothing better than the farmcarts and diligences which he himself uses, cannot resist an oligarchical impulse to take that farmer by the scruff of his neck and teach him that he must adapt his farmyard to my higher civilization instead of dragging down my civilization to his farmyard. I do not believe there is a single member of the Fabian Society who would face the consequences of placing the government of England in the hands of the vast majority of the English people: that is to say, of the laboring classes, unless his real object were to achieve a *reductio ad absurdum* of democracy and have done with it for ever. The staunchest and most eloquent democrat of our day is Mr Gilbert Chesterton; but his finest political poem is that one in which he tells us that the English people have never really spoken yet—that none of the political revolutions and religious reformations and social developments have been the work of the people. And he is quite right. The people of England have had no more to do with it all than the sheep of England, not because they were dumb or gagged, but because they had nothing to say; not because they were eyeless or infirm, but because they looked on without interest and struck as they were paid or bidden to strike.

To come to the root of this part of the matter, real democracy is impossible without public opinion. And in our system the difficulty is not, as we so often say, that public opinion is not enlightened. The difficulty is that public opinion does not exist. There is literally no such thing. Opinion means a view of the world; and a view of the world means an income. There is the view of the man with 18/- a week and the view of the man with £30,000 a year. Both may call themselves by the same name: Liberals, Unionists, Socialists, Church of England, Catholics, Baptists, or what not; but it is utterly impossible that their views should be alike. Not even genius can attain a common human position: Morris and Tolstoy in their intercourse with peasants and mechanics could get over the obstacles of personal intercourse that baffle the ordinary snob; but they could not get over the difference in knowledge and outlook that was the result of the difference in income: the Socialist League was a hopeless failure from that point of view. Nothing wider than class opinion is possible; and every different income means a different class. What we call public opinion is only the greatest common measure of all the class opinions. This greatest common measure is not an average: no such thing as an average man exists, just as no such thing as an average income exists. The average of 18/- a week and £30,000 a year is £15,023:8:0 a year, half what the one man has got and 326 times what the other has got. The greatest common measure is so very common that it represents not only the opinions common to the two men but probably to dogs and cats and sparrows as well, including nothing more heterogeneous than the cupidities and resentments and terrors and concupiscences that are felt by most vertebrate animals. The moment you carry political action into the more highly evolved planes on which Man appears not only as distinctively human but as a member of a complicated civic organism, no public opinion is possible; and the organization and administration of the community must necessarily be done by a class securing the consent of the lower classes either by honest autocratic or oligarchic coercion or by pseudo-democratic humbug. It is hardly worth laboring a point so obvious. We all know in this room that a Fabian Society of laborers is an utter impossibility, although we are very far indeed from being a society of rich men.

This is the real reason for the failure of democracy to work democratically. And there is no remedy except the abolition of class by the abolition of inequality of income, and the consequent substitution of a solid public opinion for a chaos of conflicting class opinions. Democracy would really work then, and would be irresistible and permanent, instead of being what it is at present, a doubtful and discredited recent political experiment, which has achieved its successes, such as they are, only because it is not really democracy at all.

I do not of course suggest that equalization of income would abolish differences of temperament. On the contrary, it would set them free to operate; and we should have real political conflicts instead of the sham fights with which our oligarchic factions keep us amused and submissive at present. But the greatest common measure of the disputants would include the whole field of economic interests. The fight would be for ideas, not for bread and butter at one end and for corrupt domination and stolen luxury at the other.

If equality is fundamental in economics and a life or death condition of democracy, it is no less indispensable in our sexual institutions. I have dealt before with this question so fully that I do not propose to elaborate it here. Briefly, the argument runs thus. The real obstacle to the very complex and active organization and co-ordination of society which we Fabians propose is not any unsoundness in the logic of Socialism, nor any want of the most appalling evidence of the need for it. Nor, since the Fabian Society undertook the task of devising ways and means, can it be said that there is now much difficulty about practical methods, or at least of practical beginnings. What stops us is that the work is beyond the political capacity of the human animal as he exists today. We are like the crowd at the street fight mentioned by Dickens, which told the small boy to go in and win: "an excellent thing," said Dickens, "if you are able to do it." The Fabian Society is very like that crowd; and the governments of Europe are very like that small boy. I have preached Socialism for nearly thirty years; and I have never yet met a hostile audience; yet Socialism seems no nearer than if I had preached in a continual shower of rotten eggs. For more than 2000 years our best people have admitted the superiority of Plato's social ideals: but the Platonic republic is still waiting for a population of Platos. The old statement that every nation has got the government it deserves may not have much meaning; but we may say pretty confidently that no nation can have a

better government than it is capable of comprehending and conducting. In short, we must improve the nation if we are to improve its institutions. An improvement by direct breeding is
impossible, not because there is the smallest rational objection
to a human stud farm, but because if we set up a stud farm we
should not know what to breed. The Eugenic Society feels
quite sure, apparently, that it can make a beginning by at least
breeding out tuberculosis, epilepsy, dipsomania, and lunacy; but
for all we know to the contrary, the Superman may be tubercu-
lous from top to toe; he is quite likely to be a controlled
epileptic; his sole diet may be overproof spirit; and he will certainly be as mad as a hatter from our point of view. We really
know nothing about him. Our worst failures today may be
simply first attempts at him, and our greatest successes the final
perfection of the type that is passing away. Under these circumstances there is nothing to be done in the way of a stud
farm. We must trust to nature: that is, to the fancies of our
males and females. No doubt some of the fancies are morbid;
but they must all have some meaning: that is, some purpose;
and the purpose must be in the main a vital one, or it would
hardly have survived. At all events, that is the best we can make
of the situation.

If, then, we have to depend on fancy, we must give it the
widest possible field. To put it practically, we must make the
whole community intermarriageable. We must also mobilise
our population so as to facilitate to the utmost the institution
which the Germans call the Year of Wandering; for it is no use
making us all intermarriageable if we cannot wander in search
of a mate. Already the people in our villages are intermarriageable; and they belong to a very large class; but because they live
in isolated groups and often spend their lives within ten miles of
a big town without ever visiting it, they breed in and in until
the stock is ruined. We are appalled to find among peasants
living under apparently ideally healthy conditions all the dis-
eases of degeneracy. Every young man and young woman
should wander widely in search of a mate. Old Age Pensions are
far less important than a year's travelling at a suitable age—a

sort of eugenic travelling scholarship—having as its main object wider opportunities of falling in love, and a standard of humanity founded on actual observation of all existing types.

But as long as we have classes, all such arrangements are Utopian. In London locomotion is cheap and easy; and everybody has the habit of it. A population of several millions provides a choice sufficiently large to exhaust the variety of nature. If we cannot find our affinity in London, or Paris, or New York, or Vienna, or Berlin, or Rome, we must be rather hard to please. The real difficulty in such places is that when the affinity is found he or she is inaccessible through difference of class. If your father owns a coal mine, you cannot marry into the family of a coal merchant; nor can a coal merchant's daughter marry an attractive coal-heaver. The difference between a duke and a dairy-maid, a duchess and a chauffeur, does not greatly matter: there are too few dukes to bother about; and they can always add to the romance of the peerage by marrying beneath them. What does matter is the difference between the wholesaler and the retailer, the mechanic and the car-man, the docker and the railway porter, the doctor and the chemist, the chemist and the pork butcher, the curate whose grandfather was a country gentleman and the curate whose grandfather was a pawnbroker, between Kensington and Islington, Hampstead and Camberwell: that is, not so much the large differences as the small ones, and not so much the small ones as the imaginary ones. I remember my father being shocked to find me playing with the son of an ironmonger who was very much richer than himself, his own business at that time being the sale of flour by the sack or the hundred sacks. And I have no doubt that certain abrupt and otherwise unaccountable breakings-off of my relations with other boys were due to the discovery by their parents that my father had so far forgotten himself as to engage in trade under the degrading necessity of earning his own living. Even when intermarriage does take place, you have the result described by Dickens in Dombey and Son, where Mrs Dombey's set could not be induced to mix with Mr Dombey's set, and the two occupied different ends of the drawingroom. The struggle is kept up by husbands and wives themselves to the end of their lives: the story of the lady of county family who married a cotton millionaire and could never quite get over the sense of his taking a liberty when he called her by her Christian name is quite true, if not to nature, at all events to class civilization.

How artificial these distinctions are is shewn by the fact that though hardly any of our senses gets so acutely developed as our sense of class, it fails completely in a foreign country unless it is helped out by the outward and visible sign of dress, or of the use of soap and water. Among the people who dress similarly and wash with equal frequency, we are able to perceive no distinction once we cross a frontier. Even a frontier is not needed. When I was a youth in Ireland, I could place Irish people socially apparently by instinct. When I came to England I was completely at sea. Confronted with an altered standard of income, of dress, and a new and quite strange manner of speech, I was for some years quite lost: provided only that a man did not drop his aitches and wore a tall hat I could not guess whether he was the Lord Chancellor or an undertaker. Later on I came across cases of the same class blindness on the part of Americans. An American woman will sometimes marry an Englishman whose distinction attracts her, only to find out later on that the distinction is nothing but novelty, and that she would never have thought of marrying an American of his class. When I first came to London, I found a huge black tom cat in the house one evening; and I captured it and kept it for a year, in spite of its revolting debaucheries, as a rare and curious specimen, not knowing that black cats are as common in London as they are rare in Ireland. In the same way I have seen a highly cultivated and fastidious foreigner adoring an English girl whose speech would have curdled his blood, could it have reached his ears in its Parisian or Berlinese or Viennese equivalent. How little it really mattered was shewn by the fact that [when] he married her and took her abroad, she passed off as well there as if she had been a duchess. Finally, all these class

differences resolve themselves into differences of income. In the
long run, no class can hold out against money. Rockefeller and
Rothschild are irresistible: the only condition on which a feudal
aristocracy can exclude them is by excluding itself from society,
and sulking in a forgotten corner whilst plutocracy leads the
fashion, rules the court, marries into the best families, lays
foundation stones, scoops in peerages: in short, *is* the real smart
set in spite of all hole and corner theories of aristocracy. The
same thing occurs in the other grades. The poor little firms of
wholesalers who once scorned the shopkeepers, now dare not
dream of such an honor for their daughters as an alliance with
a Benetfink, a Whiteley, a Gamage, a Gorringe, a Lipton, or a
Pearce and Plenty. If I had a son, I should urge him to make the
acquaintance of sons of prosperous ironmongers, also of their
daughters, and to shun poor and proud middlemen like the
plague. The people who will not look these facts in the face,
and persist in making XVIII century class distinctions, simply
do not get their daughters married, as the only men they will
accept cannot afford to marry them and are flying at better fed
game. Roughly speaking, anybody bred on an income of a
thousand a year, and still possessing it, is eligible as a mate for
anyone else in the same financial position, no matter what their
ranks may be. And, conversely, neither matrimony nor even
society is possible between persons whose scales of expenditure
are widely different. A man with a hundred a year may be
much more refined by nature and cultivated in his tastes than a
man with twenty thousand; but he cannot dine at the same
table at Willis's Rooms, nor sit next to him at the Opera. He
cannot even accept the rich man's hospitality, because he cannot
afford the necessary dress and the tips.

Every income, then, means a separate class; and every class
breeds in and in. With the exception of the few who can afford
to travel, or who, as commercial travellers, sailors, navvies, or
strolling actors and entertainers of one kind and another, are
mobilized by the nature of their occupation, this inbreeding is
intensified by excessive localization; so that youths and maids,

instead of having their whole class to choose from, really have only as much of that class as is covered by the field of a dance in a Hornsey villa.

It is waste of time to labor the point further. The utmost widening of the field of sexual selection involves the equalization of income, and can be effected in no other way. As an argument in favor of Socialism I believe this has a hundred times the leverage of the Surplus Value demonstrations of Marx. People desire the Superman so ardently that they will run after the poorest imitations of him, inventing him for the sake of something to worship where he does not exist. Unless this aspiration moves us, unless we believe that the life in us is a divine spark that can be nursed into a steady flame and finally into an all illuminating fire, then there is really no sense in belonging to a Fabian Society or indeed in taking the trouble to feed ourselves. We are all ashamed of ourselves as we are: we all want to reach forward to something better; but we none of us care twopence whether we receive the whole value of our labor or not, provided what we get is enough to keep us going. I therefore think that the biological argument may prevail even if all the others fail. I even rejoice at the failure of the Marxian argument inasmuch as it was not the really important economic argument. To say to a man that he has produced twenty shillings and only got ten will not move him much as long as he can live on the ten and thinks that if there is a class which gets ten without working, he may perhaps make his way into that class some day. Mankind is not revolutionary on the selfish side unless it is starved to a point to which it does not pay Capitalism to starve it. But if you put the true economic argument, and derive from that not only a political argument, but a biological argument, you will begin to go ahead. At all events, it is worth trying. Marxism clearly not only does not help Socialism now, but destroys the minds of the Marxists. The doctrine of Equality, based at every point, not on the evils of Capitalism, but on the whole facts of human society and human nature, enlarges the mind and educates the man.

The task of the Fabian Society in the future must be to work

out the practical path towards equality. I should like to put in
the basis for signature not only by all new members, but all the
old ones as well, such an article of faith as "I believe that a
cabin boy should have the same pay as a captain" or "I believe
that the king should have no more pay than the dustman." Until
we can see the expediency as well as the justice of this, we are
not Socialists: we are only pitiers of the poor and rebels against
unpleasantness. The line of practical progress, roughly speaking,
is the advocacy of a minimum wage. On that path we are already afoot. We have established in practice not only a minimum wage for laborers in public employment, but the habit of
thinking of it and calling it a *moral* minimum wage. It began in
the London County Council at 24 shillings a week. When it
rises to 38 it will have reached the level of the best paid skilled
trades in the country except those which, like steel-smelting,
are only possible for powerful men in their prime. If the rise is
accompanied by the exaction of higher qualifications from the
unskilled, so much the better. However that may be, if we
could get the wages of unskilled labor up to £2 a week, we
should achieve equality of income as between four out of every
five men in the country. But the clerk and the university engineer would be left in a helot class. For the engineer the remedy
would be not to learn his trade at Oxford, but at a Polytechnic.
For the clerk I see no remedy but either to make clerking a
criminal offence or to resort to legal regulation.

At the other end of the scale we must proceed by taxation as
Mr Lloyd George does; but our object should not be the vague
one of recovering site values and other ultimately undefinable
figments of abstract economics, but the reduction of all excessive incomes to the normal standard. As to the professions, we
should work, by making education and culture accessible to
everyone, for the destruction of the present class monopoly of
such advantages. Already, however, many professional men are
much poorer than men engaged in work in which education
and refinement are positive drawbacks. The real difficulty is
how to deal with the varying attractiveness of different occupations. We may put aside as absurd the notion that equality of

pay would cause a rush for the lower classes of work—that, for instance, the born captain would insist on being a cabin boy if he could get no higher pay than a cabin boy, or that Mr Bland and I would refuse to write articles and ride round town on bicycles with special editions if we were not offered more than the bicyclists. The danger would be all the other way: the bicyclists would want to edit the paper, and the cabin boys to command the ship, until they found out what it was like and returned to their bicycles chastened. But it would be impossible to impose uniform conditions of labor in return for equal pay. There is work that men can do for 18 hours a day without breaking down; and there is work that uses a man's working powers up in 3 hours. If I were to attempt to write plays or economic essays day in and day out for as many hours a day as I could drive a motor car without being the worse for it, I should be a wreck at the end of a fortnight and possibly a corpse at the end of a month. But if I could put in 3 hours writing and a couple of hours navvying or forestering I should be all the better for it.

Before I conclude I want to anticipate a very natural question, which is, "Why didnt you say all this before?" And if I give you a good reason for not saying it before, you may ask, "Why do you say it now?" I reply that there is a practical side to my genius which prevents me from fording a stream until I come to it; and that in this case there was so much to do to clear the way to the stream that though I always recognized that our goal was equality, and was forgiven for much Fabian Opportunism by William Morris on that account, I never shaped out the case for it until quite lately. Also, the time had not come for the Fabians to break away from the ordinary Progressives so completely as this doctrine would break them. We were quite far enough ahead of them as it was. But now the situation has changed. The spread of our ideas has had the somewhat startling result that we are too small a body to handle them. The greatest triumph of Fabianism has been sweeping into the field of practical politics the proposals of the Minority Report; but these proposals have obtained a vogue that is so

much wider than any membership possible to an avowedly
Socialist body that Sidney Webb has been forced to take it out
of our hands and form a new body, which now does all our
Opportunist work and leaves us for the moment almost without
a reason for existing. If I were now a young man of 28, as I was
when I joined the Fabian Society in 1884, I should not join. I
should join the National Committee, and attach myself either to
the left wing of the Liberal Party like Mr Chiozza Money, or
to the Labor Party. I might even join the Agenda Club. As you
stand, you have nothing to offer me except the running of your
shop, which is a very excellent shop, with its tracts and book-
boxes and so forth; but it seems to me to be living on its reputation in the matter of ideas and not, as it once did, making the
pace for the general Progressive movement. The propaganda is
so stale that I am not sure that our disciples have not got ahead
of us. Taking a crowbar to a door which is really open is all
very well on the stage; but it is ridiculous in the market place.
Now against equality of income the English mind is still shut
and bolted; and there is therefore still use for our crowbar
there. We might produce a new volume of Fabian Essays working out the application in economics, in morals, in politics, in
art and so forth, not this time merely of Collectivism, as we did
before, but of Equality.

If we also took up a suggestion of Mr Bland's, and forced on
the Labor and Lloyd Georgian program some definite piece of
Collectivism such as the nationalization of the coal mines, which
could easily be attached to railway nationalization, we might
again draw away from the main body of Progressivism and
recover our lost lead. By combining such advances with a
propaganda of Equality, we could clear ourselves of that suspicion of Bureaucratic Oligarchy which attaches to us at present
and attaches with good reason; for I repeat that without Equality—that is, the abolition of classes—we can do nothing but
organize Capitalism on a more stable, scientific, and commercially profitable basis than at present. And as that would be a
great improvement of the present system—so great in fact that
we cannot refuse to help it forward if nothing better may be—

we are all the more bound to keep its dangers constantly before our converts to Collectivism; and this we can do only by making them converts to Equality.

Finally, Equality is the best touchstone for distinguishing your real Socialist from your virtuously indignant pitier of the poor. It would be interesting to see what would happen if, as I have suggested, we introduced it into the basis and made all future and present members sign it. I throw that out as a point on which we might learn something from the discussion.

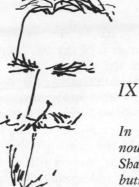

IX   Redistribution of Income

In the fall of 1914 Fabian News announced a series of six lectures by Shaw on the subject of the "Redistribution of Income" on Wednesday evenings beginning October 28. No syllabus was included because Shaw had been "compelled to turn aside from their preparation to deal with the more pressing subject of the war." Shaw's Common Sense about the War *appeared as a supplement to* The New Statesman *on November 14, 1914. For a discussion of the complex relation between the Fabian lectures as given by Shaw and the long essay below the reader is referred to the textual notes at the end of the book.*

The existing distribution of income is merely a fact, not defensible and not defended as corresponding to any political or ethical ideal or fulfilling any human intention. In our own time it has become so absurd and mischievous that we may assume to start with that it will soon be found unbearable. As it does not tend to right itself automatically, but, on the contrary, to become more anomalous with every increase in population and improvement in production, its regulation by public action is a necessity of the situation. Indeed, in one form or another, it already enters into the program of every political party, conservative or revolutionary.

The first modern attempts to lay down canons of distribution aimed only at canons of taxation, under which title we find them in Adam Smith's Wealth of Nations. If income were equally distributed taxation would be very simple: poll taxation would cover everything. The fact that poll taxation had been ruled out for centuries until the Insurance Act partly reintroduced it, and that poll taxation violates the canons, shews that taxation, both in theory and practice, has always been imposed with some regard to the effect on it of the distribution of income. The real difference between the old budgets and those of Sir William Harcourt (with his death duties), Mr Asquith (with his differentiation of taxable incomes into earned and unearned) and Mr Lloyd George (with his supertax) is that the old budgets aimed merely at raising the required revenue in the way most convenient in the view of the existing distribution, whereas the new budgets aim openly at altering that distribution by taking income from the rich and spending it on the poor, or, as in the case of Old Age Pensions, actually transferring it directly to their pockets. As such a process, unless based on a canon, seems purely predatory and provokes that comparison to "robbing a hen-roost" which has already been made by the aggrieved rich, we must endeavor to formulate such a canon; and the present lectures are tentatives in that direction.

Clearly we must begin by ascertaining what the existing distribution of income is, and making up our minds as to what is wrong with it.

And at the first step we have a surprise. Expecting to find a chaos of anomaly and inequality, we actually do find an overwhelming prevalence of simple equality of income. For every millionaire we find a million men receiving equal incomes without regard to their diversity in character and capacity. All human experience shews that it is impossible to escape from equality of income; that equality always has been, always will be, and is at present the rule, and that the exceptions are few and fantastic.

Why, then, should this familiar fact surprise us? Clearly because we have been thinking, not of individuals, but of classes and of persons whose income consists of some form of rent, whether of land, capital, or personal ability. For example, police constables get equal incomes and judges get equal incomes; but judges get about seventyseven times as much as constables. An imbecile landlord or capitalist may get two hundred and fifty times as much as a higher mathematician. A specially skilled surgical operator or a specially attractive actress or a specially acute and eloquent barrister may become very rich whilst persons of no more than average powers in the same professions may find it difficult to make both ends meet. Special skill in finance or the organization of industry, aided by luck, may secure relatively monstrous gains: say two or three thousand times as much as the stipend of a highly educated and hardworking clergyman. The dramatic effect of these contrasts blinds us to the vast plateaux of equality above which they tower, much as people look through telescopes at stars and ships and not at space and the sea; but the plateaux are there all the same, flat as pancakes, and must be taken as the typical and natural economic surface of society.

We start therefore with the knowledge that equality of income is practicable and normal in human society, and that the infinite diversity of tastes, talents, characters, bodily powers and aptitudes, and the simple divisions of sex and age, offer no obstacle to its smooth working. The fox hunting squire and the astronomer, the general and the bishop, the hereditary prince and the purveyor of sausages and groceries, and all six together, associate without the least friction provided only they have equivalent incomes. The converse is also true. Without practical equivalence of income, astronomers cannot associate with astronomers, much less with fox hunting squires. Even an officer in the army cannot belong to a regiment where the average income of the mess is much higher than his own.

The inevitable conclusion is that if human society is to be stratified into classes, the basis of the class distinction must be difference of class income sufficiently marked to form an insuperable bar to intermarriage, association in private life, and similarity in personal habits. Now this stratification is as normal in highly civilized society as that equality of income which, as we see, is universal within class limits. A mining camp or a clearing of pioneer colonists may get on without classes; but no civilized nation has yet done so. And the question whether a civilized nation can must be settled before we can attempt to alter the existing distribution with any confidence.

We must therefore begin by investigating the social utility of class distinctions; for if these are necessary, income, though it must always be equally distributed in the main as between individuals, must be equally distributed at different levels, a system involving inequality of income as between the levels: in short, a system like our present one except that the qualification for the levels might very reasonably be withdrawn from the sphere of heredity and accident and assimilated to our present public service qualifications as the result of passing some test of fitness for prescribed functions.

The question "Can a stable society be maintained without classes (or castes)?" sounds trite. But its essential form is more surprising. Can subordination be maintained without idolatry? For the whole use of class stratification is to produce an illusion that certain persons are naturally superior in themselves to certain others who have to act under their direction, and whose respect and obedience could not be secured without this illusion. All sorts of quaint ways of producing the illusion are practised. In primitive tribal society a person of superior ability as a lawgiver or a military leader may make himself chief; but he cannot make the others understand his proceedings (indeed he may not understand them consciously himself) sufficiently to secure an intelligent obedience. And the simple conditions of tribal life do not admit of his living very differently from the rest. But he can wear a special head dress and forbid anyone else to wear it. He can inculcate reverence for it in the young. If he cannot build a much better hut than his neighbor, he can give it an imaginary sanctity by burying people alive under its foundations. He can make it a capital crime to touch his person, and have servants who sneeze in his presence savagely beaten. In short, he can make himself fetish (in English, make himself an idol). And he can then declare that on his death his sanctity will be inherited by his son and thereafter by his son's son. It may be objected that he will not be the only clever person in the tribe, and that the other geniuses will refuse to be imposed on and shew him up. But exactly the contrary will happen. These clever ones, though just not clever enough to make themselves chiefs, will be only too glad to attach themselves to the illusion he has created and share its authority and prestige. When he dies and is succeeded by a commonplace son, these clever ones can rule in his name. They can even finally create the illusion that his commands are valid only when they are given by the advice of his councillors, thereby creating the curious illusion which we call a constitutional monarch and which the Belgians call an India Rubber Stamp. But in the meantime, as authority has to be delegated more and more as the community grows in size and complexity, a whole hierarchy of idol castes will have to be instituted until a complete class system like our own is evolved, and the most hopeless fool or incorrigible blackguard in a high caste will be treated with greater respect than a saint in a relatively low caste.

Now though instituting differences of income as between the idols and the idolaters is the most obvious way of establishing and maintaining the system of idolatry, it is not the only way. A naked beggar in the east may intimidate a prince. A poor priest in Ireland may take precedence of the richest man in his parish. A navy captain may enjoy a dignity and authority beyond the reach of commercial millionaires. Kings are no longer the richest men in their dominions. Bishops and judges are "poor devils" in the commercial scale, and yet are richer than many Generals and Colonial Governors. Making money is so often dirty work done by dull fellows that the deference paid everywhere to the rich is now much more a fear of the power that money gives, and a desire to obtain some of it, than genuine idolatry. Besides, circumstances are making genuine idolatry much more difficult than it was. For example, when the House of Lords was known to the people only by galleries of painted portraits or engravings of them, elegance, impressiveness, and a noble cast of features were associated with peerage in the public imagination. Photography, especially snapshot photography, errs in the opposite direction. An endless shew of snapshots of popular idols is kept up by the illustrated press; and in these our aristocrats frequently figure as grinning hopping lads with loutish bearing and fatuous faces, accompanied by baronial fathers who seem quite eligible for coalheaving and dust collecting, and jolly vulgar mothers with daughters who, if they have any pretension to good looks, seem to aim in a silly amateur fashion at being mistaken for the Sisters Somebody at a music hall.

Much more important as a means of disillusion is the fact that when our aristocrats are really fine people and look it, they do not reflect the average idolater's ideal. It is not everybody who knows a gentleman when he sees him; and now that all men above the rank of casual laborers dress alike when they are out for a holiday, and that well bred men have a nervous horror of "swank" and "side" and pretentiousness or abnormality generally, it is easier to idolize a beadle, a drum major, a judge on the bench, or even a rank-and-file soldier or policeman than a duke. Add to this the multiplication of the numbers of the idle rich and the consequent frequency of newspaper revelations as to their private life made in the divorce court and in libel actions; and take account at the same time of the fact that the splendid costumes, the imposing equipages, and the long retinues of the days before the French Revolution are now gone quite out of daily use, and you will see that idolatry is in difficulties nowadays. In fact, the surviving attempts to inculcate it often have the opposite effect. The bishop's apron, the barrister's wig, and the judge's ermine make their wearers ridiculous as far as they have any effect at all; and liveries, from the court to the kitchen, are imposed as badges of servitude rather than as symbols of authority.

Nevertheless we cannot pretend that we have learnt to dispense with idolatry; for classes are as distinct and idolatry as prevalent as ever. But the idol is now the rich man; and the idolatry is founded on the belief that income is a measure of character and talent; that character and talent are hereditary; and that as the cost of production of a prime minister is higher than that of a hewer of wood and drawer of water, the man who costs most is the best man. We must examine these beliefs closely.

When we say that income is a measure of character and talent, we are clearly dealing only with earned income; and as it is unearned income which creates the difficulties that have led to a demand for redistribution, no generalization that applies only to earned income is relevant to the case. But the generalization is not sound even within its limits. If certain qualities of character and talent lead to riches and consequently to political dominance and the power of manufacturing public opinion by means of privately owned newspapers, the owners of these qualities will identify them with virtue and productivity even when they are demonstrably nothing more than unscrupulous ambition and callous destructiveness or conscienceless laziness and greed. The German Emperor, by making Majestätsbeleidigung a criminal offence, and flattery a road to promotion, made it difficult and disastrous for anyone to characterize any of his acts or words as other than highly virtuous. But in this case the publicity and *naïveté* of the coercion undoes a good deal of its effect. The idle rich, who are far more mischievous than the official rich, have no laws to protect them from denunciation; but not even the literary genius of Ruskin could secure him a hearing in the press for his exposure of that mischievousness, although attacks on the Kaiser in German papers are quite common. There is a steady propaganda of the superiority and gentility of the rich and their habits, and a steady suppression and persecution of all really fundamental criticism of them, which ends in making us ashamed of genuine virtue, and ready to accept income as a measure of talent and character because we have been persuaded that a man's talent and character are, in effect, his income. Such idolatry leads finally to national disaster, because men who are merely rich not only thrust themselves into high positions of national responsibility which they seek because they have no sense of the responsibility and a good deal of vanity, but provide for their relatives or gratify their friends by finding public jobs for them, with the result that national emergencies find us unprepared and without leaders.

The notion that character and talent are hereditary need not detain us. If they were, Richard Cromwell would have become King of England; and his descendants would still hold the throne. And George V would be just like George IV. And no good man could ever have a scapegrace brother. It is true that acquirements are transmitted from parent to offspring by infinitesimal increments; but the effect in each generation is so slight and confused as to be negligible for practical political purposes; indeed a whole generation of biologists denied its existence. It is also true, and much more important, that a family tradition of public service is of great value, and ennobles those who live up to it. But here again we find not only that the tradition is to be found in families of moderate means rather than in rich ones, and that the rich are making a tradition of idleness and social worthlessness. The presumption is now against the rich as far as heredity goes.

The third bulwark of the idolatry of riches, namely, that the man who costs most is the best man, requires more disentangling. In some aspects it is contemptibly untrue: for instance the imbecile who inherits a million and squanders it in a couple of years is clearly not, even during those years, better than the men who are living within moderate incomes. The famous million dollar American baby is not a prize baby. But the plunger's millions and the baby's dollars are not their cost of production. The plunger has not really cost more to produce than his footman nor the baby than its nurse's baby. If the community is foolish enough to throw money away on them in the form of monstrous incomes it does not alter their cost of production any more than throwing the money into the Thames would alter the cost of production of the embankment. That is so obvious that it is a waste of time to discuss it, though it is worth stating because so few people can see what is obvious.

But if men be regarded merely as instruments of production, as our commercial system regards them, differences in cost of production and maintenance at once spring to light. Scavengers and ragpickers are cheaper than valets and lady's maids. Croupiers are cheaper than chancellors. Clerks are cheaper than chemists and astronomers. If two babies of equal natural capacity be taken with the intention of making one of them a shepherd and the other a director of the Bank of England, it will be found necessary to spend a good deal more money on the education of the one than of the other. But who are you that you should arrogate to yourself the right to use babies in this fashion? Leaving the feelings of the babies out of the question, and assuming that all that is needed is a shepherd and a bank director, it still remains desirable that you should get the best possible shepherd and the best possible bank director. Suppose the result of your predestination of the two babies is that the bank director would have made a very good shepherd, but wrecks his bank, and that the shepherd loses all his sheep because his natural bent is towards finance! It would have been wiser to spend just the same money on both babies by giving them an equally good general education and then allowing them to develop their natural aptitudes, which is just what we do with our doctors, clergymen, and barristers. The commercial mind will immediately object that a shepherd with a liberal education represents a shocking waste of money. The human mind perceives that if the shepherd is a better man for his education the community is a better community for his existence, and that this is the true and only real value it can get for its money. And from this point of view the illusion that one man costs more to produce than another suddenly becomes a reality; for here you can see that though one educated man does not cost more than another, an uneducated man costs more than an educated one, a drunkard than a sober man, a rogue than an honest man, a murderer than a kindly person, an underfed unseemly ragged vagrant than a well fed, well clothed, well housed citizen. The boot, in short, is on the other leg; for your commercially cheap man does not pay his way socially, and the commercially dear man does. This indeed is the very centre of the eternal conflict between the human point of view and the commercial, between Capitalism and Socialism.

The moment you give up regarding a human being as a mere instrument for producing commercial profit, and decide that every Englishman shall be a decent, healthy, educated Englishman, you reach a point at which an astronomer does not cost a penny more to produce than a ploughman, and costs less to maintain, as he is likely to eat and drink less, and his boots and

clothes last longer. As an Englishman and a human being he
may cost as much as you like: the more the better; but as an
astronomer, a prime minister, a poet, a philosopher, a general,
or a managing director, he costs absolutely nothing, specific
talent being the free gift of Nature.

Prejudice and perversity, driven out of the proposition that
the talented man costs more, falls back on the proposition that
he produces more. Of course he does: otherwise the world
would be none the better for him, and he would be none the
better himself, as he has to live in the world and cannot get
above its level. It is true that if he has had a commercial training and has no sense of the dishonor of trying to make money
out of Nature's free gift, he may try to make his fellow citizens
pay him for exercising his talent. It is also true that his fellow
citizens may shoot him for refusing to exercise it, as Admiral
Byng was shot. But Admiral Byng was in the public service and
under the control of those whom he served: in short he was
Socialized. In commerce a man of commercially lucrative talent
can take advantage of the competition among capitalists for his
services to sell his talent for something less than it adds to the
product of the business he engages in (for if he demanded all
there would be no profit in employing him), which is usually a
good deal more than the payment made to men without exceptional talent. This process, which is inevitable under competitive private Capitalism, seemed to the late Lord Furness so
natural and proper that in claiming for the organizer of industry all the difference that his work made to the product, he
offered no apology for it, concluding that it would appeal to
every reasonable man as obviously fair and reasonable. But in
doing so he immediately raised the question whether he was
really more indispensable than the workers he organized. He
said truly, "Without me, you could not carry on a shipbuilding
business." But they replied, equally truly, "Neither could you
without us." "Remove me," he said; "and what becomes of your
profits?" And from this deadlock there is no escape. The product of organized industry is a joint product of the organizer
and the organized, to which each is equally indispensable; and

as it would be as irksome for a man with organizing talent to leave it unused as to a navvy to have his hands tied, there is nothing natural or necessary in the practice of paying the organizer more than the organized. Even as it is, the organizer often gets less than the organized. A surgeon blackmailing a man with a broken leg for a large fee for setting it is liable to a reminder that the patient has contributed to the operation by breaking his leg just as indispensably and much more painfully and hazardously than the surgeon does by setting it. A military surgeon taking advantage of a battle to refuse to operate on the wounded until they paid him all they possessed to staunch their wounds would very soon find himself past all surgery. These military examples are all the more elucidatory as we have so recently seen how ruthlessly war exposes the pretences of private capitalism and forces a nation to prompt recourse to socialistic measures. Thus we find General Bernhardi, the evangelist of Prussian militarism, suddenly realizing at the end of his gospel that the civil measures he has been postulating as necessary to the national safety are all nakedly socialistic, and rather feebly pleading that he is an officer and a gentleman, not a vulgar Social Democrat.

Now let us have another look at distribution of income from the commercial point of view. From that point of view it is not worth while keeping a manual worker alive after he is forty: it pays better to replace him by a younger man. Employing elderly men is like using worn-out machinery. Probably it is a commercial mistake to employ men as old as forty. It would pay better to work them much harder and wear them out at thirtyfive or earlier. The old Manchester tradition of wearing out nine generations of men in one generation made many fortunes for cotton lords. Before the introduction of electric traction tramway companies sometimes estimated that the most economical way of working tram horses was to work them to death in four years and then buy new ones. Similar calculations were made by slave owning planters, who accordingly worked their slaves to exhaustion and death in a few years and then bought new ones. The substitution of so-called free wage labor for chattel slave labor does not abolish this system: it intensifies it, when it is not prevented by humane uncommercial laws. That is why the man over forty is not employed in high pressure industries; and the man over fifty can hardly get employed at all. The steel smelter and the coal miner is used up as such long before his old age pension comes due, and has to find comparatively invalid occupation at a reduced scale of income. These facts are the *reductio ad absurdum* of the commercial estimate of men and of the monstrous notion that a sane society could be constructed on the commercial system.

The extreme repugnance of all generous souls to face this omnipotence of Supply and Demand is natural enough. Nothing is more horrible than to be under the control of a force that has no conscience, no sense, no purpose. The modern Darwinian theory (which Darwin, by the way, did not hold) that we are all the prey of Natural Selection is so hateful that many able people, thoroughly acquainted with modern science, have taken refuge from it in medieval Catholicism. But Natural Selection, though it could not claim a purpose, at least claimed a result: the result of the Survival of the Fittest. True, as it was only the survival of the fittest to survive, it was a poor consolation when you met a hungry tiger and realized that under the circumstances the tiger was fitter to survive than you: still, it stimulated you to invent a gun and turn the tables on him. But Supply and Demand is more soulless than Natural Selection even. It guaranteed the Feeding of the Fattest and the starving of the Thinnest: a much less inspiriting warcry than the Survival of the Fittest. Everyone loathed it.

Unfortunately we have an inconsiderate habit of wreaking our hatred of unpleasant facts by denying their existence and refusing to discuss them. Mr Podsnap always swept disagreeable considerations behind him and refused to discuss them, or to associate with people who did discuss them. But that is just what all the disagreeable things want us to do. The sort of policeman a burglar likes is the policeman who turns his back and looks obstinately in the other direction. The sort of policeman he dreads is the Sherlock Holmes variety, who is interested in crime and investigates it, unravels it, exposes it. If you persist in disposing of Supply and Demand with a wave of your hand and a declaration that it is banished to Saturn, it will not go to Saturn: it will continue to oppress you all the more securely because, instead of mastering it and putting it in its proper place, you keep assuring yourself and everybody else that it has left the planet.

Now its proper place is most certainly not the place that should be occupied by your duty to your neighbor. For here Supply and Demand become the diagnostic of slavery. If a man's income varies, not according to his needs or the number of children he has to support, but according to the scarcity or plenty of the sort of labor he does, or if it rises as he approaches his prime and falls until he is "too old at forty," then that man is a slave, no matter what sort of legal constitution he lives under or votes for, because a slave is a person bought and sold for the sake of the work he does and being denied any other access to the means of subsistence. A planter may keep an old slave and an old horse out of human kindness when both are past working; and there is an old statute in England, the Poor Law of Elizabeth, which still compels our Guardians to rescue destitute persons from actual starvation in as disagreeable a manner as possible, so as to insure their sticking to Supply and Demand as long as Supply and Demand will have anything to do with them; but to delay the death of worn-out human beings is not the same thing as enabling them to enjoy life; and it cannot be pretended that this wretched last resource really redeems their lot from slavery. If we are bought and sold whilst we are worth anything, we are slaves whether the price be thirty shillings a week or three thousand pounds. We are free only when we become gentlemen of property, with an assured income from the cradle to the grave, and have within our reach a society formed by a whole class of persons in the same circumstances and having about the same income. We are all struggling to attain that position: there is no disguise about it, and no pretence that it is not the object of every man's efforts to secure a safe and honorable place in the sun.

Nevertheless the Supply and Demand system has come to appear quite natural to the middle class, because the middle class is the employing class. As a natural result, it is also an odious class. To the working class the system is disastrous and consequently abhorrent. The education and political emancipation of the wage workers puts it out of the question as a method of distributing income. The self-organization of the working class has always had for its object the substitution of a satisfactory subsistence income, continuing whether the worker is employed or unemployed, for the commercial competitive wage which ceases the moment the employer can find nothing commercially profitable for the worker to do, and which takes no account of any of the worker's own needs except in so far as their denial would disable him for the employer's purpose. There is here a marked distinction between the need of the community for fully cultivated and continuously healthy men, and the need of the commercial employer for bearers of burdens, hewers of wood and drawers of water, preparing work for a minority of masons, carpenters, and other relatively skilled workers.

But we need not let our national loathing of commercialism blind us to the fact that it is quite unreasonable to ask the commercial employer to pay for something he does not need and cannot sell. If he needs only the muscular power to carry a sack, and a little coarse food and a rough shelter will suffice to produce that muscular power, he naturally objects to pay for it the cost of producing and maintaining an accomplished gentleman or lady. Yet the achievement of a community of accomplished gentlemen and ladies and the elimination of coarsely fed, roughly housed, ignorant and brutalized persons is just the object of civilization, and the chief interest of all civilized States. It is also the object of the wage workers, who all desire to be ladies and gentlemen. It is this desire that makes the wage-working class the hope of the human race, in spite of their present vulgarity and degradation. And the deliberate intention of the richer classes to keep the wage-working class in a position of inferiority and servitude makes the rich the enemies of mankind, in spite of their culture, their philanthropy, their elegance, and their frequent personal amiability. Still, the rich cannot now keep the wage-workng classes in a position of inferiority by their own will. They are too few, too feeble, too helplessly dependent on the working class at every turn, too completely subject to the working class vote in Parliament, to practise direct oppression and exploitation with any hope of success. What happens is that they find a system at work by which they profit, just as the working class finds a system—the same system —at work by which they lose; and this system is the only means by which either class can get their living. Neither class understands the system. Neither class can see any alternative to it or can imagine how it would be possible to live without it. Both of them accept it; but both continually try to modify it: the rich trying to increase the luxury and power it secures to them; the poor trying to ease its pressure on them at the most cruel points; and each resisting the other's efforts because the gain of one always appears the loss of the other, and in fact actually is so except in cases where the rich have diminished the productiveness of the poor by treating them too badly: killing the goose that lays the golden eggs, in fact. The change from the worst degradation of labor in the nineteenth century to the higher wages, shorter hours, general elementary education, and stricter sanitation and housing of the twentieth has benefited both the rich and the poor because up to a certain point the better you treat a slave the more you get out of him. But there is a limit to that sort of improvement. That point is reached when the improvement in the condition of the slaves ceases to increase his technical productivity and begins to diminish it and even to destroy it. If, for example, you wish to make use of a man or woman for the purpose of cleaning boots or washing dishes, the effect of enabling them to enjoy the masterpieces of art and literature will certainly not increase the number of boots and dishes they will clean in a day, and may quite possibly result in their declining to do such work on any terms, and leaving you to polish your own boots and wash up after your own meals unless you are prepared to pay them a good deal more for doing it, and to change your domestic habits so as to allow of its being differently organized and done largely by machinery superintended by fastidious persons with clean hands.

Changes like these have actually happened, and may happen again, under the influence of supply and demand. Forty years ago, Irish domestic general servants, or "thorough servants" as they were called, were paid £8 a year; lived squalidly in underground rooms; and were not expected to be as cleanly as their employers in their personal habits. When these women emigrated and sought domestic service in New York, they not only demanded and received much higher wages, but insisted on what were called stationary tubs, meaning housemaid's closets with hot and cold water, though they were so ignorant of everything but the names of these things that wily American ladies found no difficulty in imposing on them by nailing a common tub to a bench in the scullery and representing that device as the latest thing in domestic engineering. In this case the American hired girl appears more bumptious and the American housekeeper less oppressive than the Irish; but the appearance is quite illusory. Servants were scarcer in New York than in Dublin: that was all. In some English manufacturing towns today domestic servants are so hard to get on any terms within the means of the householders that the householders have either to do without them or be content with the services of the feebleminded girls whom the factories will not employ, though in non-manufacturing districts domestic servants are still cheap and plentiful. In any case the state of things has nothing to do with greater or less coercive power on the part of the rich or resistant power on the part of the poor. If the householders of the two neighborhoods were exchanged like prisoners of war, the price and treatment of the servants would not alter in the least. The same domestic servant who gets £8 a year in Belmullet today will get £24 in Belgravia; and the mistress who pays £8 when she leaves Belmullet has to pay £24 when she comes up for the season to Belgravia. Such changes of conditions as the system allows are wholly inhuman and automatic, and can never be carried to the point of equality.

The anxious housekeeper will ask me at this point what a house is going to be like when my ideas come into practice. The answer involves an enormous digression; but it is so interesting that I will tackle it.

To begin with, we shall not go back on division of labor. Take the case of a surgeon, for example. Today a surgeon who is too lazy or too uppish to put on his boots and pull off his trousers can find a valet who will do both for him, and will even submit to be sworn at and addressed on all occasions as an inferior, for a sufficient consideration. I am afraid this luxury will be untenable under an equalitarian constitution. All able-bodied persons will have to valet themselves; and the ladies who ring for a maid in the middle of the night to pick up a book they have dropped out of bed, will have to get up and pick up the book for themselves, or take more care not to drop it. But though the surgeon may have to put on his own boots, it does not follow that he will have to clean them. A state of society in which a surgeon would have to clean the boots and knives; make the beds; lay and light the fires; and answer the door, is as unthinkable as one in which the housemaids would have to cut off their own legs. What is quite thinkable is that the surgeon and person who makes the surgeon's bed should have the same income and be equally polite to one another. As it is, the hospital nurse is sometimes better bred, as we call it, than the surgeon; and there are periods of their respective careers in which she has a larger income. There is certainly no reason why she should at any time have a smaller one.

What will happen to the household under these circumstances is an open question. There may be a great development of what we call hotel life, as there is at present. Doctors will have offices like lawyers, American fashion, instead of practising at home as so many of them do at present. The separate family household will be modified by the difficulty of obtaining a staff and filling up its time and making the place agreeable to it. At present the parlormaid is sometimes better human material than her mistress or any of the young ladies; but then she is a parlormaid and they are ladies; consequently the young gentlemen who

come courting the young ladies do not marry her instead; and
she does not compete with the mistress for the rule of the
household and the affection of the master. At least not often.

THE PASSING OF THE IDOLS

We now see that the deference paid to the rich man today,
whether as peer, capitalist or employer, is idolatrous: that is, it
does not rest on real superiority, but on imaginative illusion.
But we must not suppose that all the submission we see is reverence. The distinction between reverence and submission is
important when we come to discuss, as we must, whether a system of idolatry, however beneficial it may be, is permanently
possible under modern democratic conditions. Galileo had to
submit to the Churchmen of his day; but we cannot now believe that he had any other feeling for their scientific authority
than one of contempt. No city mechanic shares the reverence
of the villager for the squire and his relations; but the reverent
villager sometimes compels the city mechanic to submit to his
superstitions. During the French Revolution the villagers and
the mechanics came to blows on the subject in La Vendée; but
the mechanics were victorious, and the villagers not unanimous;
for the Revolution began in earnest with the burning of the
chateaux by the villagers. Nevertheless, when the squire's relations are rich urban employers, the mechanics do revere them
in sufficient numbers to send them to parliament and to suppress
those who refuse to bend the knee. And the huge retinue of
servants and tradesmen and their employees, direct and indirect,
who live on the incomes of the rich, have an immediate interest
in keeping up their prestige, and in persuading themselves and
others that they are superior beings; so that where the rich live
the poor are more Conservative than the rich themselves.

On the whole, it is not easy to estimate how far the deference
everywhere shewn to riches and rank is mouth honor, paid
with the tongue in the cheek with a view to shop custom and
tips and the like, and how far it is genuine idolatry. But it is certain that crude personal pretension imposes on illiterate rustics

more easily than on educated men of the world. As the old saying goes, it is no use giving tracts to a missionary; and when
subordination has to be secured as between men of the same
rank and education, idolatry is useless: the man receiving an
order must understand either the need for the order itself
(which is not always possible) or the need for subordination in
social organization. And here we have a permanent basis for
discipline without idolatry. The difficulty about idolatry is that
it is hard to live up to it in difficult situations: that is, when it is
most important. Napoleon's soldiers idolized him; but they also
cursed him to his face, and even threatened him, when disaster
overtook them. The Russian peasant not only prays to his icon
for fine weather and good harvests: when the weather is bad
and the crops fail he takes the icon into the field and whacks it.
That is the weak place in the system of idolatry: the idol gets
found out, or, worse still for him, becomes idolized as a demon.
This is what happened to the marquises in the French Revolution: they were placed outside the pale of common humanity
on the guillotine by the people's hatred as they had been in their
chateaux by the people's worship.

The most extreme demand on intelligent subordination is
made by an order to commit suicide. Leaving out the cases in
which the person so ordered is convinced that he will be killed
if he disobeys, and therefore has not really any alternative, the
nearest thing to this that occurs in practice is the deliberate
sacrificing of enormous masses of men in battle to carry a position impregnable on any other terms. In these cases idolatry
is quite useless; for the most credulous soldier knows that even
if his commander or his country is invincible he himself is not
bullet proof. Only those who have never been face to face with
death believe that illusions persist under such deadly stress of
reality. Pugnacity, fanaticism, devotion, or coercion may carry
a man to the cannon's mouth: idolatry never. A soldier is still
conventionally invited to die for his king as well as for his country; but now that it can no longer be pretended that the Russian
soldier fights and dies for the Czar whom he idolizes; and
[since] the Western soldiers of Switzerland, France and Amer-

ica have never even pretended to die for their Presidents, it is clear that however politely we may assume that the monarchical soldier dies for his king or queen, that inducement is entirely superfluous. In fact, for military purposes nowadays one man with an abstract ideal to fight for is worth two idolaters.

I doubt whether anyone will contend that our industrial co-ordination depends on idolatry. The modern trade unionist, in his estimate of his employer, is far more apt to err on the side of cynicism than of credulity. As it is so hard to find in the whole army and navy a single soldier or sailor who can be persuaded even by the most convincing audit that an officer keeping canteen accounts would do so if he did not get something out of it for himself, it is not to be wondered at that in commerce, where gain is the avowed object of the whole business, and where men are remorselessly thrown into the street to starve the moment a depression in trade makes it impossible to make a profit by employing them, men may idolize classes, and courts, and owners of Derby winners, and prizefighters and party politicians, but not the men they have to obey. A mechanic has no more illusions about the foreman, or even the boss, than a private has about a corporal. Commerce, like all organizations of division of labor, is held together not by idolatry, but by the fact that the rank and file man is just as dependent on the orders he receives as the officer is on obedience to his orders. People do not resent orders: they ask for them. They resent insolence and illtreatment, excessive hours of work and poor pay; and those who illtreat and underpay them describe their resentment as insubordination; but it is nothing of the kind.

And here we come to another important distinction. Idolatry, superfluous as a means of securing subordination, is the only means of securing voluntary submission to illtreatment and bad manners as between classes. Cowardice may secure it as between individuals; but in masses it is the fear of the mob of idolaters that intimidates the boldest rebel. The object of idolatry, it must be remembered, is not to secure respect for persons of superior character and ability; for such qualities impose respect; and their possessors are always impatient and contemptuous of the ceremonies of idolatry. The object of idolatry is to secure respect and reverence and submission for commonplace or even inferior people. Since nothing can raise these people above their natural level, their position is maintained by degrading other people below it. There are many methods of doing this; but the first and most universal is insolence of speech and address. The idol speaks of himself in the plural, and addresses the idolater in the singular: the king is "we": the ploughman is "thou." The German will not deign to address his inferior directly: he decrees that his slave, in the third person, shall do such and such a service, and leaves the slave to infer that he had better do it. Neither does the inferior presume to address the superior directly: but speaks of his majesty and excellency, his highness, and so on. Finally, as these attributes are feminine in most languages, the majesty and excellency get shortened into a simple "she," with results that make a British tourist laugh when he is treated politely by a Highland gillie, and betrays him into horrible incivilities in Italy with his blunt British yous and yourses where politeness demands shes and herses.

Manner of speech is added to verbal forms. Nothing is more disagreeable than the deliberate insolence which is the rule of our naval and military services when an officer addresses a private or an able seaman. But it runs through society from end to end. Every rank passes it on to the rank beneath. Inferior food, inferior clothes, inferior accommodation of every kind, rub in degradation. Even when it becomes intolerably troublesome and saves nothing to give servants cheaper food, as in restaurants, a lower price is charged for it: that is to say, a higher price is charged to the servant's employer. And when it is a question of railway travelling, though the engine cannot go slower for the humble man than the haughty, special carriages are set apart for different classes of the community, and the cheaper ones are made deliberately uncomfortable, though the cost of making them as comfortable as the dearer ones is practically negligible.

Thus we see that the system of idolatry involves a policy of deliberate insult and injury to the mass of mankind with the object of inculcating a sense of their inferiority in themselves. It works so efficiently that a poor man feels ashamed and awkward if a rich one asks him to sit down or addresses him as a rich man would be addressed, and feels sincerely shocked and ashamed if a gentleman does a stroke of manual labor instead of ordering a common man to do it for him.

A curious variant of this system is the idolatry of sex. A gentleman behaves to a lady as a servant behaves to him: hands her chairs; remains uncovered in her presence and stands until she is seated; submits tamely to treatment from her that would be held to justify him in punching a man's head or sending him a challenge; and assumes that she has no legs and no digestive apparatus. Having thus established a sort of angelic status for her, he has gone on to assume that she can have no property, no rights, no soul, and no other purpose in life except to be the angel on his hearth and the fulfiller of his sexual destiny and her own.

Now it is evident that all this idolatry is breaking down in practice. Second class carriages are being abolished; and everybody travels third class except those who have ulterior motives: for example I travel first class because I write in the train and like plenty of room and comparative solitude; and other men do so because their standing in society or business depends on their seeming to have more money than their neighbors. Women hold property independently of their husbands; sit on public bodies and royal commissions; and bathe with men as avowed two legged animals.

Let us now note carefully how this change takes place; for it is very important to know whether it comes by levelling up or levelling down. In the main, it comes by levelling up. Take the case of the railway carriage. Fifty years ago, when I began to travel by rail, it was not possible for ladies and gentlemen to travel third class without degrading discomfort. The third class passenger sat on a hard plank; inhaled the fumes of cheap tobacco (there were no smoking carriages; but everybody smoked in the third class); sat beside men who had not changed their shirts for many weeks and who expectorated freely on the floor of the carriage; and acquired vermin. Nowadays the company in the third class carriage is much more agreeable than in the first class: all the letters of complaint in the newspapers refer to smart ladies deluged with scent and fussing about their lapdogs. And the third class carriage has been levelled up too. When I last travelled from Edinburgh to London, I began the journey in an old first class carriage. On exploring the train through the corridors I found a new third class saloon carriage; and I finished the journey in that for the sake of its greater comfort and cleanness. The process for both the carriage and the man has been one of raising the minimum, not of lowering the maximum.

Though this is obviously the sensible method, it is not the first that occurs to men, because they seldom try to alter the order of the world until they are angry with it; and anger is a bad counsellor. Thus, when the poor can no longer endure the slums they live in, they rush to the rich end of the town and begin to burn the good houses there. This is silly: if they resort to incendiary methods at all they should burn their own houses, and insist on their being rebuilt more commodiously; and the process should be repeated at frequent intervals until Stepney is as comfortable as Belgravia. But the poor will not go as far as this until they have come to think that they ought to be as well off as the people in Belgravia, which means that they have acquired self-respect and cast off idolatry. There is no absolute standard of what is befitting in any class of life. King George's valet would probably flatly refuse to submit to the sort of accommodation that satisfied Solomon in all his glory, though it does not follow that a modern valet is healthier or happier than an ancient king. Up to a certain point he thinks himself as good a man as the king and up to that point accordingly he is treated as well as the king: has the same number of meals, the same quality of bread, as good clothes or better, the same roof to shelter him, and so forth. The poor man is creeping up and up; and it is impossible for the rich man to climb away from him, because the rich man is already at his limit. It is true that the king could make himself a Lama, and never be seen or spoken to by common persons, remaining an awful divine mystery, as in Tibet. But the result is utterly miserable for the Lama: he is a prisoner in solitary confinement, and envies Peter the Wild Boy. We try to do something of the sort with our navy captains. They also must not speak to anyone or be spoken to except in a profane manner under irresistible provocation, with the result that all admirals, representing the survivors of the system, are a little mad, like kings. The man who is artificially secluded after an elaborate training as an idol, and so placed that he cannot escape from his horrible situation, may become a multi-millionaire; but he finds it impossible to differentiate himself in any conspicuous manner from the mass of what are called carriage folk, the carriage folk being themselves, when they are not, so to speak, harnessed to their carriages, indistinguishable from any other well dressed and well spoken folk. We are all sansculottes nowadays; and the strongest barrier that now hedges off the social idols is the barrier of speech. There are still four main dialects in use: the dialect of the university man, the dialect of the merchant gentleman, the dialect of the lower middle class, and the dialect of the wage workers. But now that everybody is taught to read, and speech is beginning to be taught scientifically by phoneticians, a double movement is abolishing the class monopoly of dialect. One of these movements is discussed by everybody: we all notice how the vocabulary of the wage workers is being enlarged by elementary education and cheap reprints of classic literature, accustoming the poor to literary grammar, and introducing to them a large stock of words which have no traditional vulgar pronunciation and therefore come into use with no prejudice against the accepted educated pronunciation. We hear less about the other movement, though it is much the more important of the two. The idiom, the grammar, the pronunciation of the lower middle and laboring classes are entering into literature and imposing themselves on the university and public school. The most widely circulated newspapers today are not written in the university dialect, but in the dialect of the public elementary school and the workshop, of the office boy and the Clarion cyclist. The pronunciation of the newly acquired vocabulary is not the accepted university pronunciation, but a pronunciation guessed from the spelling, a most misleading plan in a country with an absurd orthography like ours. And this dialect and this pronunciation is being forced on the whole community by sheer weight of numbers, gradually making the old accepted speech of educated men so scarce as to sound ridiculous and affected, and finally making it unintelligible. I sometimes have to incorrect myself before I can get what I want in a shop: when I am asking for an envelope, for instance, because I pronounce it in the French manner just as my great grandfather used to pronounce the word oblige. The initial h is kept alive by Ireland, Scotland, America, and the Colonies: without them it would perish in the south of England as completely as it has perished on the continent.

Thus the class dialects are sweeping from both ends to a common centre. Already, even in a country so aristocratic as Sweden, there is no class dialect: porters talk as prime ministers do. Indeed wherever the current spelling is practically phonetic, class differences of speech are mainly differences between roughness and delicacy of utterance. People speak roughly when they live roughly: and as life becomes gentler speech becomes gentler.

On the whole, the farsighted statesman must conclude that idolatry has had its day, because the workers will no longer submit to the systematic degradation it involves when the idols, being for the most part ordinary men and women, cannot raise themselves above the masses and must therefore try to depress the masses below the common level. And there is no other way of keeping up the idolatry now that its pageantry is gone. The retinue, the distinctive dress, the monopoly of literacy, have passed away with the sword and the culotte; and everybody who can save a few pounds can live like a duke for at least a week end. You can impress the populace by possessing thirty pairs of trousers if you can walk abroad with twentynine footmen at your heels. Cut off the footmen; and for all the idolatry they will win you, you might as well have only the one pair you are wearing.

DISCOURSE OF A TRAFFIC MANAGER
AND A RAILWAY PORTER

Stratification of workers' incomes according to the sort of work they do is produced automatically by the action of commercial supply and demand. That sounds a trite dry sentence; but it opens up a tremendous question for those who propose to put an end to that automatic system and substitute for it a conscientious system. For, if you propose also to go on paying men wages and salaries and fees for their work, you will find yourself confronted with a new task which will seem to you in contemplation to be familiar and easy and matter-of-course, but will prove in action to be the most grotesquely impossible absurdity ever conceived by the author of a fairy tale. That task is the valuation in money of human beings and their services to the community. You have been brought up under a system in which an inferior person lives in a kitchen or a laborer's cottage or a dosshouse, and gets from thirty to fifty pounds a year, whilst a superior person sits in a drawingroom or handsomely furnished office and gets from five hundred to fifteen thousand a year. You have found this commercial valuation of them ready made, and have regarded it as a natural valuation which would always assert itself and be easy to determine. Suppose you snatch the commercial system away! You are at once confronted with your inferior and superior persons informing you that they no longer have a commercial value, and that in future they are to be paid according to your notions of right and wrong, justice and injustice, and the hard cash value of their respective attainments and virtues and performances.

If you are a wise man you will give it up at once as hopeless. In fact you must do that anyhow sooner or later; for you will

not know even how to begin. Suppose you try an apparently
simple case to start with: say a traffic manager and a railway
porter. You are clear that the traffic manager should have more
than the railway porter. The railway porter will not unreasonably ask why. You will say—having no other answer—that it
has always been so. The porter will then ask you with some
heat why the devil you did not leave things alone if you meant
them to remain as they were. To which you will have no reply
at all. You will perceive on reflection that the only reason you
had for discarding the commercial system under which men
were bought and sold in the labor market at prices fixed by
supply and demand was that it resulted in the porter getting too
little and the manager too much relatively, and that it also
handed over a huge surplus to idlers which you now have to
redistribute between the porter and the manager. You must
make a new valuation; and the two, being citizens and voters
equally with yourself, will have a say in the valuation. It occurs
to you to pay them according to their merits; but you suddenly
remember your Shakespear. Polonius also proposed to use men
according to their deserts. "Zounds, man," said Hamlet, "use
them much better. Use every man according to his desert, and
who should escape whipping?" It may be very difficult to prove
on any rational system that the world would be any the worse
if the train solved the difficulty by running over both the porter
and the manager: you could probably replace them with
younger and better men.

An argument begins. The manager instinctively eschewing
Polonius, tries Menenius, and repeats the old parable of the
revolt of the hands against the belly. The porter replies that a
revolt of the belly against the hands would be just as disastrous
for the organism as a revolt of the hands against the belly. He
will add, being a highly educated Socialistic porter, that no porter outside the columns of a class newspaper in the nineteenth
century ever questioned the necessity of having a manager as
well as porters on a railway. He will hint that a man noodle
enough to use such an argument ought to be a ticket collector
and not a manager. And the discussion will become so heated

that you will have to concede hastily that the notion that any one necessary operator of a public service is any more or less dispensable than any other is untenable.

The porter will then suggest that the sensible thing is to pay according to the hardness of the work, and that the man who sits all day in a comfortable chair in an office ordering other people about can have no claims comparable to those of the man who in all weathers on draughty platforms shoulders heavy trunks and hoists them on cabs, or wrestles with bales of merchandise and milk cans, besides being the friend of the unprotected female who without him would have to carry her own luggage. To which the manager will reply, in more or less injurious and contemptuous terms, that if the porter is ready to take on the job of managing he is welcome to try it, and that he (the manager) is prepared to bet him a week's wages that before the end of the first half hour he will be glad to offer to do a fortnight's portering to be let off the rest of the day's managing, and be so hungry into the bargain that he will need a second breakfast before he can do another stroke. All of which, being immediately verifiable by experiment, forces the too uppish porter to moderate his pretensions and fall back on the safe position that the manager would not enjoy portering any more than the porter would enjoy managing.

So far, honors are even. The manager has made a fool of himself and the porter has made a fool of himself, each in the same way, by claiming that he should have more than the other. The problem remains unsolved.

The manager tries again. He falls back on the need for idolatry to secure obedience, and claims that if he is not paid more than the porter and set apart from him thus as a superior being, the porter will not obey him. The porter replies that he had no illusions about the manager in the days when he had only a twentieth of the manager's pay; that he obeyed him as far as there was any need to obey him, because he shouldnt have known what to do if the manager hadnt told him, and had sense enough to know that somebody had to do the thinking and somebody else the shoveling, and that, far from idolizing him, he had habitually spoken of him to the other porters as Flat-nosed Jerry and knew that his mother-in-law's addiction to drink was the talk of the town.

Further discussion being hardly bearable on these extremely personal lines, idolatry has to be hastily ruled out of the controversy. You are thrown back on a vague idea that a man of many accomplishments should be paid more than a man of comparatively few or none. On your hinting at this, the porter, having been stationed for some years at Dover, pleads a sound working knowledge of French. The manager does not know French but planks down his golf handicap. The porter challenges him to a game of knurr and spell, at which he is a champion. Neither you nor the manager have the faintest idea of what knurr is, much less spell; and you rule out games; but the porter comes up again undaunted with an unsuspected proficiency in cultivating standard roses (he has taken a Daily Mail prize), in breeding pigeons and pigs, and in the fine art of faking common barn-door fowls into the semblance of rare and exotic birds. The overwhelmed manager, feeling that it would be useless to plead cycling and some boyish practice in photography, flatly declines to accept the accomplishment test on the ground that it would lead to a plutocracy of acrobats; and the triumphant porter says "I thought so."

You feel that the apparently easy and obvious case for under-paying the porter and overpaying the manager is crumbling in your hands. In desperation you ask the porter how much he wants. He evades the difficulty by saying that he wants "enough," thus ingeniously putting the manager in the position of having to ask more than enough if he is not content with equality. And here the porter utters the first and last word of wisdom on the subject.

But you will not give up your old habits of mind without a longer struggle. You are still possessed with a quite unreasonable, and indeed anti-reasonable notion that the better man should have the bigger income; and you make a last stand for payment according to character or genius—or you do not quite know what, but you feel that everybody will understand. They will not; but they will agree, which is another matter, good enough for you. Alas! When you come to business you are in worse difficulties than ever. First you have to decide whether the porter or the manager is the better man; and you at once foresee that if the porter should bear off the palm, your preconceived notions of the proper payment of managers and porters will receive a more violent shock than if you paid them equally. Yet that is a trifle compared to the problem which will arise even if the manager wins the prize of virtue; for you have to decide exactly how much better he is, and express the result in shillings and pence. You are asked to enter on a mad rule of three like a schoolboy in a nightmare. If A's word of honor is worth twopence how much is B's teetotallism worth? If Georges Carpentier's punch is worth ten pounds, how much is the Archbishop of York's Christian charity worth?

You give it up with a secret shiver of amazement at the glimpse you have had of the monstrous things you used to believe in the days when you concluded, because men were paid different sums, that they were different sorts of men. You admit that though the Christian doctrine that all souls are equally valuable before God has always seemed to you impracticable and rather out of taste anywhere but in church, yet it certainly is confoundedly difficult to escape from it when it gets fair play.

You have to confess apologetically to the manager that though you think he ought to have more you do not see your way to giving the porter less, and to the porter rather indignantly that though you think it ridiculous that he should not have less yet you do not see your way to giving the manager more. You suggest to them however, as reasonable men, that if their wages are made exactly equal the porter will want to be a manager, and the manager will refuse to do anything more brainy than porter's work. The porter will then tell you that he wouldnt stick in an office doing sums and dictating letters not if you gave him an extra ten bob a week for it; and the manager will declare passionately that if the elementary decencies of business are to be cast aside and a porter is to be put on a level with him he would rather do manager's work for less money than porter's work for more. You are driven back on equality more hopelessly than ever.

Yet you feel that equality is not a solution. And you are quite right. An equation between men and money is an absurdity. You can express commercial profit in money: in fact, money is the form of commercial profit; and when men are regarded solely as instruments for producing commercial profit, you can compare their respective productivities in terms of that profit and pay them accordingly. But if you abolish commercial profit, this is no longer possible. You can still ascertain that one very exceptional man can (for a bet) set type as fast again as another, or run a hundred yards whilst another is running ninety-nine, or you can fix his golf handicap in figures. But you cannot express these differences in money because you cannot express the value of the invention of printing to the community in money, nor that of sprint racing, nor that of golf.

It is true that men do attempt this impossible equation, and find, like the higher mathematics, that impossible equations will produce working results. You can induce a man to run a hundred yards at the top of his speed by offering him a money prize if he succeeds in doing it in less time than the fastest man who has tried before. You will find him refusing to attempt it for five shillings and consenting to attempt it for twentyfive pounds. Apparently he has found a money value for his ability as a runner. But you will find other things as well: for instance, that if he has an income independent of his racing, he will race for the sake of being known as the fastest runner, and will indignantly refuse money as a gentleman amateur. And when he is not so circumstanced, his estimate of the money value of his exertions will depend altogether on the standard of income among his neighbors. A village laborer at the local sports will run himself to exhaustion to win a prize of a shilling; and his brother the bricklayer will fight any man for a sovereign or less, whilst a champion pugilist will refuse to step into the ring for less than several thousand pounds, win, lose, or draw, plus cinematographic rights.

226 THE ROAD TO EQUALITY

INCENTIVE

The great incentive is necessity. Nature says bluntly to you, "Eat or die." To eat, it may be necessary to slave at the toils of agriculture; to torment your brains until they invent the bow and arrows, and the gun; to brave the terrors of the sea in frail canoes; to fight the wild boar and draw leviathan with a hook. Nature will not give you everlasting life even on those terms. She says, "You are for an age only, not for all time; therefore replace yourselves or the race will come to an end with you." To replace ourselves, our women must martyr themselves by a tedious and painful travail. But all these things are done. Laziness and selfishness, inertia and fear, are swept away by necessity. There is no difficulty about the incentive, and no danger that men, any more than bees, will strike against necessary work.

But in all the parts of the earth which are worth inhabiting at all, it is possible, even in primitive stages of production, for a single person to produce more than is sufficient to keep him alive. The women of the North American Indian tribes are able to produce not only the children needed to replace the dead, but enough subsistence to enable their husbands to devote themselves entirely to sport, which means hunting and fighting. And as the productiveness of the hunting is probably cancelled by the destructiveness of the warfare, it is doubtful whether the men can be said to produce anything at all except amusement and romance and admiration and so forth; excellent things, but producible by less questionable methods. They are what we call Kept Persons: men kept by women.

When we come to modern division of labor in huge populations, and modern machinery, keeping on a gigantic scale becomes possible. I do not lean on such facts as that a Nottingham lace making machine is said to be able to produce fourteen thousand times as much lace as a hand worker, nor that a single shell of the kind known as a Jack Johnson can in a second of time kill a large family and knock down its house and dig its grave into the bargain, which would be a day's work for a whole Indian tribe; for I am aware that man does not live by lace alone, nor can the means of death be counted as food and raiment. All the same, the machinery and organization of modern agricultural, textile, and building industry, enables the people engaged in them to feed, clothe, and house a prodigious number of people besides themselves.

The enormous moral significance of this fact arises from its creation of the crime of theft. Let us consider a state of things in which a living creature can barely keep itself alive by incessant work. Under such circumstances robbery means murder; for the man robbed of his food perishes: therefore he fights to the death in defence of his precarious gains. In a society of such persons theft would be a capital crime. The Esquimaux, who are more nearly in this situation than any other settled body of people, are honester than we are simply because if they robbed one another as we do the robbed would starve to death and the robbers be compelled by necessity next day to work as hard as ever after risking their lives in a fierce fight with honest men.

Take the case of the moles and the bees. A mole, which is the strongest creature on earth in proportion to its size, has to work continuously like a steam navvy to get food enough to maintain its monstrous energy and rapacity. If it meets another mole of its own sex, it kills it or is killed by it as a matter of course. Theft and all minor injuries are ruled out by the simple fact that a mole cannot produce more than it must consume to keep itself alive. A kept mole is impossible. In strong contrast stands the bee. The bee wants but little here below, nor wants that little long; and it can produce immense stores of honey over and above what it need consume except in rare climatic emergencies from which it can be artificially protected. Accordingly a whole class of human beings, called bee farmers, live wholly by robbing bees. They breed them, house them, and supply them with blankets for the purpose of robbing them. Those bees who do not notice that the hives and cells and blankets are paid for out of the money received for the stolen goods probably regard the bee farmers as their benefactors, and regard the

notion that bees could live without bee farmers as an unpractical, ungrateful, Utopian dream.

But even if there were no bee farmers to be kept, the bees
would keep other bees. They would not only rob one another,
but make an institution of the robbery, and insist on its being
done in prescribed legal forms, killing all disorderly, casual,
unlicensed robbers. There is a curious female instinct, already
alluded to above in the case of the North American Indians,
which leads women to regard men as luxuries and playthings,
not as productive, industrious, sensible creatures like themselves.
This has produced in advanced human societies such complicated reactions that its origin is obscured, and many people
imagine that men have seized their privileges by superior muscular force. But if that were possible, the men who oppress
women would themselves be oppressed by prizefighters. The
bee, instinctively held up by all nations as an example to mankind, shews us the truth in its simplicity. The male bee is not
allowed to meddle in the household work: he is set up in idleness as an ornament and nothing else. He wears gorgeous
armor, but does not fight. He flies about amusing himself in the
sun, and produces, not honey, but emotion in the breasts of the
female bees, who, with a psychological refinement that is utterly
beyond us, have by a suitable diet deprived themselves of the
material part of the sexual appetite and function, and can therefore romance about the males Platonically. To perpetuate the
race, they educate one unfortunate infant bee for the duties of
maternity. This astonishing insect has no such weakness as the
individual preferences which lead to so many aberrations in
human choice. Strictly eugenic and Darwinian, she selects her
mate by starting on a pretended journey to the sun at such a
speed that only the strongest flyer can overtake her; and she
probably has to wait for him when he has outstript all the rest.
As the result of the adventure is that she spends the rest of her
life producing about four thousand infants every day, she
clearly cannot be bothered with an idle male hanging about the
hive; so she providently kills him. When she returns to the hive,
the other bees quite agree with her as to the superfluity of the

male in winter time, when the season of romance is over, and the business of looking after four thousand babies per day becomes overwhelming. So they kill all the other males out of hand, and settle down to business until romance is again kindled by the return of spring. This would be impossible if the individual bee could not and did not produce more than it consumes.

But the case of the bee tells only half the story. When instincts are described as female, we are on dangerous ground. Most of the primitive instincts are necessarily female in origin, because it is now fairly clear—unless evolution is a dream—that the first comer in the garden of Eden was Eve, and that she, finding that it was an economic mistake to combine two separable functions in one person, differentiated and threw off Adam for her own convenience and delight. But as long as man continues to be born of woman, he will get his male instincts mixed up with female ones. Accordingly, when we get far away from the garden of Eden into modern civilization, we find men trying to do to women what the bees do to the drones. Women, said Napoleon, are the occupation of the idle man, the relaxation of the warrior, and the stumbling block in the way of kings. Therefore both the idle man and the warrior seek to withdraw their women from productive work; to decorate them and pamper them; to make them frightfully expensive and industrially helpless and useless: in short, to treat them, not as human beings, but as seductive and deleterious luxuries. Two of the most remarkable plays of our time dramatize this curious sexual tendency. Mr Granville Barker, in The Madras House, dramatizes the revolt of our men against wives who are very expensive, very charming, very demoralizing, and nothing else. Ibsen, in Little Eyolf, shews the rich idle woman who keeps a husband as a Sultan keeps a Sultana. In both cases a sort of domestic life is produced which is refined, luxurious, charming, artistic, beautiful, gentle, costly, destructive, abominable, and finally so unbearable that the most attached and amiable couples end by hating one another.

What has all this to do with our subject of Incentive? Simply this: that there is in nature an incentive to idleness not only on the part of the lazy who wish to impose their share of the burden of necessity on others, but on the part of those who wish to take on the burden of others in addition to their own in order that they may use them as instruments of luxury. This incentive is so powerful that in all the classes which receive superfluous incomes women are exempted from work so extensively that at last a convention arises that they should not work; and the practice that began with the uxorious man pampering and idolizing his wife ends with all sorts of men finding themselves obliged by the custom of their class not only to exempt their wives from labor, but to provide the like exemption of their daughters. You find also that married women are divided between their need for the subsistence earned by the work of their husbands and their jealousy of that work as withdrawing his time and attention from themselves, and bringing him into intimate relation with persons who are strangers to them.

Domestic difficulties of this kind are becoming intensified by the revolt of women against idle dependence, and by their claim to a share in all human activities, public as well as private. When the sexes were severely segregated to such an extent that women never meddled in the city and only curates meddled in the parish work that women were allowed to undertake, the wife's jealousy of her husband's occupation and the husband's of his wife's were seldom exacerbated by sexual jealousy. The man-milliner with his dressmakers and shop assistants, the doctor with his lady patients, the artist with his models, the curate with his district visitors, the playwright with his actresses, have always had to weather domestic storms which were formerly unknown to city men and solicitors. But today city officers are full of women. Women act as managers; sit on committees and boards; are indefatigable in political associations; and cause Sir Almroth Wright to declare publicly, like Constantine Madras in Mr Barker's play, that work is being made impossible by the sexual disturbance produced by the unaccustomed presence of women. And these women, who formerly would have had only the most distant relations with any men except their husbands and brothers, are now brought into intimate working partnership with numbers of men, often to the extent of spending much more waking time in their company than in that of their husbands. Not only, therefore, does the old jealousy of the occupation became embittered by sexual jealousy, but husbands and wives make all sorts of discoveries about one another which they never made in the days when they knew no other women and men intimately enough to make critical comparisons. That is why divorce, which is merely a method of enabling badly assorted couples to re-sort themselves, occurs in inverse ratio to the segregation of the sexes. Also why it is so fiercely resisted by the disagreeable people who are left in the lurch by it.

The bearing of this apparent digression on our theme of the sexual or romantic incentive to idleness is that it shews that there is an antidote to it in the instinctive revolt of the Kept Person against it.

But the main importance in our society of the possibility of making one set of persons keep another in luxury and idleness instead of everyone maintaining himself by his own exertions lies in the fact that it is now not a voluntary arrangement thrust on the idle persons by the workers, but an involuntary one forced on the workers by the idlers by means of laws which denounce any other arrangement as dishonest, and are enforced by violent and cruel punishments. Such a legal system, when it is first imposed on a free people, is called slavery, and is an admitted denial of equal human rights to the enslaved. This is not a creditable course when the enslaved are of the same blood as their masters: that is why no tyrant will for long allow anyone to call him a tyrant. He insists on being called The Father of his People, or The Commander of The Faithful, or something else equally honorable and reassuring. Slaves may be called slaves when they are black; but the white slave is declared a freeborn Englishman, and his relation to his master is described as freedom of contract. He is taught to sing that he never never will be a slave; and persons who exhort him to throw off the yoke are persecuted for inciting him to dishonesty; and the free condition they are advocating for him is called The Servile State.

Now for the exact method by which all this has been brought about I must refer you to any textbook of Socialism. Fabian Essays will do as well as another. In the first essay I have explained how, even if men start free and equal on virgin soil in a new country, as pioneer colonists mostly do nowadays, the simple act of allowing each colonist to appropriate the plot of land he cultivates will in the course of time, without any other change except increase of population, produce a class of idle landed proprietors; secure them a monopoly of capital; and finally place the entire burden of production on a destitute proletariat without hope of ever rising above the level of a bare subsistence wage, the only possible escape for them being the pooling of the entire return from land and capital in the hands of the whole community, and its redistribution as personal income in the interest of the whole community: in short, by Socialism. All this is the mere ABC of modern economics; and I take it for granted without further explanation or argument, as I must assume that I am addressing an educated audience and not teaching in infant school.

However, the process has one feature of which I must remind you, because a gentleman asked me last week how I proposed to defeat or do away with the individual selfishness which, he supposed, has brought about the present admittedly deplorable misdistribution of income. Human selfishness has a great deal to answer for; but it must be clear that the one thing it must be innocent of is a system under which the many sacrifice themselves abjectly to the few, and the word duty has no other meaning than self-sacrifice. The result aimed at by those who instituted private property in land was exactly the opposite of the result they achieved. They did not want the idle to be rich and the industrious to be half starved. They did not want the Duke of Westminster and Lord Howard de Walden to have a thousand times as much money as a couple of agricultural laborers of equally estimable private character; nor did they consider that children should die of cold and starvation whilst Pekinese dogs were luxuriously fed, protected from the east wind by quilted silk coverlets, and decorated with gold collars. Though they were not saints, they were not fools and madmen. They honestly thought that if every man's homestead were made inviolable, and the harvest secured to the man who sowed and reaped it, men would flourish in proportion to their industry and sobriety and suffer in proportion to their laziness and drunkenness.

It is therefore an error to blame human nature for the monstrosity of our existing distribution of wealth. You might as well blame an ignorant woman for the results of feeding a baby on herrings, beer, and strawberries. She means to feed the child well and wants it to grow up strong and healthy. When it dies you have no right to call her a murderess, and declare that there is no use in trying to feed babies properly because the desire of their mothers to kill them will always defeat your attempts at reform. If you can persuade her to change the child's diet, and it flourishes in consequence, she will be pleased and continue the new regimen.

Now there is no reason to suppose that it is impossible to make men understand how the private property system of securing a wholesale distribution of wealth is as delusive as the apparent motion of the sun round the earth. They know already that if a change produces greater happiness and prosperity their selfishness will save them from perversely going back to the old system. After all, selfishness aims at wellbeing for the self; and as nobody proposes a change of system with the object of diminishing the wellbeing of individuals, selfishness is on the side of Socialism. Thus the fact that men are selfish—in other words that they desire to have more abundant life—does not shake my argument: it supports it. The real difficulty is that men are so warlike and ascetic that they seek suffering and mortification, and take an interest in death and destruction that they refuse to birth and creation. But if we are finally a race of born suicides, why have we already travelled so far on the road to Socialism? Anyhow, my selfishness leads me to desire Socialism; and the existence of several millions of people in Europe who are of the same mind proves that in this respect at least I am not unique.

But please note that the operation of private property has one very important effect. It reduces the whole mass of laborers to the Esquimaux condition in which the men can escape unbearable privation and actual starvation only by continual exertion. The pressure of Nature in the Arctic circle is reproduced in the temperate zone by taking away from the British laborer everything that he produces in excess of what an Esquimaux produces. In the twentieth century, surrounded by the triumphs of modern civilization, we preserve the farm laborer and shepherd, precisely as they were at the time of the Norman Conquest, by cutting them off from all share in the benefits of the improvements in production discovered since the eleventh century, and thereby maintaining the pressure of mere Necessity on him at the same pitch. In short, we have maintained slavery as the basis of our civilization long after we were producing enough to make every slave a free, educated, well-to-do man.

This, curiously enough, is the very result that has reconciled to our system many eminent and public spirited men who thoroughly understood it, and were under no illusions as to its evils. It is quite a mistake to suppose that Henry George's Progress and Poverty was the first book in which the worst results of private property in land were exposed. The Benthamite Individualists and Tory Squirarchists of the first half of the nineteenth century supported our system expressly on the ground that it secured the existence of a huge proletariat kept continually at work to keep the wolf from the door because they could never hope to gain more than a bare subsistence from week to week, no matter what improvements were made in production, or how rich the proprietary class became. It maintained the incentive of the fear of starvation; and they could not see how men could be induced to work without that incentive. Macaulay foresaw clearly the horrors of modern American capitalism, in which whole States are devastated, not by German armies under the command of the Kaiser, but by American forces maintaining the legal rights of Mr Rockefeller to everything the inhabitants produce except a pittance which the aboriginal redskin would have scorned. Austin, in his lectures on Jurisprudence, warns his students not to be turned against our system by its horrors and injustices; and for the better steeling of their hearts, he paints those horrors more luridly than Henry George. De Quincey, in his Logic of Political Economy, faces the slavery of the proletariat as calmly as Aristotle did, regarding it, like him, as the necessary basis for a superstructure of high culture. Nobody at that time shrank from making these concessions to Socialism, because as a politically practicable Socialism, as distinguished from a Utopian or monastic Communism, had not then been proposed, no feasible alternative to the Capitalist system was in sight. The early Socialists, notably Lassalle and Marx, made vigorous use of these admissions. Lassalle branded the levelling down of the masses to bare subsistence, which the economists had explained as a blessing in disguise, as The Iron Law of Wages, and contended that the disguise was altogether too perfect for human endurance. Since that time treatises on political economy have been either socialistic or disingenuous. But the old difficulty remains in people's minds. If you free people from the fear of starvation, what will be their incentive to work?

The reply is that the fear of starvation is simply the fear of death; that there are fifty ways of killing a man if he refuses to work; and that of all the fifty ways the very worst and most mischievous to the rest of the community is starving him. What is more, it is not effectual. The idlers, the drunkards, the cadgers, the tramps do not starve to death: they have in so many ways a better time of it than the industrious people that it is hardly too much to say that all the external incentives in operation today are incentives to idleness rather than to industry, with the result that some four or five millions of our population are classed hopelessly as "residuum." They steal; they beg; and when they cannot steal or beg, and the hammer of necessity is poised above their heads at last, we dare not let it fall, and open the casual ward to them as a refuge from it. Our system is contrary to human nature: when it comes to the crucial point we dare not go through with it.

And now suppose you say that we ought to pull ourselves together and go through with it, closing the workhouses; forbidding all charity; and ruthlessly allowing the idler to perish in his idleness. I sincerely wish you would make the attempt; for the moment you grasp your system firmly it crumbles to dust in your hand. Ruthlessly enforced, it will condemn the man who will not take an available job to die; but it does not provide a job for the man who is willing to work: on the contrary, it depends for its commercial practicability on the power of the employer to discharge men in slack seasons without providing for them until he can again find work for them. Consequently you cannot leave a man to die merely because he is idle: you must first try him on the capital charge of idleness, and acquit him and make honorable provision for him if he proves that he has sought employment and found none because, trade being slack, there was none to find. If he is a voluntary idler you can find him guilty, and hang him or shoot him according to your established method of execution. But you really must not throw him into the street to starve even if the charitable public could stand the spectacle. You would not do that to a murderer: such a method of execution is unknown to our law: besides, an execution produces no moral effect if it is not formal, public, intentional, and justified.

But if you proceed thus directly and legally, troublesome questions will come up. Counsel for the defendant will ask you to be clear as to what you propose to hang his client for: whether it is for idleness or simply for having no money: two quite different things. If you say it is for having no money, he will challenge you to hang all your babies. If you say for idleness, he will threaten to lay an information against half the west end of London. Either way your system is reduced to absurdity. The mere fact that idleness is almost always a symptom of riches, and toil a symptom of poverty; and that your incentive to a man to work is also an incentive to him to make idlers of his posterity and to become an idler himself as early in life

as possible instead of as late, knocks what is left of the ethical
pretensions of your system into a cocked hat. It is a practicable
system up to a certain point, just as brigandage is practicable. It
can be legalized just as the robber barons who were the rogue
elephants of the feudal system legalized their thefts by calling
them taxes and tolls, making laws to regulate their exaction and
bequeathing or selling their powers of exaction and calling their
men at arms (gendarmes) police agents. But the moment the
legal disguise became so old-fashioned and consequently so
effectual that economists and sociologists, accepting it as natural
and honest, sought to reduce it to a system, they landed themselves first in the impossibly inhuman and dangerously anarchic
doctrine of laisser-faire, and finally achieved an exposure of the
brigandage that had underlain this grotesque disguise of law and
sham political economy, and a rediscovery of the true base of
human society in Communism, without which personal property and security is impossible.

Private property is an evasion of Communism. It is actuated
by selfish greed, ambition, poverty, and the fear of poverty, and
was largely produced by them. But it was not, and is not, sanc-
tioned by them. The intention with which we maintain it is to
provide encouragement and security for honest industry and
conscientious service. Men have often pumped water vigorously
on burning whiskey to extinguish it, and have thereby spread
the conflagration they meant to extinguish. It by no means follows that if you wish them to work vigorously you must appeal
to their incendiary instincts. They will learn in time to smother
such fires with sand. No doubt a good many towns will be
burnt first; for men are unteachable creatures. But if you proceed on the assumption that they really want to burn down
their towns, even to roast their pigs, you will gradually get
civilization into a mess from which it will never recover. I forget how many civilizations Mr Flinders Petrie counts as having
arisen and perished since the first syllable of recorded time: I
think about two dozen. They all died of stupidity and ignorance. None of them wanted to die or meant to do it. Their
statesmen tried to nourish their infant States on herrings, beer,

and strawberries: that was all. Our own statesmen have as yet added nothing to that diet but thistles.

This paving of hell with good intentions is not peculiar to the private property system. History is mostly a record of the tragedy of politically uneducated citizens giving their loyalty to equally ignorant rulers and politicians for the maintenance of shallow and obvious moralities which defeat their own purpose so completely that at last even professional sociologists are driven to set up Anarchism as a political principle on the ground that nothing worse can possibly come of it than the results of the laws and creeds.

THE INCENTIVE TO THINK

We now see that the Private Property system does not supply the incentive to work. It takes the incentive supplied by Nature and distributes it in the most disastrous possible manner, relieving a small class from it altogether, with the result that they become lazy, idle, useless, and enormously expensive, and throwing it on the mass of the community with such severity that only by constant drudgery can they escape starvation, the result being that they become degraded by overwork, illtreatment, underfeeding, injustice, and the drink they consume in order to create artificial happiness for themselves.

This we all know; but we are less conscious of the more disastrous fact that the system not only abuses the natural incentive to work, but almost destroys the no less important incentive to think. This incentive in its natural form is direct and clear enough. The hungry Esquimaux, with his life dependent on fish and seals, has the strongest incentive to set his brains to work and invent the fishing hook, the line, the kayak, the spear. He builds a weather proof house out of snow: he discovers how to make fire and to burn blubber. He invents the sledge, and tames and breeds the reindeer. Such devices as the wheel and the arch he does not hit on; but that is because they are of no use in the snow, not in the least because they are beyond his inventive capacity. I harp on the Esquimaux because Nature drives such a hard bargain with him for bare life, and so much of his energy is consumed in mere sleepy resistance to the cold, that under his conditions an idle class or an enslaved class or a criminal class is a physical impossibility. The natural incentive to work presses equally and severely on everybody; and the natural incentive to think does the same thing, with the result that we stand amazed before the number and ingenuity of the contrivances by which they live in a manner which, relatively to their resources, is more comfortable and civilized than the life of our own people in a temperate climate with coal and iron in abundance at our doors and all the materials the earth can produce, from cotton to diamonds, within our reach.

Turn from this admirable spectacle to our European proletarians. They invent nothing directly useful to themselves. They are paid, not to think, but to do as somebody else tells them. If they begin to think, they are marked out as dangerous men and deprived of their employment; for the first thing Nature drives them to think about is the means of extricating themselves from the wretched and degrading conditions in which they find themselves. And the result of that is that they invent something the Esquimaux never dreams of: to wit, a Trade Union or a Socialistic scheme for upsetting the whole system under which they live. This activity is described by their masters as sedition; and as it most certainly is highly seditious, the rash thinker is burnt alive, or hanged, or shot, or battered with a policeman's club, or, like Mr Tom Mann the other day, simply imprisoned until the emergency which has stimulated him to intellectual activity has passed by.

In the end the proletarian ceases to think of thought as an activity that concerns him. He digs the foundations of a temple exactly as he empties a dustbin, shifting so much dirt from one place to another just as he is told to do, without knowing why. He is glad not to have to know why, because knowing such things means reading and thinking; and nowadays he has almost always made a laborious and unsuccessful attempt to read, because everyone tells him he ought to. The man who has done ten hours manual labor, or even eight, falls asleep over a book in less than a minute and a half, just as Sir Isaac Newton does if, by some incident of travelling or sport, he happens to put in a few hours hard physical muscular exercise. Physical overwork and underfeeding are fatal to thought; and so are idleness and overfeeding, because the idle man has nothing real to think about: he lacks experience of anything but his own fancies and vanities; and he has no incentive to make simple mechanical inventions and devices like the Esquimaux, because an idle man gains nothing by having work made easier. I have more than once talked to William Morris in the company of a manual laborer intelligent enough to have been attracted by our ideas. We always had him snoring within five minutes, though we were fairly lively company for thinking people; and Morris's language in private life—sometimes even in public life when he was displeased—was by no means lacking in the flowers of invective which give emphasis to the dialogues of navvies.

In short, a system which compels men to live by selling themselves as instruments for making money for other men with no public aims inevitably leads to some men being specialized as thinkers and others as diggers and hewers and machine minders; and as, for the purposes of profit making, the proportion of thinkers to manual workers doing simply what they are told without knowing why is very small, one Napoleon being sufficient for a whole army, our system not only withdraws the natural incentive to thought from the mass of mankind, and concentrates it on a few superior employees, but concentrates it in a corrupt way; that is, it bribes the thinkers to think out means of increasing commercial profits, and forbids them to think of the interests of the whole community on peril of starvation.

The thinkers who are not directly engaged in industrial concerns as technical experts are equally corrupted by finding that the way to make money in their very precarious professions is to prove that the biggest commercial profits carry with them the greatest prosperity for the entire nation. They provide, not thought, but whitewash for the system. Yet even they cannot persuade the exploiters of the system to make good their conclusions. For example, since they cannot pretend that it was good for mankind that the Lancashire cotton mills should have used up nine generations of men in one generation, they point out that as men working eight hours a day actually turn out more and better work than men working twelve hours a day, the interest of the employers will, if they are only let do as they please, lead them to reduce the hours of labor from twelve to eight of their own accord. Unfortunately, this simply does not happen. The employers are either incapable of thinking along such lines at all, or else they are clever enough to see that though if you must employ the same man all his life it will not pay you to break him down with overwork, yet if you can work him until he is used up and then throw him into the street and begin the process again with a fresh man, it may be extremely profitable. Accordingly, hours have been shortened by Act of Parliament or by Trade Union pressure, but never by voluntary commercialism. A few apparent instances to the contrary are found on examination to be either philanthropic, not commercial, or else the reduction in duration has been accompanied by an increase of intensity and continuousness which makes a comparatively short working day more exacting and destructive to health than the work of petty traders and servants of one kind and another who have nominally no leisure at all, and are at call all their lives except when they are asleep.

In short, the penalty of thinking about the private property system is that the thinker finds out that it should be promptly extirpated, abolished, eradicated, and held up to abhorrence in every school and at every mother's knee; and the penalty of making that discovery is the agony and shame of keeping it to oneself and then becoming an accomplice in all sorts of baseness, or being prosecuted and imprisoned for sedition and blasphemy. Under such circumstances, poor men take care not to think.

Thought is not, however, entirely baffled. A man with private property enough can write and say what he likes, because it is assumed that he will not saw off the branch on which he is sitting. But a highly intelligent proprietor may realize that a branch does not necessarily make a comfortable seat because it is so high above the level of the ground. He may see that it is easy to make the ground comfortable, and impossible to make the branch either comfortable or even safe. He lets himself think, and says what he thinks. Thus, what with your thoughtful Thomas Mores and Shelleys and Ruskins and Morrises and Tolstoys and Kropotkins whom nobody dares interfere with because they are carriage folk or nobles, and your Marxes who cannot help thinking and cannot hold their tongues, however miserably they are starved, the cat is let out of the bag often enough to discredit the notion that it is a holy spirit. Though even then plenty of us are Egyptian enough to worship a cat.

Now the good of the community requires that everybody shall be not only a worker to the full extent of his capacity for work, but also a thinker to the full extent of his capacity for thought. And this means that he must have leisure for culture. His day's labor, if it is bodily labor, should leave him in such an unexhausted condition that after a couple of hours rest and refreshment he has plenty of time and energy for art, literature, philosophy, society, sport, or whatever activity his natural impulses may make enjoyable to him. In short, he must be a cultivated gentleman as well as an instrument of production; and it may be added that a cultivated gentleman is capable of using methods of production (laboratory methods, for instance) that an ordinary commercial proletarian can no more handle than a black slave on a cotton plantation can handle even so rough an instrument as an ordinary English iron plough without smashing it.

THE INCENTIVE TO BODILY LABOR

But there is another side to human requirements. The professional thinker or brainworker, as he is sometimes rather invidiously called, needs bodily exercise as much as the manual worker needs mental exercise. Charles Dickens and George Meredith desperately taking long walks, like postmen, and Mr

Lloyd George and the Lord Chief Justice paying a professional golf player to go round the course with them on Walton Heath, are melancholy and ridiculous subjects of contemplation. The spectacle of men involving themselves in tedious and expensive games and exercises to enable them to sleep and digest their food whilst at the same moment other men are being paid to do useful, enjoyable, productive muscular work, and not enjoying it because they have to do a great deal too much of it, is not one that reflects much credit on our social organization. Quarrying, road making, railway making, telegraph construction, forestry, gardening, ploughing, harvesting, docker's work are only a few of the physical recreations that should be open to a poet or a mathematician or a barrister or an accountant driven to desperation or squash rackets by a sluggish liver. They are all capital fun for an ablebodied intellectual man after two or three hours of high pressure brain work.

But he never gets a chance of doing them, because our system remorselessly specializes us all as mere instruments of production, that being the most profitable way commercially. If the navvy and the barrister share their work, a navvy, who for mere navvying purposes costs only sixpence an hour when he is working, and nothing when he is not, would cost as much as a barrister, who is a much more expensive article, because he has not only to know a good deal more than a horse or a dog, which a navvy need not, but to associate with rich people and impress juries and even judges as a person to be treated with consideration. Thus the navvy's body is exercised and his mind left like an unweeded garden. The barrister's brains drudge until he hates the sight of a brief, until his digestion is wretched, until he has to take one drug to make himself work, and another to make himself sleep, and half a dozen more as antidotes to the two first.

In a healthy nation the monstrous idea of taking exercise could never arise. Men taking exercises may preserve a certain air of health, just as troops wearing gasmasks preserve much activity and effectiveness when the enemy poison the air they breath. I dare not compare them to bottle fed babies; for our

health is so bad that when you convert a mother from bottle
feeding to breast feeding, you sometimes discover that our
European civilization has actually succeeded in making a woman
inferior to a bottle and a packet of Infant's Food from the shop
as a nurse to her own child. I have known invalids who cursed
the day when their mothers were persuaded to nurse them. If
the maternal breast is to have a fair chance it must not be the
breast of nervous idleness or of starved drudgery. In the same
way the gymnasium, the fencing school, the hunting field, may
turn out finer physical specimens than the docks, the quarry or
the turnip field; but all this means is that an absurdity is better
than an abuse. If our social system robs a man of his natural
opportunities for healthy physical activity, he must either decay bodily or else make himself unspeakably ridiculous by tug-
ging at india rubber ropes attached to his bedroom door, and
lying naked on his back in his bathroom and trying to touch his
eyelids with his toenails with a solemn face that would be
wrinkled with merriment if he saw an Arab genuflecting in
prayer. And if the same social system compels him on pain of
starvation to do nothing but drag and lift and pull and wield
heavy implements for ten hours a day, then he must do what
he can with doctors' stuff to make his sciatica and rheumatism
bearable, and go from the coal mine and the steel foundry to
the furrow, and finally to the workhouse as he wears out. But
whether his natural incentive to activity is baffled or abused, it
still remains part of the life within himself, something that no
political constitution needs to supply, tending on the whole
rather to excess than to defect, and needing rather to be restrained by a school of laziness than stimulated by athletic com-
petitions or the whip of the slave driver.

THE APPETITE FOR DISTINCTION
AS AN INCENTIVE TO PRODUCTION

The appetite for distinction does not affect the question of distribution of income except so far as it leads to an appetite for

an exceptional income. The two objects are by no means the same: men frequently sacrifice income to distinction, and strive after honors they cannot afford. Money cannot confer personal distinction: it can confer class distinction only, because no man can live at a given rate of expenditure unless a whole class of persons are also living at that rate. The demand of one man cannot create an industry or a market: he must be content with what the existing industries produce: in the shops he can find nothing to buy that has not been produced to meet a more or less general demand. Once, in a town of 66,000 inhabitants, I wanted to buy a cap, for which I was quite prepared to pay the London Bond Street price of a guinea or thereabouts. But I might as well have been a working potter; for the most expensive cap I could buy in the town was a potter's Sunday cap, which cost me one shilling. And a multi-millionaire trying to buy a five guinea cap in London would have been equally baffled. To spend this sum on a single article of headgear he would have had to buy a Panama hat; and this he could not have worn in London for eleven months out of the twelve. He could of course give special orders regardless of expense. He could have made to such special order a sugarloaf hat two feet high, covered with cloth of gold, and encrusted with diamonds. He could order a coach like the one used by the Lord Mayor on state occasions (profanely called a gingerbread). He could obtain a team of cream colored ponies, or even zebras, to draw it. And any theatrical costumier would make him a set of coronation robes to wear. But the distinction he would acquire thereby would be that of the laughing stock of London. The utmost he could do in the way of extravagance would be to adopt the habits of the most extravagant class catered for by the west end; and though this class is not numerous, it is not a millionaire class; and it is numerous enough to deprive its members of the very essence of individual distinction: uniqueness. Five country houses and a town mansion, two or three yachts, six motor cars, and all such mere multiplication of common things, may leave their owner indistinguishable in Piccadilly from his own valet, and indistinguishable in society from dozens of other persons burdened with similar possessions.

The rich man in quest of individual distinction must buy a title; an easy matter, for, since Queen Victoria very sensibly said that she would not give titles to people who could not afford to keep them up, money has become the master key to the House of Lords. But here again the distinction is not personal: others enjoy it equally: the baron finds himself surrounded with other barons, and at a disadvantage with an infant viscount. A baron is already less impressive than a mere esquire was a century ago. Already it is a sign of humility to value a knighthood. Thus genuine personal distinction is now more than ever a matter of personal quality. Those who possess it sometimes refuse titles on their own account, because the title obliterates the name they have made distinguished; merges them in a class; and actually imposes on them an artificial inferiority to nobodies with purchased or inherited titles of precedent rank.

Yet, when the title is hereditary, it is not so easy to refuse. There is one's son to be considered, and one's wife. To them the title may make all the difference between distinction and obscurity. It is the only way in which a man of genius can share his eminence with those he loves; and as they have the power to make his home more uncomfortable for him by a domestic grievance than a title can make it, he succumbs, and condescends to a baronetcy or a barony much against the grain. This, however, only emphasizes the fact that the real use of titles is to distinguish the undistinguished and confound the distinguished: just the opposite, that is, of what titles are supposed to do to justify their existence. People ask who on earth is Lord Chatham, and are told William Pitt. If they ask who Lady Chatham is, they are told "Oh, only Lady Chatham." When the title becomes merely hereditary, nobility makes men acquainted with strange bedfellows. The spectacle of hopelessly undistinguished and even cretinous people absurdly overloaded with hereditary titles becomes so common that when an emperor or grand duke happens by chance to be a man of average ability he has the greatest difficulty in getting credit for it except from pure idolators who regard him as a divine being.

And so we find on examination that though the appetite for distinction is so strong that where titles are abolished they reappear unofficially in such forms as Mrs Professor Smith and Mr Penny Steamboat Commander Jones, it cannot be used as an incentive to social service either by the device of exceptional incomes or hereditary titles. Fundamentally the only sort of distinction that is socially useful is the natural distinction of the individual who does distinguished things well for their own sake. But it may be not only convenient but necessary to make this distinction visible. For example, we should never get on without uniforms or insignia of some kind. As a naked colonel or police constable looks exactly like a naked dean or a naked burglar, and as the soldier must know a colonel, and the civilian a policeman, when he sees him, it is necessary to distinguish colonels and police constables by special dresses, and to make a law forbidding deans and burglars to assume these dresses so stringent that even on the stage an actor who impersonates a colonel must not wear a correct uniform. Not for one day could any conceivable society of any complexity be kept in order without the establishment of a multitude of ranks compared to which those represented by the handful of people in the House of Lords are negligible. To abolish the office of Astronomer Royal on general levelling principles would make no serious difference in the work done at Greenwich; but if you abolish the office of foreman in industry you would wreck civilization.

Thus, on Socialism and Unsocialism alike Nature imposes a huge multitude of necessary distinctions, all of which imply orders and titles, privileges and exemptions, responsibilities and obligations. The bishop is exempted from blowing the organ, the brigadier from blowing the bugle, and the butler from brushing the boots. The privilege of making decisions is indispensable; and it is the cardinal privilege in civilization. A wise society must hold all such privileges sacred, and develop their full value, which can be attained only when they are independent of differences in income, and can neither be inherited by the commonplace, bought by the rich, nor withheld from the poor.

THE INCENTIVE TO IRKSOME WORK

We may then dismiss the idea that inequality of income is needed either to maintain distinction or authority. But on the general question of incentive it is to be noted that the necessary work of the world may be divided into work that needs no incentive, as it can only be done by men in whom a natural incentive to do it is so strong that they will do it for nothing rather than do other work for money, and work which would not be done at all unless the doers were bribed, or forced, or convinced of its necessity: in short, interesting work and uninteresting work. If a liner is to be sent across the Atlantic, the competition for the post of captain may easily be sufficient to induce individuals to secure it by offering to accept a smaller income than anyone else in the ship. But when it comes to finding men to stoke the furnaces or clean the boots the difficulty of inducing men to undertake such work may be so great that it may prove necessary to fall back on the need of the passengers to get to America, and tell them that they must clean their own shoes and take it in turns to do the stoking if they wish to cross the ocean. Here our own habits suggest that the difficulty should be got over by tempting men to become professional stokers and stewards by giving them a larger income than the captain. The creation of a plutocracy of stokers, scavengers, sewermen, ragpickers, and miners would be immensely more sensible than our present plutocracy of idlers; but a moment's consideration will shew that it would not work; for a plutocracy of idlers is the only sort of plutocracy in which a man gains anything by being a plutocrat. If the stoker has to spend his day toiling in the stokehold whilst the passenger is in the saloon, and the captain on the bridge or in the captain's cabin, what does he gain by the fact that his income is greater than the captain's or the passenger's? He can enjoy his income only when he is idle. It comes to this then, that you compensate him for the irksomeness of his job, not by extra income but by extra leisure. You make his day's work shorter, or his week's work shorter if he prefers it that way, or give him longer spells of holiday; or you allow him to retire at an earlier age.

Under any circumstances there must always be wide differences in the conditions on which men work. These conditions must finally be fixed by supply and demand. If stokers are not forthcoming, the inducements must be increased. If no inducements will induce men to do the work, the world must get on as best it can without it, or people must do it for themselves under pressure of their direct personal needs, as the unvaleted now wash and dress themselves, and the servantless clean their own boots. No tariff can be drawn up beforehand; for in working as in eating one man's meat is another man's poison. The old proposal of Fourier, that dirty work should be done by children, as they seem to have a taste for it, might be applied to a good many adults. There are men who enjoy tending furnaces and exercising great muscular strength. There are men who like bookkeeping and women who like washing clothes or hearthstoning steps: at least they like them better than the lighter and more elegant occupations. Even the bored guardians of picture galleries do not commit suicide or seem desperately unhappy.

MONEY AS AN INCENTIVE

The whole record of civilization is a record of the failure of money as a higher incentive. The enormous majority of men never make any serious effort to get rich. The few who are sordid enough to do so easily become millionaires with a little luck, and astonish the others by the contrast between their riches and their stupidity. In fact it is the complete breakdown in practice of the sufficiency of the pecuniary incentive that has compelled us to turn our backs on Adam Smith and Cobden, and confess that both the old Tories and the modern Socialists are right, and that there is no salvation for the world in Free Contract and Free Trade.

The belief in money as an incentive is founded on the observation that people will do for money what they will not do

for anything else. Careless observers think that men will
do anything for money; but this is clearly not true: if it were,
the majority would not be poorer than the minority. They say
also that everything men do is done for money; and this also is
obviously untrue: if it were men would be always earning and
never spending. The most important, arduous, and painful of
normal human activities is the bearing of children; but when
I try to persuade women that they should refuse to do it unless
they are handsomely paid for it, they are shocked, and persist
in doing it for nothing even when the result is starvation for
themselves and the children. We must therefore keep strictly to
the terms of the proposition, which is, that people will do for
money what they will not do for love or for anything else except money. For instance, an immense mass of the work of the
modern community consists in the oppression of the poor. To
take a crude instance, no man will go into the house where
naked and hungry children are crying for food and warmth,
and extort from their mother four shillings to pay a slum
landlord who already has more money than is good for him,
unless he is paid to do it. Consider the relations between the
sexes. When they are dishonorable they are paid for. The old
generalization that the love of money is the root of all evil is
founded on the observation that you always have to pay people
if you want them to serve your selfish ends, though good is
done largely for its own sake and often at a pecuniary loss. It is
true that the best of men must live, and must therefore demand
subsistence of some kind to keep him from dying of hunger;
but he does not ask a premium in consideration of the virtue
of his conduct: it is the evil doer who does that; and though
the evil doer sometimes spends part of the premium in bribing
journalists and moralists to invent virtuous excuses for his evil-
doing, and uses his political influence to persecute those who
expose its true character, he cannot alter the fact that men do
not begin to press you for money until you want them to sell
their souls. Curates are cheap: persuasive salesmen are dear,
because the curate is not expected to say anything that most
curates do not believe (rightly or wrongly), whereas the per-

suasive salesman seldom ènjoys the luxury of believing everything he says.

But even within these limits the money motive is far too weak to work a commonwealth. To get any strength into it you have to reduce men to such utter destitution that they must have money or die. Thirty years ago a great depression of trade reduced masses of the population to this extremity. The result was that they became revolutionists. They crowded into the churches and interrupted the sermons of bishops, who naïvely bade them remember that they were in church, though they had obviously suddenly remembered what a church means, and the bishop had quite forgotten it, if, indeed, he ever knew. They broke windows; they looted shops; they held continual revolutionary meetings in Trafalgar Square. All this they did because their customary supply of money had been cut off. They were turned into harmless drudges again at a moment's notice by a revival of trade, which enabled them to earn from eighteen to thirty shillings a week by from sixty to ninety hours of work. They wanted a little money badly enough to make an insurrection for it; but they did not want much money at all. I do not say that there was one of them who would not have taken a million if it had been offered to him for nothing: what I do say is that the man who was prepared to break windows and even cut throats for eighteen shillings was not prepared to cross the street to raise that sum to thirtysix; and the man who was accustomed to thirtyeight shillings would not take as much trouble to get fifty as he would to learn to ride a bicycle. When money is made the only incentive to improvement, every reformer raises the same despairing cry. Half a century ago Ferdinand Lassalle retired from his campaign beaten by what he called the damned wantlessness of the workers; and today Mr George Lansbury echoes him. Karl Marx's elaborate demonstration that from every pound produced by the labor of a worker ten shillings is legally stolen from him, left the worker absolutely indifferent as long as the ten shillings left to him was as much as he was accustomed to. In startling contrast to the failure of Marx's demonstration is the success of Garibaldi's celebrated offer to the Italians of "starvation, wounds, and death," at which his nation rose and rallied round him with irresistible enthusiasm.

In short, except when money represents an escape from crude bodily starvation, its incentive power is negligible; and this is why modern commercialist nations like our own, depending wholly on the incentive of money, never rise above bare subsistence wages for the masses.

HOW THE CHANGE TO EQUALITY OF INCOME
IS ACTUALLY HAPPENING

Let us now consider the effect of sticking a ramrod into this huge automatic machine for the degradation of humanity and the ruin of civilization. It is a dangerous business, for, infamous as the machine is, the existence of the community depends on it until it is replaced by a better system. We must not throw out dirty water until we get in clean. A violent overthrow of our system in a single and sudden catastrophe is an extremely desirable event, and one which would afford the keenest satisfaction to every honest man and woman who really understands what is going on; but most unfortunately it is a physical impossibility; and an attempt would be so terrifying and destructive in its consequences that the most probable result would be a precipitate reaction, and the restoration of the *status quo ante* with some amelioration and some aggravations.

I do not propose here to study an ideal method of getting rid of our system, because that is not a practical way of going to work. If the system is not repugnant to humanity it is useless to propose a change. If it is, then it is certain that an attack on it is already in operation; and what we have to do is to find that attack and develop it on the lines it has discovered by instinct and corrected by trial and error.

Let us turn therefore from the middle class literary Utopias and schemes of so-called Scientific Socialism to the actual campaign of the working classes against the system. There is no difficulty in finding the battle field. The only working class organizations which do anything against the system except write and talk and collect subscriptions to enrich capitalist printers and the landlords of public halls are the Trade Union movement and the Co-operative movement.

The Co-operative movement is not what we are looking for. What it has done is not to challenge and limit the private property system, but to explode the delusion that the organization of capitalist industry is a matter quite beyond the competence of the working classes, and must therefore remain a monopoly of the middle class upon whom the working class must depend for it in an attitude of galling servitude. In it we see working class consumers organizing the supply of all the services and commodities they require, from fried fish to building and banking, without drawing on the propertied classes for capital or submitting to the direction of middle class organizers except such as choose to accept employment from them at salaries which may seem handsome to men with working class standards of expenditure, but which seem absurdly small to the grandson of the younger son of a duke, or to a big city man. They divide the profits among themselves; and they strive to become their own landlords by acquiring freeholds when it is worth their· while. All this is excellent: there is no reason why the working classes should pay the middle classes exorbitant profits for doing managing and clerical work when they can get it done for moderate salaries, and have the goods and the profits into the bargain. But these transfers of an economic function and a share of commercial profits from the middle class to the working class leave the system untouched as a whole; and though it effects a redistribution of income to some extent, it must in the long run, unless other forces come into play, simply reduce the market price of industrial managers and thus leave more surplus for the landlord and capitalist. It is based on the exploitation of the proletariat quite as much as ordinary commerce is; strikes occur in the Co-operative factories just as they do in commercial ones. At such moments we see the Co-operative movement coming into sharp conflict with the Trade Union movement; and it would be in continual conflict with it if the

Co-operators paid the lowest supply-and-demand price for the
labor they employ. The fact that it mostly maintains a truce
with Trade Unionism by conceding to it something more than
the bare market price of proletarian labor does not differentiate
it from the better class of commercial enterprise; for all decent
employers now pay Trade Union rates when there is any sort
of serious and responsible Union in their trade. Consequently
it is fair to say that in so far as the Co-operative movement
repudiates the commercial system it does so at the suggestion
of and on the lines of Trade Unionism. We may therefore pass
by Co-operation, and seek for the plan of campaign against the
system in the Trade Union camp.

THE LAW OF MINIMUM

The Trade Union plan has been quite instinctive; for it has
come naturally to men with no knowledge of synthetic political
science: often, indeed, with no knowledge of reading or writing.
Struggling on a precipitous slope of degradation, privation, and
contempt, with their backs to a bottomless central crater of
absolute death by starvation, these men have at last made a
stand and drawn a line below which they have said they would
not be thrust. And when they were told that they must give
way or starve, they have replied that they would in that case
starve, but that at least their employers should suffer with them;
for they would do no more work, and thus teach their oppressors that the working class is the goose that lays the golden
eggs. In other words they struck for a minimum wage which
was at least something more than their supply-and-demand
price in the labor market.

At first the employers used the power of the State to suppress
Trade Unions by force. The Trade Unionists were transported,
imprisoned, and ridden down by dragoons. Their combination
was treated as a treasonable conspiracy. They retorted by
burning ricks, wrecking machines, concealing canisters of gun-
powder in forge fireplaces, bringing down factory chimneys
with bombs made of fulminate of mercury and other risky

explosives, and shooting blacklegs with air guns. In agricultural districts they held secret courts in which they tried and condemned their landlords and hired executioners to shoot them. They maimed cattle; burnt stables; made their landlords afraid to light their lamps before the curtains were drawn or to throw a shadow on the blind lest it should be shot at; withheld their rents; and finally invented the terrible weapon of the boycott, which made life almost impossible to its victim except in cities. They fought the police and the soldiery in pitched battles in the street. And always their most hated enemy was not the employer who offered wages below the Trade Union minimum, but the proletarian who offered to take them. He had to go about escorted by police and soldiers, always in bodily fear, and with very good warrant for it, as he had reason to be thankful if he escaped with his life when he allowed himself to be caught unprotected. This sort of civil war was almost incessant during the nineteenth century except at periods when trade was so good that supply-and-demand price of labor rose to the Trade Union minimum, and employers offered what the men asked or more. But the main weapon was the strike; and the authorities were generally strong enough to keep order and reduce the strike to a test of endurance between the employer [and his men], the employer having to go without profits and see his capital eating its head off and his machines rusting or his pits filling with water, and the men's families having to go on short commons and finally to starve. It was an unequal contest; but the men asked so little, and the productivity of labor increased at such a rate through the introduction of new methods and the discovery of new sources, that at last Trade Unionism became a recognized part of the British constitution. Trade Union wages were imposed on contractors by public authorities, and then made generally compulsory in certain industries by parliament, new authorities called Trade Boards being set up expressly to determine and enforce them; the proletariat secured representation in the House of Commons by a separate independent party; and Trade Unionists for the first time in history received seats in the Cabinet.

At a very early stage in this long conflict, the Trade Unionists discovered that the private property system was too strong
for them, and that whatever gains they might achieve from
time to time, they lost them again at the next spell of bad trade
unless they had induced parliament by a vigorous political agitation and by the pressure of their votes to secure the advance
by legislation. Parliament was obdurate on the point of the
minimum wage: its economic experts assured it that the sale of
labor at supply-and-demand prices was the basis of our whole
social system, which was perfectly true; and it was not until the
influence of those who loathe our social system and want to upset it became felt in parliament that at last parliament very re-
luctantly began to establish local authorities for the purpose
of ascertaining the current rate of wages and prevent employers
from nibbling at them. It still refuses to fix an absolute minimum
except in the form of Poor Law relief and the old age pension.

Therefore until very lately the Factory Code did not touch
wages directly, and always kept up a pretence of not interfering
with adult men. But under cover of protecting women and
young persons, it regulated the hours of labor and the sanitary
conditions in certain industries, enforced precautions against
accident; and forbad certain abuses such as the payment of
wages in kind instead of in coin. Parliament also provided and
enforced general elementary education at the public expense;
cleared insanitary areas in towns and built working class dwellings to be let on uncommercial terms; enforced sanitation on
private landlords and penalized overcrowding; and in many
ways deliberately substituted public law for the pressure of
supply and demand. And by means of the taxation and super-
taxation of income, added to the old system of local rating
which falls finally on the landlords, it confiscated part of the
incomes of the rich by force and without compensation, and
applied them to improving the condition of the proletariat.

I have summarized this encouraging page of history in order
to bring out the fact that the parliamentary method was
throughout essentially the Trade Union method. It prescribed
a definite minimum of humane dealing and enforced it at all

costs. When the employer said to the Trade Union, as he always did, that they were cutting their own throats by asking another farthing an hour, as it would eat up all his profits and drive him out of business, they seldom believed him; but in any case they refused to listen to reason and stuck to their determination to have a better life or perish. Then parliament became conscience stricken at the spectacle of little children working from twelve to sixteen hours a day in factories under savage conditions, and threatened to cut the hours down, the factory owner engaged distinguished economists to demonstrate that all their profits were made in the last hour, and that utter ruin must overtake the whole industry if they had to stop the machinery even half an hour earlier. Parliament replied, in effect, that they must learn how to make their profits in some humaner manner, and might have added that the demonstration of the distinguished economists was at best a venal equivocation; for though it is true that every industry may have on its extreme margin a few businesses so poor that only by ruthless sweating can they be kept going, most of the businesses would not exist at all if they did not return a handsome surplus to the proprietors.

I repeat, there was nothing new in the method of proceeding by successive minima, or drawing successive lines nearer and nearer to the ideal by making everybody toe them. Legislation always proceeds by that method. We do not say "All or nothing" like Ibsen's hero. Sane legislators do not make a law that men shall be honest or gentle or decent or temperate. Ignorant amateur legislators do that in American States, with appalling consequences. Tyrants do it in order that they may be able to imprison and execute their subjects at pleasure. But practicable and honest legislation always prescribes some definite thing that you shall do or shall not do. There may be a hundred other things just as good that you are not required to do, or just as bad that you still may do with impunity as far as the law is concerned. It may be unlawful for a starving man to pluck a turnip whilst it is at the same time lawful for the owner of the turnip field to turn a family out of house and home because they prefer a Methodist chapel to the parish church. The law may compel the citizen to supply the country's soldiers with ammunition and subsistence whilst it leaves it to his own choice whether he will feed the country's hungry children and clothe its naked ones. But such inconsistencies arise only because the law has to be definite and has to do one thing at a time. Indeed it very often has to do things by halves at a time. But its positive method is always to prescribe a definite minimum of good conduct. A law commanding people to love their neighbors as themselves is no use; but a law enacting that if you kill a man maliciously you will yourself be hanged makes you think twice before you commit murder. This is one of the earliest of civilized laws, and is really a law imposing a prescribed minimum of neighborly conduct. Trade Union Law proceeds in just the same way. A law to forbid sweating in general terms is no use. A law prescribing a definite minimum wage or a definite maximum number of working hours per week does actually abolish sweating to that extent, and bring into comparatively healthy cultivation a plot of humanity formerly abandoned to the anarchy of commercial supply and demand.

Here then we have found the way in which the commercial system is being actually fought and destroyed. It is not an ideal way: it is simply the way in which the thing is happening. Let us follow it imaginatively into the future. Beginning with the sweated trades, you raise their wages and shorten their hours until the persons employed in them are no worse off than unskilled laborers who are not classed as sweated. You have thus levelled up the lowest class until it has attained to economic equality with the one next above it. You then proceed to raise the wages and shorten the hours of this amalgamation until the unskilled laborer is as well off as the skilled artisan, a proceeding which will probably fill the artisan with such indignation that he will try to escape from the equality thus imposed on him by trying to get a move on the legislation already in operation for his own benefit. I need not pursue the process in detail. The rising flood of public regulation will float all labor up to its common level, overtaking one stratum after another, until—well, until when? For clearly the process cannot go on for ever. It would seem a fairly jolly thing to pass a final Factory Act raising everybody's wages to £50,000 a year, and restricting the hours of labor to ten minutes a day with two half holidays a week and six months vacation. Unfortunately, one indispensable preliminary to paying wages of any sort, high or low, in cash or in kind, is that they should first be produced; and if you distribute more than you are producing, or work shorter hours than are needed to produce what you are distributing, you are burning the candle at both ends, and will presently be bankrupt.

But long before the whole community reaches the limit set by the product, a good many separate establishments, and some entire industries, will have reached it. As it is, many an employer can hardly make both ends meet by sweating himself and all his employees both by low wages and long hours. When he has to pay his women eighteen shillings instead of eight, and stop work daily after eight hours instead of after sixteen, his miserable situation will become impossible. There are mines in the country which yield so little that they are just barely worth working under existing conditions; the least addition to their working expenses would lead to their being abandoned or closed. There are canals which have been abandoned because railway competition reduced their takings below their expenses; and some of the railways barely pay their way. All such businesses are called marginal, because they are so close to the brink of bankruptcy that a touch will push them over.

That touch will be the impact of labor legislation. Old Trade Unionists will laugh, and say that this is an old alarm and a false one; and their experience warrants them in saying so, because during the nineteenth century the advances imposed by Factory legislation were so small, and the cheapness of labor had left employers so ignorant, dull, and slovenly, that all the advances were easily met by putting more brains into the business, smartening up the organization, and speeding up the machinery. Indeed it happened over and over again that when the worker was paid more, and worked for a shorter time, he produced more: enough indeed to pay the increase in his own wages with a profit for his employer to boot. But this only delays the day of reckoning. Sooner or later, if the raising of wages and shortening of hours go on, the time must come when, though every business may be tightened up to the maximum of possible efficiency, the marginal shops or mines or factories will not produce the minimum wage imposed on the whole trade, though the trade as a whole may be able to produce it easily. The whole trade must therefore be pooled in some manner. How, exactly, will it be done?

Clearly if the threatened businesses are marginal and the Factory legislation is to stand, the Government must come to the rescue if it wishes to save them. It may not so wish. The trade may be one which the country on the whole would be better without; and the restriction of supply and consequent rise of price which would follow the cutting off of the marginal establishments, or even the destruction of the whole trade, may be, on the whole, a good job. About the public execution of deleterious trades in this way we need not trouble ourselves. What we want to know is about the necessary trades which the Government would have to save just as it would have to save our railways or collieries for strategic purposes if they became commercially bankrupt. Well, how could the Government save the marginal establishments, or the whole trade if all the establishments were marginal from being pushed over the margin by the advancing Factory Code? Quite simply, either by nationalizing the industry as it has nationalized the letter carrying and telegraph industry, or by making grants in aid of wages.

This is already done in many forms. For instance, the building trade. In this enormous and important industry there is a section which is not merely on the margin: it is over the edge. It is not worth the while of any private builder to build houses for laborers within reasonable distance of their work. Consequently the poor have to live in decayed streets, in houses built for well-to-do people long ago, and now fallen into disrepair and disrepute, and quite unsuited for use as tenement dwellings, or crowd into already overcrowded cottages in the country, until the local governing body subsidizes the building of blocks of new dwellings or laborers' cottages *ad hoc*, and charges the commercial deficit on the rates.

Take another case. When the war suddenly thrust the financial industry below the margin, the Government promptly saved the situation by a grant in aid and by a drastic alteration of the terms of existing financial contracts.

Thus there is nothing new in the support by Government of socially necessary industries which would become insolvent without such support; and there is therefore no reason to anticipate that the process of raising the minimum standard of subsistence for the whole community by enforcing successive minima of wages and maxima of hours will be stopped for want of grants in aid of wages to marginal establishments or by nationalizations of whole industries like the Post Office.

The net effect of such operations is a redistribution of income. The Government sends to a millionaire or a great ducal ground landlord a tax collector, backed by a sheriff's officer, backed by the police, backed by the army, and takes from him a part of his income without compensation by simple physical force, flatly confiscating it without the least concealment or apology; and it adds the income so confiscated to the income of poorer men. It can in this way confiscate and redistribute all that part of the national income which consists of rent of land and interest on capital, and may be lumped together as unearned income. It has hitherto done so without understanding anything of the process beyond its immediate effect in providing public money. If the Chancellor of the Exchequer is ignorant of economics, and has a traditional Radical notion that landlords are wicked people and that rent should belong to the people, he may begin by concentrating taxation on the landlords; but the landlords will very soon open his eyes to the fact that considering how country landlords manage their own estates, administer justice, distribute coals and blankets, organize cottage hospitals and collect subscriptions to maintain district nurses, whereas the mere capitalists are so absolutely idle in respect of their property that very few of them have ever seen the factories and workshops and mines from which their dividends are

derived, all the reasons for confiscating rent apply *à fortiori* to
interest. Thus a fund of many hundreds of millions annually
will be available for grants in aid to industry before industrial
profits or wages are touched by the tax collector. The war has
opened the eyes of the nation to this prodigious reserve fund,
and to the fact that a taxation of between thirty and forty per
cent of the large incomes of which it mainly consists has actually increased production as well as improved distribution.
There will be no remorse about pursuing the process to its
logical end.

But the war has shewn also that public opinion, which re-
sents the accumulation of riches by tradesmen more than by the
aristocracy and gentry, is much more clamorous for the taxation
of "profiteers" than of capitalists and landlords. This is easily
explained by the fact that the employer and shopkeeper, by
their daily effort to keep down wages and keep up prices, are
the oppressors with whom the people are engaged in a hand-to-
hand struggle, whilst the territorial landlords and opulent capitalists come in contact with the people only through their
expenditure, which is popular and apparently beneficent. Be
this as it may, what is called by economists "rent of ability,"
including employers' profits and the big fees earned by individuals with exceptionally lucrative talents of one kind or another will rather be taxed more mercilessly than rent of land
and interest (rent of capital).

Let us therefore trace the process, not in its logical order of
expropriating the idle rich first and the industrious rich afterwards, but as it is actually happening: that is, by labor legislation which hits the employer first, and leaves it to him to shift
the burden to the shoulders of the landlord and capitalist as best
he can. Assuming that he has already pushed scientific management as far as it will go, and that there is no further means of
increasing the product, how will he try to carry the last straw
of State regulation before giving up the game in sulky despair.
If his business is big enough he will almost certainly first try
to save the situation by turning it into a joint-stock company.
His reason for this will be that instead of receiving as inde-

pendent employer the residue after everyone else is paid, he will, as a company manager, have a fixed salary which, like the wages of the workmen, will be charged on the product before any dividend is paid. The landlord must still be paid or he will sell up the business and turn it out of doors; but the capitalist, in the form of the unfortunate shareholders, will have to do without a dividend if the manager's salary and the workmen's wages eat up all that the landlord leaves; and thus the item of interest on capital is saved. In this way a commercially insolvent business may be carried on for years without paying a farthing interest; and the shareholders cannot get out or get their money back, as their shares are of course unsaleable.

But this ingenious device, which has ruined many a widow and starved many an orphan, is not always practicable; and in any case the next stride forward of the minimum may eat up the manager's salary. Then the game is really up at last. The employer and the capitalist are both cleaned out: the capital which figured so bravely in the prospectus has turned to withered leaves, like the magician's gold in the eastern tale.

But the business is still supporting the workers at the full minimum standard; and it is also yielding rent to the landlord. A business that is doing this is not insolvent from the point of view of the community. Let us suppose that the manager, being on his beam ends, would be willing to go on managing if he were relieved of the burden of rent, and might pocket what the landlord now exacts. All the State has to do in that case to keep the business going is to make an annual grant in aid of wages of superintendence equal to the amount of the annual rent, and levy it from the whole body of landlords by an Income Tax on their revenue from land. The industry is saved; the trick is done; and, as Karl Marx would have put it, the expropriators are expropriated.

Incidentally, the business, from the moment it received a grant in aid, would be audited by the State, to guard against appropriation by the manager of reserve funds, depreciation funds, sinking funds, and the like.

But long before the whole private property system will have

consummated this process, its garment of thought will have begun to wear out and drop off. For example, though people will go on for a long time talking about wages in the coal industry or the textile industries, and separate Trade Boards will establish separate minimum wages in each separate industry, the introduction of grants in aid will relieve the Trade Boards of all necessity to consider the actual product of their particular industry in fixing the minimum wage in it; and from that moment they will have to fix the wage either according to their fancy, which is ridiculous, or adopt the general standard of the whole country. After that, the mere habit of talking about wages in the coal industry and wages in the textile industry may persist for a while; but it will become plainer and plainer to everyone that what the collier is getting has no more to do with coal than with cotton, and what the spinner is getting has no more to do with cotton than with coal or marmalade or dolls or performances of Beethoven's symphonies or anything else that the whole country produces. It will really not be a wage at all, but a quota of the national income.

Still, for some time it will have in common with wages the condition that the worker will not get it unless he works. This, however, implies that a man will be free not to work if he does not choose to; and that freedom he will certainly not be permitted to enjoy when the loss of his labor impoverishes the whole community instead of merely leaving an extra job available for his neighbor, and not hurting the employers. There is nothing new in compelling a man to work: on the contrary, there are laws in every country to punish the masterless man, the tramp, the loafer, the sleeper out, the sturdy rogue and vagabond, the beggar or whatever else the idler may be called. It once seemed quite natural in England to brand such a person with hot irons, to cut off his ears, to whip him through the town, and, if he was incorrigible, to hang him. The reason such laws fell into abeyance was, first, that the commercial system failed to provide employment for all who were willing to work; second, the presence of large bodies of unemployed men acting as a reserve army of labor was necessary to the working of the commercial system; and third, the system created a class of idle rich commoners, and the prospect of becoming one of those was treated as the incentive to industry: so that it became rather invidious to punish a tramp for trying to live like a gentleman.

These reasons for tolerating idleness disappear as the commercial system is eaten away by the advance of the minimum. Idleness will again be treated quite directly as crime. No doubt for some time it may seem natural to thoughtless people to punish it with poverty. Unfortunately, the poor man suffers much less from poverty than the community does, just as a man who never washes his clothes is unbearable to his neighbor though quite tolerable to himself. It is positively delightful to be naked in warm weather: we are forced to dress for the sake of our neighbors against our own inclinations. A destitute man depresses his neighbors, defiles his dwelling, becomes a centre of infection, depraves morals: is, in short, a scandal. We may take it then that a man will not be allowed to be poor, whatever other indulgence may be extended to him. That is to say, he will receive his quota of the national income whether he works or not as long as he is allowed to live. He may be boycotted for idleness, or he may be laughed at and tolerated if he is an engaging sort of rogue, or he may be put into a lethal chamber and killed if his idleness is a disease that defies medical treatment of any sort. I do not myself think that idleness will ever become a serious question in a well constituted and well bred society; but at all events the practice of punishing it by a stoppage of income will have to be discontinued; and from that moment the last link between commercial wages and communal income will be snapped, and the notion of working for pay decay and finally perish.

As to the proprietary classes, long before the supersession of the commercial system is consummated by the final victory of the minimum, the game of private property will have ceased to be worth the candle. The proprietor of land or capital does not, as such, cultivate land or organize industry. He lets his land or lends his capital to the middle class man of business, who organizes production with them, and distributes the product in wages to the worker, rent to the landlord, and interest to the capitalist, keeping what is left to himself as profit. Thus both the proprietary classes and the workers are wholly dependent on the employers; and if these throw up the commercial game, the commercial game is up for everybody.

So far, the gradual encroachment of Factory legislation on the employer's profit has been met by devices so successful that the employers have actually gained more money than the workers by the new legislation. Employers are like other people: their exertions are proportionate to the pressure on them; and they never do their very utmost unless the pressure is a matter of life or death. A man walking to a railway station will walk at his usual pace, no matter how early he is; but if he is running it too close and must run to catch it, his pace will depend on how late he is; and even when he is running as fast as the fear of losing his train can take him, you can get another mile an hour or so out of him by sending a bull after him. Before Factory legislation began no employer made as much money as he might have done if he had been hard put to it. For example, railways were content to start express trains within ten minutes of one another until the Government, for the protection of the public, imposed the block system on them, when they found that under this restriction it was quite safe and practicable to start express trains within two minutes of one another. The opponents of such legislation were never tired of pointing out that it very often produced results diametrically contrary to those intended by the legislators: for example, that laws against usury enable usurers to charge higher rates of interest, and laws to restrict the sale of drink led to increased drunkenness and higher profits for the distiller. This did not prevent them from prophesying disastrous results from Trade Union legislation, nor from being surprised when the actual results turned out to be quite the opposite.

Up to a certain point, employers benefit by labor legislation automatically, by the simple increase in the product due to the workers being better fed and less exhausted by excessive hours and drink and despair and demoralization. When that effect is exhausted, the employer has to do something to meet the further encroachments of the minimum. For instance, if the working day is shortened to eight hours by legislation, or at the demand of a Trade Union enforced by the threat of a strike, he may agree on condition that the workers produce as much in the eight hours as they did before in nine or ten. This is the usual course with coal miners, who cannot be speeded up mechanically. In a factory the worker can be driven harder by simply making the engine turn faster, or making the person who has been tending two machines tend three. From America we have received an interesting and amusing system of so-called scientific management in which the movements of the body in manual work are recorded by the cinematograph, and measured and timed by various instruments, until the most economical technical method is ascertained, the determination being so nice that at last the precise orbit of a cobbler's elbow as he stitches is determined with astronomical exactitude. By these means it is possible that the worker whose hours of labor have been greatly reduced and his wages doubled by Trade Union action confirmed by legislation, may find himself worked to exhaustion in a few years; so that his last state is worse than his first, unless the too scientific exploitation is countered by a still further reduction in the length of the working day and by an increase in the number of holidays.

Besides putting the screw on the worker, the employers can put the screw on the public. They can take a leaf out of the Trade Union book, and instead of cheapening their wares to the bare supply-and-demand price by competing with one another for customers, they may combine and fix a minimum price below which they pledge themselves to one another not to sell. They often begin by lowering the price to such a point that all the marginal businesses are ruined or compelled to sell out to the combination; but when this is effected the price goes up to the point at which the loss by the reduction in sales would be greater than the gain by increase of price.

The abandonment of competition in price makes it easy to effect further economies by amalgamating different businesses and thereby saving the cost of several separate managements. When the business is large enough, its products can often be standardized and turned out by machinery at a cost of production so low that the rate of profit can be considerably increased and the price startlingly reduced at the same time. American motor cars are cases in point.

Thus we see that the trust, the combine, the kartel, the unprecedented fortunes of millionaires, are all products of the first onslaught of Trade Unionism and Communism on the commercial system. All classes are the better for it; and a delusive truce is made. In businesses where no Trade Unionist was formerly allowed inside the walls, they are not only welcomed but insisted on. The Trade Union, no longer persecuted, becomes a national institution.

Note that the economy which is affected by great combinations of capital in joint stock, and finally in trust and kartel, destroys the personal independence of the middle class, and turns Mr Pickwick into Mr Wilfer. The man with a capital of a few hundred pounds, who formerly went into business for himself, or into a private firm of two or at most three partners, has now no chance of competing with the big concerns, and must become their employee, as a manager at best, but oftener as a clerk. And though the view of Marx and Buckle that the history of mankind is essentially an economic history may be open to much criticism, it is beyond all doubt that when you change a man from an employer into an employee, you change not only his clothes and his address, but his mind, and consequently his politics and his religion. His abhorrence of Trade Unionism and Socialism changes to a conviction that they alone can save society from ruin; and the energy with which he once resisted the advancing minimum is now expended in shoving it vigorously forward.

Thus we see that if the minimum is pushed steadily upward it will absorb not only all the modern machine made economies, all the landlord's rent, all the capitalist's interest, all the profits of the employers, and all the fortunes of the renters of exceptional ability, but will meanwhile convert bit by bit the whole body of opinion and conscience on which these institutions rest.

We see, in short, that if there were no such thing in the world as a conscious and loquacious Socialist, the movement of civilization towards Socialism would be accelerated rather than retarded or reversed; for the Socialist doctrinaire often contributes nothing to the process except friction.

THE INCENTIVE TO USE MONEY AS CAPITAL

Capital used to be described by corrupt economists as the reward of abstinence. This was obvious nonsense. The reward of abstinence is death. Capital is not even the reward of privation: Nature rewards that by ill health and misery.

Capital has also been called the result of saving. It is, on the contrary, the result of spending. The whole world might save for a million years without producing a single railway or excavating a single mine. A thing that is merely saved produces nothing: it simply rots and is wasted, or poisons the air until it is buried. Mere postponement of consumption ends speedily in there being nothing to consume.

Industrial capital is not a negative thing: it is the present value of the spare money, or rather the spare time and energy devoted to making work easier and shorter. It cannot possibly arise unless men, when they have provided for the day's needs, have still time and energy left to make something that will make tomorrow's work more productive: say a path or an irrigation canal or a water butt or a wheelbarrow or a spade or a fiddle to accompany a chanty or what not. Here there is no question of abstinence or privation: the better a man is nourished the more spare energy he will have.

Therefore the condition for producing capital is not that men should be abstemious or stingy or otherwise shortsightedly suicidal or mean, but that they should have more than enough time and strength to keep themselves alive from hand to mouth.

Now this condition is produced by Nature in the more fertile zones up to a certain point without any special organization or much social co-operation, every worker making his own implements and his own paths and water courses. But it cannot be carried even to the village stage of civilization without division of labor, at least one man being specialized as a carpenter and another as a blacksmith; and the carpenter cannot do much without a lumber industry somewhere, nor the blacksmith anything at all without a mine and foundry at work within reach of him. Every village is thus dependent on a mine and a railway for the simplest metal implements.

Now a mine or railway represents a quantity of time and energy that could not be spared by the strongest man. Therefore as long as there is no other provision for capital but what individuals can do for themselves in their spare time, civilization cannot be carried even so far as a blacksmith's shop. At this stage the problem would seem to be how to produce an individual of supernatural strength, having the spare energy of five thousand men. That problem is solved by the invention of money, which not only makes division of labor possible, but endows the individual with as much energy as he has money enough to buy in addition to his own. If the money is equally distributed the problem will not be solved, because no man will have enough to make a mine or construct a railway or an ocean liner. For that, Socialism would be necessary: that is, an organization representing the whole community would have to collect the spare money of all its members and make a common capital fund of it. But the same thing can be achieved by a distribution of money sufficiently outrageous to leave certain individuals with spare money enough to command the spare energy of thousands of men for years after they had spent their utmost on their immediate wants. Single persons thus circumstanced will make mines and railways and liners just as single Pharaohs made pyramids. Combinations of such persons will result in whole railway systems, whole fleets of liners, and Channel tunnels.

This way of doing it is so manifestly grotesque that no community in its senses would contrive it purposely: it occurs, as we have seen, as an unforeseen and unintended effect of private property; and when people find out what is actually happening they abolish private property and adopt the Socialist system. At present we work both systems. The naval, military, and air services, the roads and bridges, the postal and telegraph services, the lighting of the streets and so on: in short, all the services which cannot be doled out to us in exchange for individual money payments, and therefore benefit the community without making profit for their owners, have to be provided by the Socialist method. The others are provided by private capital. In this division Socialism has encroached a little on the sphere of private capital, as in the case of the posts and telegraphs. But private capital most carefully keeps off the unprofitable grass of Socialism. Nonetheless we are still trusting for most of our civilization, not to the saving of money by private individuals, for as we have seen, mere saving produces nothing, but to the spending of the spare money of private individuals on the establishing of great industrial enterprises. I say the establishment of them, because, once established, they pay their way with a profit to the capitalist. Once established, they either maintain themselves or perish as far as the capitalist is concerned; for he takes no part in the daily work by which they live. Many people imagine that when they are buying shares they are encouraging industry. This is true only of the original shareholders in a concern, or those who take up a fresh issue of shares for the extension of its operations. The man who buys shares today in, for example, the London and North Western Railway is simply purchasing somebody else's legal right to a share in the money paid by travellers for the use of the railway: he is not calling an inch of railway line into existence, nor adding a farthings-worth to the efficiency of the line as it already exists.

It will now be seen that the advance of the minimum, by gradually squeezing the idle rich dry, and bringing down the incomes of the working rich to the common level, will destroy the present provision for capital expenditure.

Let me repeat, the commercial system of private property provides for this by making the rent appropriating class so rich at the expense of the rest of the community that it has more money than it cares to spend. The fact that the spare money thus accumulated can be lent on hire and thus become a source of additional income acts paradoxically as an inducement to saving. I say paradoxically because it seems odd that the effect of giving a man more money than he wants should be to make him want yet more. The explanation is that the additional income brought in by his capital is unearned and perpetual. The future is always uncertain: however little a man wants he may want more later on; and however much he may have, he may lose it in the general insecurity of the system. Therefore he will always save when he can do so without privation.

Now when we begin to supplant the commercial system by a Communist system we soon discover that capital is very nervous, and that its normal commercial secretion can no longer be relied on. For consider what we are doing. Under the commercial system in its older form of private firms, the first charge on the product of an industry is wages, the second rent, the third interest, and the residual fourth profits. The employer comes last. This is the most advantageous position for the middle class man when there are any profits: that is, when what is left after paying rent, interest, and wages, is more than the salary of a hired manager. But when the advance of labor legislation forces up wages, and restricts the quantity of labor that can be exacted for those wages, profits are gradually cut off until there is nothing left for the manager but a hired manager's salary. At this point, as we have seen, he transforms his business into a joint-stock company and thereby turns the tables on the capitalist, who now has to take what the manager leaves instead of coming in front of him. The next advance reduces dividend; further advances extinguish it.

Meanwhile, what is becoming of the incentive to capitalize? Remember that under the commercial plan the capitalist becomes so rich that capital "saves" itself: he has more than he cares to spend. A little is capitalized by the poor, incited by fear of the future, desire to provide for daughters and widows, and so forth: just enough to make the poorer middle class desperately defend the very institution which has produced their poverty. But advancing Communism will remove the fear of the future by giving widows with orphans "mothers' pensions," and securing employment on honorable terms for everybody. Thus, as the capitalist becomes poorer and poorer he will also find that the reasons which drive poor men to sacrifice the present to the future by capitalizing are disappearing as fast as his income. He will have less and less to capitalize; his bank, instead of taking charge of his money and paying him interest on it, will make a charge for keeping his account; and it will no longer be imprudent to say "Let us eat and drink; for tomorrow we die." Under such circumstances the private man will not capitalize; and even if you take the trouble to convince him that he ought to, you will find that he has no spare money to capitalize.

The Government must come to the rescue again. The grant in aid of wages must be followed by the grant in aid of capital. Take a marginal business in which the rise of the minimum has caused the rent of the premises, the wages of the workers, and the salaries of the manager and his staff, to eat up the whole product; so that nothing is left for reserve fund, sinking fund, depreciation and so forth. At first it seemed that the Government must stop short of this point. But we saw a further consideration that this does not follow from the Communist point of view. The industry as a whole may be producing a surplus sufficient to provide on the most lavish scale for depreciation and renewal long after the separate establishments on the margin of it have come down to bare payment for labor and rent of land. Nay, even if the whole industry becomes insolvent, the industry of the country as a whole may be gaining so much more on the swings than it is losing on the roundabouts as to make it perfectly sound finance for the Government to make grants in aid of reserve and depreciation funds, or in any other way to maintain and extend the capital, not merely of marginal firms, but of whole industries, long after they have ceased to pay their separate ways. Nobody proposes to abandon the telegraph system because it does not make both ends meet, nor to allow London Bridge to collapse in ruin because its upkeep would be called "a dead loss" by a commercial firm.

The final limit of the financial resources of the Communist

system is the entire national income. The final limit of its capital resources is the aggregate spare energy of the whole community. A fully organized community can keep redistributing both up to the last penny, despite the shrieks of the unenlightened. But they cannot redistribute more than the community is producing; and they cannot capitalize more than it can spare after satisfying its current needs. Within those limits, the Government will make grants in aid of reserve funds and depreciation funds, and advance capital with all the liberality of Jack Cade, whose economic instincts were much sounder than they were held to be by Henry VII, Edward VII, and the intervening monarchs.

But what of the landlord, whose rent we reserved as one of the charges on the marginal industry? His turn will come. Already he is being taxed to provide wages and salaries, and to maintain the capital of the concern from which he draws his rent. Already he receives it with a rueful consciousness that a good deal of the money he is receiving has come straight out of his own pocket. Still, he gets something; and what is more, if it is not paid he can sell up the whole concern and resume possession of the land. Sometimes indeed the capitalist possesses this power; for he may have begun by investing capital in the purchase of the freehold, thereby making himself both landlord and capitalist. In this case he is either the simple owner of the land, or, if the capital is in joint stock, and he has given a lease to the company, both lessor and lessee. In either case he has the power to shut down the business by simply turning the workers out and letting the land as a deer forest to an American millionaire, or using the premises as a cinema theatre, or in some other way escaping from the net of labor legislation. We must not include among the alternatives open to him the starting of another ordinary industrial firm, as that would take him straight back into the net.

The remedy is obvious. The Government will save the business, if it be worth saving, by a further grant in aid for the purchase of the freehold at such market value as their previous operations may have left it. Thus the last idler is bought out; and the trick is done as far as that business is concerned.

WHY STATE MORALITY AND STATE ECONOMICS ARE UNIQUE

In all these minimal transactions the Government is redistributing income, not producing it. Governments do not produce material wealth: they organize and render services, many of them very expensive services, and compel the community to pay for these services. They force expenditure out of one channel into another. They come down on the citizen who wants to spend sixpence on more beer and more tobacco, and compel him to spend it on sewers or schools, chaplains or chemists, food or trinitrotoluene, bibles or bayonets, and what not that, in the opinion of the Government, the community needs more than it needs more beer or another smoke. They abolish property in land and capital and redistribute the control of it, forcing landlords to sell their land so that it may pass into other hands and be devoted to other uses, and forcing capitalists to surrender their capital with the same object.

Now these proceedings on the part of a private individual or corporation would be stark robbery with violence; and a community in which they were tolerated would fall into anarchic ruin. In fact to the very considerable extent to which at present private individuals and corporations do these things incidentally in the course of their commercial operations, they do commit robbery with violence (in forms which they have themselves made legal), and the community is actually in a condition of anarchic ruin. Why then is it right for a government to do that which it is wrong for private individuals and corporations to do, and what it would be criminal for them to do if they had not corrupted the laws and perverted the police by using them to make their property secure instead of to establish justice in human affairs? Is the Government to be exempted from moral law merely because it has the power to flout it? Certainly not;

for an unrighteous government is a far greater evil than the most unrighteous individual can be. Why, then, may it send a tax collector to do what it imprisons a highway man for doing?

The handiest answer is that the tax collector is transferring capital from a worse employment to a better. But highwaymen can do this, and have, as a matter of fact, often done it. The popularity of Robin Hood was based on the belief that he ran his business of redistributing income on philanthropic lines. On the Stock Exchange capital is daily transferred from worse to better employment. True, it is also daily transferred from better to worse; but for that matter Governments often make such transfers. Clearly then, if the Government is in a unique moral position, it is evidently not so in respect of a power that is exercised every day by private persons.

The correct answer is that Governments may do what individuals may not because they can do things that individuals cannot. They enjoy a unique power in virtue of which they are allowed a unique license. The Government is the only body that can distribute the cost of a change and the benefit of it over the entire community, or throw it on any particular section of the community. This is why Governments can do things that private enterprise, individual benevolence, and personal righteousness cannot touch. It is why Socialism must be State Socialism, and not Guild Socialism, nor Syndicalism, nor moralized Capitalism, nor private and sectarian eccentricity. You cannot redistribute income without taking from B and giving what you take to A. If A and B are individuals and acquaintances, the transaction is simple enough: A simply begs, borrows, or steals from B; and the thing is done without any necessary Government intervention. But if A is a whole class, each consisting of individuals unknown to one another, and scattered throughout the country in different occupations and places, the operation is clearly beyond the power of any organization smaller than the Government. If a body of a thousand workers in a single factory found that the deduction of rent from the product of their labor left too little to maintain them in a decent condition, they could help themselves only by refusing to pay rent to the land-

lord of the factory. By doing so they would do a double
wrong: they would throw the whole burden of the change
ruinously on the shoulders of a single man who was no more to
blame for our land system than any other landlord, and they
would add the value of the land to their own earnings, though
they would have no more right to the land (if no less) than their
neighbors, thus making themselves the landlords. The only body
which can effect such a transaction equitably is the Government, which can buy the landlord out with money raised by a
tax on rent which falls impartially on all the landlords, who are
thus compelled to share the loss of the individual landlord whose
particular piece of land is in question. Still more justly, the tax
can be levied on all unearned or excessive incomes, whatever
their immediate source. No smaller body or agency can do this.
No other body can do it in the name of the whole community,
with no interest in it but that of the whole community. This is
why all private philanthropic bodies, however pious and charitable, are fundamentally useless, and indeed aggravate human
misery by obscuring and delaying the real remedy, which is
redistribution of income.

We now perceive that we are engaged in a transition of our
commercial system based on private property in land and capital, without conscience, or honor, or sense, automatically producing every conceivable moral and material evil, to a system
in which land and capital are conscientiously, honorably and
sensibly communized, and income is distributed intentionally in
such a way as seems wisest from the point of view of the interest of the entire community.

The method of the transition is not an ideal method: it is one
which has been evolved under pressure of necessity by the instincts of common men without theories to verify or doctrines
to justify. It is in actual operation; and its results so far have
been encouraging. It does not call for any new quality in human
nature; it does not involve the application of any new principle
in law; it asks legislators to do nothing they are not already
doing; and the equality at which it aims is the old and tried and
perfectly possible and familiar equality of money income and

not an impossible levelling of genius with stupidity, strength
with weakness, and vice with virtue. It is not an automatic system: it can be stopped at any point, resumed at any time, reversed to any desired distance if it has gone too far or too fast;
in short, controlled as completely as any political process ever
can be. Thus it meets every demand of the really practical man
(most so-called practical men are doctrinaires and dreamers
when they are not simply people who do not care how poor
others are provided they are themselves rich); yet it makes
Utopia possible.

Note how in this process all question of compensation is
avoided. The only form of confiscation employed is the familiar
one of taxation. Just as the squeezed out capitalist retains his
shares and suffers nothing more unusual or revolutionary than
the too familiar experience of receiving no dividend and finding
his shares consequently so depreciated as to be unsaleable, so the
landlord never has his right to his land challenged or his property in it assailed. It is bought from him at full market price,
with the usual added percentage for compulsory sale. He becomes a landless man; but his pockets are full of money. The
tax collector takes from him only the smallest fraction of that
money, lifting the rest from the other renters, who all share the
burden. There is nothing to complain of: the thing happens
every day. As times goes on he contributes to the purchase of
other men's property as they have contributed to the purchase
of his. And in the end he finds he has neither land nor money,
and must work like other men, though at no point in the whole
process can he say that any wrong has been done him, or claim
a penny compensation. He has sold his land and paid his taxes:
that is all.

X　Socialism and Culture

In the spring of 1918 the Fabian Society presented a series of three lectures on "The Labour Party: Its Programme and Its Possibilities" by Arthur Henderson, Sidney Webb, and Shaw at King's Hall, Covent Garden. Shaw's lecture, given on May 10, was announced as "The Climate and Soil for Labour Culture." The manuscript, on the other hand, is headed "The Climate and Soil for a Labor Party." Since Shaw's subject is much broader in scope and of more lasting interest than his original title suggests, I have retitled the lecture "Socialism and Culture."

SIDETRACKING THE LABOR MOVEMENT

Nothing in politics is more feasible than to organize a political party and call it a Labor Party. It costs work, a good deal of which will be done for nothing by enthusiasts, but some of which, like the stationery and the committee rooms, will have to be paid for. Still, given enough money and enough enthusiasm (and the Labor Party can command sufficient of both) the thing can be done under experienced direction as surely as a canal can be dug or a house built. Everything will be in order at the general election: voters canvassed, registers marked, candidates standing, committee rooms open, addresses printed and circulated, cards filled in, conveyances borrowed, and possibly seats captured even to the extent of a majority in the House of Commons. The King, on asking whether he is to call on Mr Asquith or Lord Lansdowne or Sir Edward Carson or Mr Lloyd George to form a government, may be told, to his astonishment, that none of these gentlemen command a majority

in the House and that he must send for Mr Henderson. A Labor
Cabinet may be formed; and the leaders of the old parties may
have to crowd together on the front Opposition bench, united
at last by a common adversity, and glower at a Treasury bench
filled with men who have worked for weekly wages, and learnt
to read and write at public elementary schools at the expense of
the ratepayers. All this may happen and nobody outside parliament be a penny the better or worse. The verdict on the apparently revolutionary change at the end of five years may be
"Plus ça change, plus c'est la même chose" ("The more parliament changes, the more it resembles its old self").

Let us illustrate this possibility by the alleged conversion of
the Roman Empire (which meant virtually the world) from
paganism to Christianity under the Emperor Constantine, whom
we call Constantine the Great, and our comrade Anatole France
calls Constantine the Apostate, in the fourth century. Constantine was, if possible, less a Christian than Mr Asquith is a Socialist; but he dished Christianity very effectually by simply agreeing
to call himself a Christian and his Government a Christian
Government and his temples Christian temples and his gods
Christian gods. To this day, though sixteen centuries have
elapsed, his pagan Imperialism is in all its essentials more widely
and powerfully established than it was in his time; and the
preaching of genuine Christian doctrine is a punishable offence
in all the empires.

It is just as possible to sidetrack Labor as it was to sidetrack
Christianity. Socialism has already been extensively sidetracked
in Constantine's way. In the leading European states ambitious
journalists and barristers have labelled themselves Socialists and
Republicans to secure election and obtain office. In office, they
have behaved exactly as the ambitious journalists and barristers
of the old parties behaved, except that, knowing the people and
the real Socialists better, they have feared them less and oppressed them more. They have had as colleagues genuine proletarians from the factories, the mines, the docks, the fields, the
ships and the railways. When such men have graduated as Trade

Union secretaries, no one can deny their right to call themselves Labor members. Yet many of the ablest of such men have been more imperialistic than any emperor, more militarist than any field marshal, more plutocratic than any millionaire, more bigoted persecutors than Archbishop Laud.

Against this danger of sidetracking mere party organization affords no protection whatever. It even intensifies it; for the more the party falls into the hands of electioneering experts, who are among the most hopelessly demoralized classes in the country (and nobody who has been through the bluff and chicanery of an election will wonder at it or blame them), the more its principles will be thrust into the background, its attention concentrated on election tactics, and its votes reserved for candidates who are good winners.

ROOTLESSNESS OF LABOR MOVEMENTS

There is another danger. Labor movements are like flowers without roots, stuck in the ground by children. Their life is much shorter than human life. Our experience with Prime Ministers is very much the experience of Napoleon with generals: they are worn out in six years. For example, Gladstone made his reputation by his term of office from 1868 to 1873: all the rest of the time he was an obstruction and a nuisance. The political generations in the House of Commons pass very rapidly, and ought to pass much more rapidly. The consequence is that no policy or cause can survive in parliament longer than a decade at most unless it is taught to the children in the schools and associated with public credit and good social standing in everyday life. Now the education in our schools and the standards of gentility in our families have not been touched by the modern democratic humanitarian movement. The conventional European gentleman or city merchant of today, instead of being more advanced than his greatgrandfather, is positively less so; and the cause of this retrogression is the spread of education. I had better explain this apparent paradox.

THE PERILS OF SO-CALLED SECONDARY EDUCATION

As modern ideas are not taught in the schools, they can spread only among those who are not at school, or who, being at school, are neglecting their school work and reading books which are either forbidden or else hinder their readers instead of helping them in the school work of winning scholarships and passing examinations. On the other hand, feudal ideas, mercantile ideas, snobbish ideas, are steadily inculcated and embraced. Thus secondary education is an obstacle to modern culture and therefore a danger to the Labor Party. The "ladder to the University" is much less encouraging than the ladder to the gallows as far as Democracy is concerned; for those who climb it are enriched and lost to the modern movement instead of being simply hanged. The case of primary education is somewhat different. Without primary education we cannot educate ourselves, or communicate our ideas by the pen, or support ourselves in a city. With primary education we can do these things on condition that we are set free to read what we like and learn what we want to learn, and are not persecuted for following the modern democratic bent. But this freedom is just what our secondary education destroys. The secondary school imprisons the growing citizen, and keeps him or her at dictated task work under the social influence of feudalism, plutocracy, and ecclesiasticism, with the result that only incurably cantankerous and recalcitrant persons, or geniuses, or idlers, come out of the mill with any political ideas and social standards except those of the country house, the mess table, the Stock Exchange, the Chamber of Commerce, and race course. The more thorough the secondary education becomes and the longer it lasts, the more reactionary and ignorant the secondarily educated class (a class continually increasing) becomes, and the wider becomes the gulf between the university man and the wage worker, who is lucky enough to escape from his school prison when he has learnt only to read, write, and cipher. His one chance of giving himself a democratic secondary education is to keep out of

At first, when I sent the letters, I spent time wondering about Kate reading my words. Standing at the mailbox on a beautiful California morning. Smiling, or not smiling, as the case might be, alone in her bathroom, door locked, afraid of what I didn't mention. But slowly, as the years passed along, I didn't think any more about Kate reading the letters. It didn't much matter. They weren't for her anyway.

On a Monday morning I went to work as usual, and as usual, the office door was locked and the lights were out. Most of the time I was the first to arrive. On this particular Monday morning, I flicked on the lights to see my co-workers standing in the lobby around a large cake on a table. Balloons were tied to the four corners of the table and somebody had written on a white poster: HAPPY BIRTHDAY OLD MAN.

It was my sixtieth birthday. I was sixty years old. Sixty years had passed since my moment of mis-conception.

They began to sing, off-beat, awkward, most of them wishing they were still in bed. And as they sang, I thought about how much I hated everyone in the room. Keith Perkins with his nasty little secret. Debbie Cunningham with all those extremely black nose hairs. Chad Driskall and his political comments on everything under the sun. "I believe beavers would be Republicans if they had a choice, don't you? I mean, they're industrious, conservative creatures."

I didn't really hate them, and so we all stood in the lobby at seven in the morning celebrating my sixtieth birthday and ignoring the absurdity of it all.

I turned my head away from Debbie Cunningham as she gave the obligatory birthday hug, and then as we parted, tried to stare directly into those dishwater eyes and keep myself from glancing at the newest nose hair sprouted overnight. Keith Perkins wanted to wink at me so badly his face twitched, and I swear to God I heard Amber Sullivan pass gas standing next to the cake during a quiet moment. I imagined her stink absorbing into the white frosting and almost dry-heaved at the idea.

I had dinner that night with Allen and his family. Emily cooked a grand meal. Little Early was a young man, grown up before my eyes. His sister, Jessica, looked just like Gretchen to me, which was genetically impossible of course, and made me feel I might be losing my mind.

During dinner, I started to think again about killing Allen Kilborn Sr. It would flash in my mind, and I'd try to switch quickly to something else, but it would come back again and again, making my head actually hurt. There was really only one question left. Would I tell Allen I'd killed his father or not? Would I go to my grave unforgiven, or risk losing the love of the person in my life who probably loved me more than anyone ever had?

How would Allen react if I told him, and would his reaction be a product of who he was born to be, or who I made him? After all, ultimately, don't we become a combination of every important person in our lives, taking pieces of them as we go?

I looked around the dinner table. They had no idea who I was. To them I was Early Winwood, old man, builder of doghouses, stockbroker, ex-savior. They didn't see me at night at my desk next to a glass of brown whiskey, scribbling pitiful letters to a woman who never loved me. Or sitting in my office wishing Keith Perkins was dead. Or remembering my fingers on the inner thigh of the whore in the motel room. They didn't know how much I missed my mother and needed my father. They didn't know because I didn't tell them, and there was no way for them to know such things.

For days after my birthday I sat around thinking about telling Allen. I decided it wasn't a choice. It had to be done, maybe more than anything I'd ever done before. So I smoked and thought, thought and smoked, and tried to work out the details of my confession.

It would be done in person. A letter would be too cheap and easy. I should leave out gruesome details and not provide too much explanation either. It wasn't a moment for justification or self-pity. It was my gift to Allen, for him to do with as he chose, and I would need to be prepared for the worst. Prepared to spend the rest of my life without him, or Emily, or Jessica, or Little Early's baseball games. In some regard, it was much like one of my suicide scenarios, with less finality and more serious consequences. It also happened to be real life instead of volcano fantasy, and for months I couldn't think of anything else.

Kate,

A long time ago, in high school, we left a party one night to take you home. You made Jake drop you off blocks from your house late at night under a streetlight. I can still see you standing there under the light. We drove away and I watched you out the back window of Jake's car.

You waited until we turned the corner.

I'm sixty years old.

Early

It happened around midnight.

I was alone at home, as usual. The house was quiet. I remember standing slowly from the wooden chair at my desk.

It was like the lights went out. It was like God turned off all the lights in the universe with no warning except a tingling sensation in my brain.

I woke up on the floor beside the desk. I knew where I was, but I couldn't seem to move my body. The inside of my head pounded and pounded like my brain was swollen against the bones of my skull. It was very hot, and I tried to decide what had happened to me.

I couldn't collect my thoughts, almost like being on the edge of sleep, or drugged, or chained to the floor of a smoke-filled garage watching blackbirds fly against the walls.

I would tell my arms to move, but nothing would move. I would tell my mouth to speak, but no words would come out. The room smelled like burnt hair. There was a telephone on the small table a few feet away, but a few feet was like a mile, and I began to imagine ants on my body. The same ants that bit Gretchen's feet and legs, leaving raised white welts on her skin and wet tears in her little eyes. I could feel them crawling on me, in my cracks, under my shirt.

Maybe it was a heart attack, I thought, but my chest didn't hurt. Maybe I'd been shot or struck by lightening. Maybe I was in Heaven and this was what Heaven was like, lying on a floor with my head pounding and ants crawling on my body, unable to reach the phone two feet away, as helpless as the day I was born into the world.

I could hear a clock somewhere, ticking, ticking. After a while the room began to lighten, the morning sun rising outside somewhere, and I guess I started to cry. I could feel the cold teardrop slide downward from the corner of my eye and slowly across the skin on the side of my face to a resting place in the hair around my temple. I knew I was crying, but it was more like someone else was crying and I was only watching.

My arm moved. Not so much moved as jerked, spasmodic, knocking my hand into the leg of the small table, the phone falling to the floor. The dial tone was a relief at first, a noise, proof I was still alive, but then the noise changed to a beeping sound, and I was trapped in the shell of my body. Unable to defend myself. Unable to separate my thoughts from the beeping sound.

Two days later, they tell me, I woke up in a hospital with Allen above my bed. It was a stroke, the doctor said, and I could hear him but couldn't answer his questions. I was in my house for twelve hours on the bloody floor. I'd cracked my head on the desk on the way down and bled all over myself waiting to be found, jerking on the hardwood.

It was Allen who found me. Keith Perkins called him from the office. Said I was never late, never missed work, something was the matter. The black-nose-hair lady and her farting friend were worried. Everybody was worried about Early Winwood. So Allen went to the house and found me on the floor next to the desk. He said he thought I was dead.

When the doctor left and we were alone, I looked up at Allen. The words came to me from nowhere. The perfect words to tell him what I had done and why, written neatly across my mind, words I'd never found before in all those moments of thinking and smoking, smoking and thinking.

I opened my mouth to tell him what needed to be said, knowing he might turn and walk from the room, but the words wouldn't come out. Nothing came out. Nothing at all. And I wasn't even sure my mouth had opened because Allen looked down at me in the way my father must have looked down at me in the white crib of the hospital the day I was born, wearing the t-shirt he wore in the picture I kept in my sock drawer.

I absolutely know my father's last thought was of me. Nothing else, and no one else but me. I absolutely know it, but I waited too long to tell Allen the truth, and now I'd come full circle. Back to the beginning.

seven

I so longed for my chance to die, and then it got complicated. I woke up in a hospital unable to speak, with the right side of my body basically useless. When Allen's family had gone home, a nurse came into my room. She talked to me the way people sometimes talk to pets.

"Well, does somebody need a little bath?"

I watched her scurry across the room, marking off chores on the checklist inside her mind. She was short, but her ass was wide and flat. I think she preferred to work with patients who couldn't possibly blurt out, "No, I don't want a bath, and by the way, your ass is wide and flat."

"It'll feel really good," she said. "Nice and cool," she smiled and wrapped her arms around herself pretending to shiver when she said the word 'cool'.

The woman pulled back the blankets and began to

undress me. I didn't have the energy to stop her and heard myself mumble a few words. Not really words.

"You're welcome," she said, misinterpreting my sounds.

I was naked and had the feeling drool was escaping the corner of my mouth and dripping off my cheek to the pillow.

The cold sponge touched my chest. I stared directly into her face. There were lines around her eyes. A fever blister on the top lip was visible under a smear of skin-colored makeup. She was lonely. No wedding ring. Her hair was going gray despite the best efforts to dye and pluck, probably standing in front of a mirror until she was sick of who she was, memorizing every blackhead and undesirable blemish on her generic face.

When I was young I was so sure my potential lay in a special awareness I possessed. The ability to notice and dissect other people and the world around me. Somehow, I'd lost touch with it through the years of my life. Too busy to notice, I suppose.

The wet sponge, no longer cold, slid across my arms and beneath my neck. She wouldn't look at me. All work. Just another chore to mark off the list, her eyes following the sponge as it ended up at my hips and then gently wedged between my thighs. I felt the beginning of an erection.

I was far beyond the point of embarrassment. What would be the point? Naked, spread out in the bed, unable to feed myself, shitting in a pan, drool most certainly in a thin clear line from the corner of my mouth to the white pillow. But regardless, being cleaned by a woman not remotely attractive, my body prepared itself for procreation anyway.

"Something seems to be working just fine," she said as workman-like as possible, hopefully finding an ounce of joy in the idea she could still cause such a reaction in another living thing.

She avoided any further contact with my private parts, dressed me, pulled up the covers, and left the room humming a song I didn't recognize. I was left alone to think about the irony of spending each day imagining my death, even wishing for it, only to find myself with a reason to live. I wondered how long it would take in rehab, how many months, to speak the words clearly to Allen. Because once they were spoken, I would be free to go, one way or the other, with or without forgiveness.

Doctors and nurses came and went through the night and into the next day. After lunch, the door opened slowly. A head, Gretchen's head, appeared, and as the door opened I could see Kate behind her. They'd come from California. Allen must have called. They'd flown together to see me. If things had been different, my wife, Kate, would have been the one to find me on the floor, waking in the other room to the sound of my head cracking against the wooden desk. She would have cried quietly at the kitchen table when they took me out on a stretcher, afraid of the idea I might die and leave her all alone.

My good hand tried to pat down my hair and once again I had the feeling of drooling. Gretchen stopped a few feet away from the bedside, unable to hide her shock at my appearance. If I could have seen myself, I imagined

I looked like the Hunchback of Notre Dame, eyes bulging, saliva glistening on my thin lips, strands of antenna-like, wiry gray hair in every direction.

Kate stepped up ahead of our daughter. She seemed strong, prepared, and took my hand in hers with no reaction to my appearance except a soft smile. Even if I had possessed the power of speech, there is nothing I would have said.

"Allen called," she whispered.

Behind Kate I could see Gretchen lost in the situation. It was the first time in her lifetime she was alone in a room with her mother and father, just the three of us, and it had to happen in a hospital, with her father drooling on himself like an idiot.

Gretchen roamed around the room, in and out for a few days, never knowing what to say, a ball of anger and sympathy rolled tightly together. She left to go back home. Something about her job. "Inventory," she said. It wasn't true, and it didn't matter. Kate stayed.

She hugged Gretchen and sat back down next to the bed. It was outside the realm of possibilities, so I'd never taken the time to imagine such a thing. She read out loud to me deep into the evenings from books she knew I loved. She talked to me like we'd never been apart. Like I'd dreamed all the bad things and we'd been married forever. Smiling. Taking care of me. Telling Allen and Emily she'd be staying a while longer. Whatever I meant to her, she was afraid of losing it.

I watched her face as she read out loud. It was a pretty face. The years hadn't changed it all that much. Still full of mystery and surprise. She'd been the love of my life, my whole life, and I wouldn't have it any other way, because either you believe in the concept of love or you don't. There's no middle ground. No compromise. It's all or nothing, and if it's all, there are no limitations other than those you set yourself, and a broken heart doesn't count.

She was reading from *The Catcher in the Rye*, and it was making me feel the way it always made me feel, how difficult it can be sometimes to squeeze any real purpose from the day. I started to think about finding her on the street that night, sitting on the curb, her head resting on her knees wrapped in her arms. I watched her face as she read the words, and at the same time I saw Kate as I'd seen her that night, from the back, unsure if it was her at all. She was humming softly to herself. I couldn't hear the words. And when a car passed, the lights showed me a part of her cheek, just enough for me to know it was Kate Shepherd I'd found, and rescued.

Those days and nights she stayed with me were dreamlike, and I can't be sure they ever happened. On the day she left, Kate kissed me on the cheek and touched her hand to my hair.

"I have to go home now, Early."

She said it like she knew it was the last time.

"Through the years you probably thought I was crazy or something."

I just listened, glad I couldn't speak. Glad I was able to listen without expectations. She struggled with the words.

"I guess…" she stopped herself.

We both waited a moment. I knew I'd have plenty of

time to cry after she left. "I guess," she said again, "I just didn't understand how you could love me so much. It was more than I could figure out. Maybe it still is."

Sometimes it's harder to identify the problem than it is to solve it. If I hadn't had a stroke, if I wasn't speechless and bedridden, I don't know what I would have said or done. Probably nothing. She figured it out. There was a hole in each of us, and I watched her pick up her purse slowly and then walk out the door for the last time.

It was what it was, and I'd cried about it too many times. There was only one thing left. One thing left to do. I went home to Allen's house. Emily quit her part-time job to stay with me and they turned the guest room into a place they hoped I'd like to be. Pictures of the kids were on the walls and Allen had thoughtfully packed up everything in the little house, selecting certain items to decorate my new room.

Little Early made the high school baseball team. Every evening after practice or a game he'd sit down in my room and tell me everything that happened.

"It was the last inning. We were tied six to six. Toby Raines was on third. There's two outs, and two strikes on me. The first one was high, but the second one I just missed it. No excuses.

"Anyway, the kid pitchin' was the coach's son. He throws about eighty-five. Some people say ninety, but I don't think so.

"He pulls up in the stretch, and you wouldn't believe it. The ump calls a balk, with two outs, two strikes, tie game, the ump calls a balk.

"That kid wouldn't come out of the dugout to shake our hands. He just sat in the dugout."

I went through rehab every day. I didn't give a shit about walking across the room or holding a fork. I just wanted to talk again. Coherent. Make my tongue move the way I wanted it to move, and my mouth, and the muscles in my face, to form the words.

The wheelchair didn't bother me. They even loaded me up in the car and took me to a few baseball games. I tried not to look at the people who looked at me. Especially Samantha. It would have been better for someone just to stand up and clear the air.

Someone could say, "This is Early Winwood. He had a stroke. He's not the man he used to be. Now, who wants popcorn?"

Everybody could look at me openly for a few minutes, get it over with, and go back to watching the game. Little kids could ask, "What's wrong with your face?" or "Why does your hand look like that?" and I'd have Allen answer their questions calmly.

My speech therapist was named Jackie. She had more patience in the tip of her nose than I had contained in all my bones combined.

"Say corn."

And I would make a noise similar to "corn," but since the word corn wasn't likely to appear in my conversation with Allen, I really didn't give a damn about the word.

I missed being alone, believe it or not. I missed my little house, and my desk, and the late-night drives to the post office.

I didn't miss my work, but I missed the office. The half-hour each morning I sipped my coffee and read the newspaper before I heard a key enter the lock and turn the deadbolt.

I missed the woodshop. The smell. The purity of cutting straight lines and hammering nails, making something from nothing, using my mind for a single purpose.

But none of those things changed my plan. At night, alone in the bed, the neighborhood quiet, I arranged scenes. It would be just me and Allen. I would give him a route to escape after the conversation. A door to walk through. A chance to think about what I said.

I'd be prepared to answer questions. Why? How? And explain if he wanted a further explanation. He deserved whatever he wanted, and I deserved whatever he put upon me. If he just chose to sit and listen, it would be relatively short. No more than two minutes to say everything I needed to say, and then I imagined a moment of silence. A moment when neither of us was sure how he'd react.

On a piece of paper I scribbled a note to Jackie, my speech therapist. "I'll give you $10 for a cigarette."

It didn't sound good to me, but I wanted it anyway. Since the stroke I'd lost my taste for meat, peanuts, and ice cream. My favorite foods were suddenly disgusting as feces and caused the same reaction. I prayed God had saved for me the pleasure of tobacco, but I didn't hold much hope.

Jackie wouldn't get me a cigarette, but I bought one from a wrinkled-up old bastard with six bypasses and a tube in his throat. He could barely draw the next breath, but he loved cigarettes with a lust rarely seen.

I waited until Early went to the grocery store and wheeled myself out onto the back porch. I struck a long fireplace match and lit the Marlboro. A wave of nausea began deep in my bowels and moved upwards. I vomited in a potted plant before I could take the second drag.

The days moved slowly. On the calendar I marked the day I believed I'd be ready to tell Allen. It was only four weeks away. I was able to talk to people, and they were able to understand, but I wasn't quite ready. On the other hand, I didn't want to make the same mistake I'd made twice before, waiting too long. The doctor said I was at a much higher risk of another stroke than the average person. He said I was lucky the first one didn't kill me, and maybe I wouldn't be so lucky the next time.

I worked on pronouncing certain words. "Sorry." "Controlling." Even small words were hard to say. "Gun." "Mom."

Emily and the kids went out of town for Thanksgiving to see Emily's parents. Allen stayed with me. I insisted he have Thanksgiving dinner with his mother, and I'd be fine. When Allen left, I decided to find a little whiskey. It was off-limits of course, doctor's orders, but I hadn't had a sip since the day I woke up in the hospital.

I found a bottle, and a glass, and sat in my wheelchair in the living room, feeling sorry for myself. I thought of Kate, and Gretchen, and the day marked on the calendar. I drank down almost the entire bottle and somehow made my way back to the bedroom and laid down on top of the covers.

I remember crying. That's mostly what I remember. Just crying, without stopping. My body shaking. Everything running together. Wishing I'd died and then feeling guilty. Waiting to reconcile the irreconcilable, a sin of the highest level, a life unlived.

I remember looking up from my bed to see Allen standing above me. His presence in the room made it full and complete, and it was clear the moment was upon me.

I looked up at him and said, "I killed your father, Allen."

That's all I said. The other words I'd practiced and performed avoided me, but those five words, "I killed your father, Allen," were as clear as any words I'd ever spoken, and as I expected, they were followed by agonizing silence.

eight

I can't be sure where the dream started and the world stopped.

The next thing I remember is the black circle. Just like before, on the floor between my bed and the door in my childhood bedroom. A deep black hole with a gray ring around the circumference, maybe an arm's-length across, no more.

In the dream, if it's a dream at all, I'm sitting up in my bed in the dark watching the closed door. I have a certainty the door will open, it's just a matter of time, and the wait is excruciating. I'm just a boy, maybe eleven years old. It's the day Mr. Walker told me my father died on the train tracks. My mother took me home from school early, and I remember it started raining right after dark. A steady, heavy rain.

I sat in my bed, waiting for my father to come home. He always came to my bedroom when he got home late from work, and I always, always, waited for him before I fell asleep. From my bed I could hear the car door slam in the driveway, and then a few seconds later the front door would close quietly. He always closed the front door quietly so he wouldn't wake my mother. She went to sleep early, and it wasn't good to wake her up, so we didn't.

After I'd hear the front door shut, I'd wait, smiling in the dark, for my father. The doorknob would turn. I could see it, and in the dream it turned so slowly, but I didn't move. After all, it was the day they told me my father died. It was the day I was asked to believe he'd never come home to me again. Never hold me. Never take my hand in his hand, or throw the football in the front yard, or tell me about baseball. It was the final test between a child's life and God's real world. A world where people die and just never come back, like a butterfly in a storm.

I can't move. It's like I'm frozen again. The doorknob turns. My father's coming home and the black hole on the floor waits between him and me.

The door opens slowly, and there he is. He looks perfectly normal. No bandages or blood. No scratches on his face from the glass shattered by the impact of the hundred-ton locomotive barreling down the tracks to places unknown.

He smiles at me. The same smile from the picture. Mischievous, like we're in on something together. A secret. But I want to tell him about the black hole. I want to warn him before he walks to my bed to hug me the way he does every night. I can't speak. All I can do is sit there and look at him.

The door opens wider and he takes two steps to me. I'm not allowed to close my eyes, only watch my father begin to fall into the black circle on the floor, and in an instant he is gone, the room quiet again, rain coming down on the roof of the house. I am alone.

The next thing I remember is waking up in the hospital. The light is dim and the window dark. Tubes are hanging down across my chest. Next to the bed, on my left, sits Allen. His face is down resting in his hands. It's just the two of us in the room.

At first I want him to know I'm awake, but then I remember what I've told him. I want to reach out and touch his hair, but I'm too far away, and maybe he doesn't want me to touch him. Maybe there's a black circle between us, unseen by me, but between us nonetheless. Just resting in the short distance between my hospital bed and his chair.

I watch Allen in the silence. The marrow of life exists in the moments in between. Those moments before and after the violent upheavals and admissions of futility. For the birth of a child is meaningless without expectation, and the death of a parent is hollow in the absence of memory. And though we are forged by a handful of events, some dramatic, it is those moments in between, waiting for life to happen, when we discover who we have become. When the violent upheavals and admissions of futility resonate, harden, and reveal themselves for what they are.

I must have fallen back asleep, or maybe not, but I am in my workshop with Little Early. He looks at me the way I remember looking at my grandfather, and I reach out to touch his face, holding my fingers to his warm smooth cheek, and he lets me do it without pulling away. Like he is me, and I am him, and we're making something together in my grandfather's basement, the smell of cedar soft in the air.

But before we can start, I am off again, in and out, coming to rest at the high school baseball field. The grass is amazingly green, and I sit in the aluminum home field bleachers, alone, on a bright blue day. Across, on the other side, sits Kate. She has a textbook open in her lap and looks out into center field, freshly mowed. We are the only two people in sight, and I watch Kate Shepherd close her eyes and take a deep breath.

I am in the kitchen with my mother, just a few days away from leaving for college. She is standing, leaning against the refrigerator, arms crossed over a long, faded blue nightshirt.

"Do you ever think of Dad?" I ask.

She studies me and then smiles just a little bit. It gets the best of her, just like he did, and she goes ahead and lets the smile remain.

"Sometimes," she says, and I know it's true, but more importantly, she allows me to know.

There's a far-off flash of light, like lightning in the distance too far away to hear the thunder, and I am with Gretchen at the ice cream parlor, sitting outside under a big white umbrella. We're waiting to go the matinee. Just enough time for ice cream. Gretchen has a scoop of birth-day cake ice cream in a cup made of white chocolate with colorful sprinkles.

She looks up at me and takes her first bite. A smile comes across my little girl's face, genuine and pure, and I start to cry. I can feel the tears roll slowly down my face, and instead of wiping them away I just let them roll down.

"Daddy," she says, "how much does the sky weigh?"

"I don't know, baby," I say. "I really don't know."

I wake up again. It's daytime. Feels like early morning. Allen is standing at the window with his back to me. We are very still, and I wonder if I am dying. Wonder if all of it has come to this, waiting for Allen to turn. Waiting for his decision.

One moment I see Allen's back, and the next moment I am looking out of the window of the hospital, seeing the world for the last time through someone else's eyes. Allen's eyes, looking across the parking lot to the build-ings on the other side, watching a tall pine tree sway in the morning breeze.

This time it goes further. This time I can feel what Allen feels. The forgiveness is an entity. It exists like a stone, heavy and solid, inside his body, and it is the only thing in this world worth knowing.

I turn from the window and look at myself in the hos-pital bed, tired and gaunt, much like my mother when I was called to her bedside, but Allen sees me differently. He sees himself in me, and as I walk slowly across the room, the past, the present, and the future melt together to form something entirely new for me. I am not alone anymore, and never will be again.

Allen places his hand upon my shoulder, and I am allowed to feel the touch on both the shoulder and the hand. A gentle squeeze. Assurance. Resurrection. With no words spoken, I am forgiven, and Allen's hand on my shoulder is the last thing I remember before the beginning of the gentle slide into light, when everything you ever wondered makes sense. When the enormously personal journey ends in the reflection of God on the surface of the cool water.

ACKNOWLEDGMENTS

David Poindexter, Kate Nitze, Sherilyn McNally, Scott Bidwell, Shauna Mosley, Steve Johnson, Michael Dasinger, Sharon Hoiles, Sonny Brewer, Michael and Jillian Strecker, Kevin and Carolyn Shannon, Kip and Shannon Howard, Frank and Virginia Hollon, Sara and Skip Wyatt, Sally Hollon, Hoss Mack, Marion Bolar, Austin McAdoo, Gladden Statom, Fred White, Rich Green, Allison, Dusty, Mary Grace, Lilly, Smokey Davis, Chris D'Arienzo, Robbie Boyd, Kyle Jennings, Aleta Dasinger, Paige Benson, Tank and Janet Dasinger, Melissa and Julie, Weber, Joel Stabler, Stephanie Wheeler, Russ Copeland, Will Kimbrough, Joyce Miller, Helene Holmes, Joshilyn Jackson, Brietta, Hilary, Anne, Pete Ware, and Pat Walsh. Thanks.

figure it out. Just tell me you'll be there.

Early

Most of the letters were never sent, piling up in the bottom drawer of my desk, but sometimes, burdened by the knowledge the sobriety of morning would dampen my courage, I'd venture out late at night to the mailbox. The same mailbox I once attempted to steal.

Kate,

Do you remember the time we were at the park for my visitation with Gretchen? She couldn't have been more than four or five years old. You and I walked away to argue about something, who knows what now, and left Gretchen alone.

When I turned around she was standing in a bed of fire ants. They were all over her sandals and biting her little legs, her eyes were filled with tears, her arms outstretched to us.

I remember the helplessness. The total and utter understanding I couldn't protect her from the bad things in this world.

Why is it our minds hold certain moments, certain conversations, certain words spoken, or visual images like Gretchen's outstretched arms, and yet dismiss huge pieces, events, entire years of our lives? Why is it we're not allowed to forget certain moments, and then not allowed to remember others?

Early

I took the death of Frank Rush as a sign from God. A sign to pursue my childhood vow of being average and invisible. My life became measured by baseball seasons. Going to work, stopping at the well-lit grocery store, locking the door behind me in my little house, not answering the phone, and then going to work again, looking forward to Early's next game, or even the next season.

I took to writing letters to Kate about virtually nothing, and she never responded. Usually the letters were written late at night, after I'd had too much to drink.

Dear Kate,

Come to my funeral when I die. I don't know why it's important, but it is, and I don't care to